*To all who suffer from abuse.*

# CONTENTS

# INTRODUCTION

*"The need for change bulldozed a road down the center of my mind."*
—MAYA ANGELOU

The decision to file for divorce is never easy. No one wants to admit that her marriage has failed, especially when children are involved. If a woman is married to an abusive man, the situation is much more complicated. There is the potential for an escalation of the abuse, which may include violence, as well as destructive and outrageous behavior and verbal harassment. If this is your situation, you need to take steps to protect yourself and your children. Things will not get better if you stay. In fact, they will probably get progressively worse. I wrote *Breaking Bonds* to help you assess if a divorce is right for you, and then, once you decide that it is, to help you navigate the process of divorcing your abuser.

You cannot live your best life or fulfill your divine purpose while being subjected to the tyranny of abuse. You also cannot truly give your best to others while being subjected to marital abuse, whether it's physical, mental, or emotional. No one else can change this awful situation for you. *You* must act while knowing in your heart of hearts that for some period of your life you gave your power away and must now take it back.

It is time to honor and protect yourself. You are worthy of being treated with dignity, kindness, and respect. You deserve to be loved, happy, and safe. So, resolve right now to stop letting someone victimize you. Decide that you are no longer going to be a victim. Choose not to live in fear and misery. If you are being abused, acknowledge that your husband is a sick and dangerous man who is causing you great harm, and then make whatever changes you deem necessary to protect yourself and change your circumstances.

By making these decisions and acting upon them, your life will improve greatly. As will the lives of your children. By standing up for yourself against abuse, you will give permission to your children to take care of themselves, and teach them to treat themselves and others with the dignity, kindness, love, and respect that they deserve. You, as their mother, are their first and greatest teacher. You are their role model. If you are unwilling to act merely out of regard for your own happiness, your responsibility for their young lives should give you reason enough to act.

For convenience, from now on I will assume that you have children rather than indicating that this may or may not be the case each time the issue comes up. Even so, I assure you that this book is for *all* women, not just for mothers. If you don't have children, simply ignore what doesn't apply to you and draw what is meaningful to you from the rest. Most of the information provided in this book will benefit every woman married to an abusive man.

Throughout *Breaking Bonds,* I am going to share my experiences as well as those of other women I know who have gone through a divorce. Not all were married to abusive men. Still, not one of them had an easy experience. Divorce is almost always adversarial. Learning from our mistakes and successes will be valuable to you.

## WAITING FOR HERCULES

*"If you can't be a good example, then you'll just have to be a horrible warning."*
—CATHERINE AIRD

If I am going to accomplish what I intend to with this book, it is necessary for me to expose very personal and humiliating truths about my life in the pages of this book to help you avoid making some of the mistakes I made. You see, I am an independent, highly educated, and successful woman. For most of my career, I have earned an income well into the six figures. So, there are a lot of reasons I should have known better than to marry this man or than to have stayed married to him for so long. I should have noticed the signs while we were dating. I should have picked a better partner. I should have ended the relationship sooner. I should have stopped making excuses for his behavior. And yes, I should not have allowed my children to see him belittle me.

The list of my "I should haves" kept me stuck in misery for many long years—even after we were divorced. And it was not necessary at all for me to do that to myself. My husband was the perpetrator of my abuse, and his behavior was awful. But I stayed, so I also did it to myself.

I refused to accept that I had no choice other than to end a bad marriage to save my children and myself. Years of being tormented without ceasing, like Prometheus chained to a rock and having his liver torn out by an eagle, only to have it grow back and be eaten again the next day, had destroyed my self-esteem. It took me over twenty-five years to realize that Hercules was not coming to my rescue.

One of my biggest mistakes was my unwillingness to accept sooner that my ex-husband was not sorry for the things he did and said, and was not willing or capable of change. I was in total denial of this fact because I wanted to believe that he was a better person than he really was. I also believed God wanted me to stay married, and that I needed to sacrifice my life for my children so that they wouldn't grow up in a "broken home." That idea was stupid. Well meaning, but stupid.

That does not mean that I am stupid, no matter what my ex-husband says.

Neither are you.

Stop waiting for Hercules.

## TO LOVE AND TO CHERISH

*"The real act of marriage takes place in the heart, not in the ballroom or church or synagogue. It's a choice you make—not just on your wedding day, but over and over again—and that choice is reflected in the way you treat your husband or wife."*
—BARBARA DE ANGELIS

God calls many of us to marriage, with all its beautiful promises of sharing, caring, and intimacy, unconditional love, and the joyful messiness of daily living. Ideally, this includes overlooking small flaws and quirks in your partner, tenderness, demonstrations of respect, and speaking kindly. Despite my experience, to this day I still think this is how marriage should be.

If you are reading this, then it is likely you are in deep pain. There is almost nothing worse than being abused and disrespected as a human being by a man who has promised to love and cherish you for the rest of your lives. That he would treat the mother of his children in this way is no reflection on your value as a person. You may be confused because your husband is not always abusive to you and he almost always seems normal and nice to others outside the home. Sometimes he is even nice to you, making you hope that things are getting better. But then he explodes again and again in private for no apparent reason. A better life awaits you once you accept the reality that your relationship is not working.

Divorce is difficult even in marriages where the partners customarily treat one another with respect. Don't mistake the subject of this book for "conscious uncoupling." Divorcing an abuser is not a normal situation where two people split because they have grown apart and fallen out of love, or discover their values are incompatible and they want different things out of life.

Leaving an abuser is scary because you are dealing with a dangerous and unpredictable man, even if the abuse in your household is not physical. You may be having a hard time trusting anyone right now, especially because at one time you thought that you could trust your husband and you were wrong. If you are married to a habitual liar who is in total denial of what he is doing to you, you may even think that you can't trust yourself and your instincts. He may want you to believe that what he did wasn't abuse, or didn't happen, or that you provoked him—so all of it was your fault. "You deserved what you got coming." He may say he's sorry, but it keeps happening over and over. He likely breaks promise after promise. If you are ever going to have a happy life, you must not believe that what he is telling you is the truth or that you deserve to be poorly treated and punished.

If the man you married is not willing to get counseling immediately, then you are putting yourself and your children in harm's way by residing with him any longer. If he is willing to acknowledge that he has a serious problem and takes responsibility for it and gets counseling, then your marriage may still have a chance.

However, if your husband is not willing to make drastic changes, it is magical thinking for you to believe or hope that things will get better. The odds are very high that they won't.

Most abusers are not capable of stopping toxic patterns of behavior. There is a dynamic to an abusive relationship that can become entrenched. Even if the abuse is "only" verbal, it may escalate to being physical. In the meantime, verbal abuse is damaging to the psyche. It is not something you or your children should be exposed to in your home.

If the abuse in your home is physical, you will need to act immediately. Deep down, you already know that you must get out, or you wouldn't be reading this book. Probably you are dreading what lies ahead, as you know the divorce is going to be very difficult. You have no choice.

Remember that your children have a bird's eye view of what a dysfunctional marriage is like and how awfully a couple who supposedly love each other can treat one another. You hurt them by staying. If you think you are hiding what's happening from them, you aren't. Children are sensitive to their parents' tension and unhappiness. Although you may be in total denial of how loudly your husband is berating you, your children aren't deaf. Looks of contempt and disgust directed at you are not invisible either. Nonverbal communication can be just as damaging to their mental and emotional development as it is to you.

My point is that they already know what is happening and see that, thus far, you are willing to accept being treated this way. If they grow up to think that this is acceptable behavior, they could lose respect for you and come to believe that you are weak because you allow this behavior to continue. In time, they might start treating you with the same disrespect as your husband. If this is the case, they are more likely to grow up to be abusers themselves, or victims of abuse, because they think that it is normal and acceptable behavior. It is your responsibility to show them that abuse isn't either customary or tolerable. You are the parent. Set a good example. Our lives are reflections of the choices we make. It's time for you to look in the mirror.

# PRACTICAL MATTERS

In this book, I will give you a lot of practical information. I will outline strategies for dealing with your abuser, your children, and third parties who could be your advocates or adversaries in court, and explain how to handle the financial and legal issues that you will have to deal with in order to divorce your abusive husband. This book will give you insights on how to prepare for what is a legal and emotional battle and show you how to deflect or minimize the damage your abuser will likely try to inflict on you and your life, as well as how to recover and heal.

The first two chapters define the problem and encourage you to take responsibility for what is not is working in your life and to make the decision to change it. The religious stigma of divorce as well as dealing with the judgment and demands of others are also addressed.

Chapters 3–5 help you to prepare physically, mentally, and spiritually for the battle that lies ahead. I believe that it is necessary to focus on healing and self-care starting now so that you will be able to handle the stress of the divorce and be at your best while you are preparing for and doing battle with your husband. You will need energy and brainpower to deal with a very manipulative and unscrupulous person over a period of many months. You will find informative material on leading a healthy lifestyle—everything from eating sensibly and staying fit, how to sleep soundly, breathing techniques to reduce stress, and how to break bad habits. It is important to have reserves of emotional and physical stamina to cope with the stress of standing up to an angry and abusive opponent day after day for as long as it takes to get your freedom. Building your mental and physical health will help you survive this challenge without getting sick. Begin making changes now in your daily routine so that you get enough nutrients, exercise, and rest to feel empowered and think clearly. This will boost your self-esteem and confidence.

I also discuss how to improve your self-regard using affirmations and mirror work. Other methods of self-care, including chakra clearing, music, gratitude, and prayer are examined. The importance of repairing and enhancing self-esteem is explained so that you do not repeat the cycle of abuse in your other relationships.

Feel free to hopscotch around these three chapters and use what is helpful to you at the moment. Some of the subsections may not be relevant to your specific situation. You can go back and review some of this information later, when you have the time and inclination. Many of these tools will also help with your recovery post-divorce.

Chapters 6 and 7 offer resources, preparation steps, and strategy to enable you to anticipate your husband's likely maneuvers and control the outcome of your divorce as much as possible. I will teach you how to prepare to leave your husband safely in a manner that positions you for the best results financially and legally when you file for divorce. Among other things, you will find a checklist for what types of financial and legal records to bring with you when you leave the house. I also discuss when to go to a shelter and how, when, and why to file for a legal restraining order. Physical protection for your children so they are not kidnapped is also addressed.

Chapters 8–10 discuss the divorce process, financial matters, and maintaining control of your financial decisions. You will learn how to hire a lawyer and work with a mediator. Investments, credit, life and health insurance, social security, and disability benefits are considered. Pensions, other retirement accounts, child support, and alimony are also explained.

Advice is given here on getting a job or going back to school so you can support yourself after the divorce.

The final two chapters address life after divorce, including recovery, boundary setting, budgeting, independence, happiness, life lessons, purpose, and forgiveness. The reason for going through this difficult ordeal of divorcing an abuser in the first place is to be healthy, happy, and at peace.

I am not a therapist, a doctor, or a lawyer and I make no claims to expertise in the fields of psychology, medicine, or the law. I have had over thirty years of experience as a financial advisor, during which time I have given many people advice while they were going through divorces. My personal experience of divorcing an abuser and of advising clients on their finances, as well as undergoing over twenty years of therapy, gives me an uncommon perspective on divorce and healing that may be very helpful to you.

Any advice that I offer here is my opinion. I offer it with the intention to encourage you to seek professional guidance, to ask good and productive questions, to do your research and make the right decisions for you, to take appropriate actions, and to heal. Some chapters may be more helpful to you than others. Take what works for you and leave the rest.

I don't expect you to agree with all my opinions, which are based on my point of view and are not meant to replace your thinking for yourself as well as evaluating professional advice that you receive for your unique circumstances.

## IN LOVE AND WAR

*"The truth does not change according to our ability to stomach it."*
—FLANNERY O'CONNOR

You will need to prepare for war when you decide to leave your husband. Because of his self-loathing, an abusive man has no moral compass. He will stoop to guerrilla tactics to keep you under his thumb or try to make sure that you end up with as close to nothing as possible. It doesn't matter to him whether you have given him the best years of your life or that you are the mother of his children. If he can pummel you with his words, his fists, or his passive-aggressive behavior, he is going to pummel the hell out of you both in court and outside of court for daring to stand up for yourself and leave him.

I have heard this kind of behavior referred to as *divorce psychosis*. This occurs when a man loses his mind and decides that his divorce is a life-threatening situation. He believes that his wife must die, literally or figuratively, for him to live. Therefore, he is going to try to "win" regardless of the cost.

And yes, if your husband experiences divorce psychosis, you will pay the price for having made a very bad choice in marrying him. Remember that your dignity, freedom, and peace of mind are worth any price that you will have to pay to get them.

Many women suffer from heart disease and cancer because they carry emotional pain in their bodies that they were not able to process in a healthy way. Ultimately, pain manifests itself as illness. If you don't get out of your unhealthy marriage soon, you may become ill or die prematurely. If you are suffering from a lot of pain, you need to put yourself first.

## CHOOSE YOU

*"If you think taking care of yourself is selfish, change your mind. If you don't, you are ducking your responsibilities."*
—ANN RICHARDS

Deciding to divorce is very difficult and gut-wrenching. Fortunately, you do not have to go through it alone. In addition to your family, trusted friends, lawyer, financial advisor, and therapist, there are many social and spiritual resources available to you. Prayer and meditation may bring you great comfort and help you to remember that you are never alone; we are connected to one another and God.

Know in your heart that you are valued, you deserve help, and you are loved. God loves you. Your family loves you. Your friends love you. Now your job is to learn to love yourself—or relearn to love yourself—by actively taking care of yourself. Practice self-care.

After my divorce, I realized that I needed to take time to reflect and heal. As I began to question everything I was taught, I saw that the abuse in my marriage continued for as long as it did because I was never taught to value myself. My mother did not value herself enough, so I did not have a good role model in childhood. In our culture, women are taught to put the needs of others first, ahead of their own, especially if they are mothers. We are taught to feel guilty for taking care of ourselves. Once I realized this was no longer acceptable, I committed to learning to value myself and take care of my needs.

In pursuit of healing, I read many books on spiritual matters. I made a retreat at a monastery, attended spiritual workshops, and became a Reiki master. Reiki is a form of gentle and soothing energy healing that we can give to ourselves and our children, friends, and pets. I tried many different types of therapy, meditation, and prayer. I sought to find meaning in my suffering so that I could transform it into something bigger than myself. My search led to a desire to research and write this book to help other women break the cycle of abuse and low self-esteem in their lives. This is important not only to help them recover their lives to live them more fully but also so that this cycle of abuse it is not passed on in to the next generation. Thank you for reading it and giving me purpose. My aspiration is that you find considerable information of value to you here throughout your divorce and recovery.

Your divorce is an opportunity for you to change, grow, and become the person God meant you to be. I hope it ends up being as huge a blessing for you as my divorce was for me. Although I certainly didn't see the divorce that way at the time because of the heartbreak and worry over financial issues that were aspects of the process, in the end it brought me much closer to God.

Your journey of recovery from your unhappy marriage will require you to let go of what is not working in your life, which is a loss that can feel like somebody died. The adjustment you will have to make to a new life paradigm will no doubt involve a period of mourning. Only by letting go of what is not working can you open a space for something brand new and better. The first step of letting go can feel like standing on a precipice and looking over the edge, knowing that you will have to take a leap of faith.

Many women who exit an abusive marriage remarry quickly, only to discover that their second husbands are abusers as well. They, in effect, end up marrying the same man in a different pair of pants. It is therefore important not to remarry too soon. Before you start a new relationship, ask yourself these questions:

- Why did I marry an abusive man in the first place?
- Did I have self-esteem issues before the marriage that made me vulnerable to being manipulated?
- Why did I continue to put up with the abuse?
- What can I do to repair my self-worth, which has been eroded over a long period, so that I can be at peace and cherish my life?

We are going to look at these and many other important questions together so that you can have a healthy and happy life, including a healthy relationship the next time you marry if that is what you want. It is necessary to take a hard look at yourself so that you can make the changes you need to make to have a better life and not repeat the mistakes of the past.

Looking closely at the choices you made is not going to be easy, but understanding and recovery are possible when viewed through the lens of compassion. Remember, you are worth it.

Although the divorce process is a painful one, it is necessary for your personal growth and welfare, as well as that of your children. Stop feeling guilty for what you have done and for what you have failed to do. Every single human being on this planet has done or failed to do things in ways that he or she later has come to regret. You are not your actions or how you were treated. You are not your past or your thoughts about your past. Your past should inform you, but it does not define you. Learn lessons from it and let it go. It is necessary for you to accept the reality of what is happening today. No more denial, no more excuses. It is time to act.

Women are the backbone of the family. As the members of our society who are primarily responsible for raising and nurturing our children, we have more of an impact on how our children are going to turn out in the face of abuse in the family than men do. It is time to break the cycle of verbal and physical violence that is so prevalent in our culture.

## FOR YOUR EYES ONLY

*"Out of suffering have emerged the strongest souls; the most massive characters are seared with scars."*
—KHALIL GIBRAN

This book contains a lot of information on legal and financial matters, available resources, and specific examples of good and bad decisions to help you to protect yourself and your children physically, legally and financially. The primary goal of this book, however, is to help you to take responsibility for your life and to heal mentally, emotionally, and spiritually so you may create the happy and fulfilling life that you deserve. You may have been too afraid or weak to end your unhappy marriage in the past, but now you are going to acquire the skills and strength that you need to do it.

This book is one of many resources that are available to you. Please keep it in a safe place where you know your husband is not likely to find it, or leave it at work.

Now, let's get started.

# PART ONE

# MARRIAGE—
# IT TAKES TWO

*"No man is good enough to govern any woman without her consent."*
—SUSAN B. ANTHONY

CHAPTER ONE

# THE TRUTH ABOUT HIM

*"Pay no attention to that man behind the curtain."*
—FRANK L. BAUM

## BEHIND THE CURTAIN

He seems calm and may even be being nice to you, then he suddenly screams at you for no reason, calls you names, or criticizes you in front of your children. This type of event can come on insidiously, like a fog slowly rolling in. You don't see it coming, but when it arrives, the air feels very heavy, damp, and oppressive around you. You are confused. You feel claustrophobic.

When you're married to an abusive man, he continues to ignore your requests for him to treat you respectfully. He never apologizes for his bad behavior—he won't even acknowledge it. He usually is good to you in public and saves the disparaging remark, raised eyebrow, or eye roll for the privacy of home. Over time he isolates you from your friends and family. He is increasingly controlling of even the smallest details of your life. Maybe he likes to invade your personal space, reading your mail and emails, going through your things, and standing way too close to you so that his presence feels invasive. Perhaps he yells and threatens you as he follows you from room to room. It could be that he judges you for every penny you spend, your weight, your clothes, your cooking, or how you interact with your kids. It might be that he insists that you spend every free minute you have with him. Maybe he controls your bank accounts and forces you to have sex when you are sick or exhausted. Or he refuses to help you and then screams at you if you point it out. After all, he has been training you through consistent intimidation not ever to criticize him. You dread being in his company because you always find yourself walking on eggshells around him.

An abusive man lies to your face, he fabricates stories, or he remembers a different past than you do, reconstructing it to make himself look good. He repeats the lies over and over until you think he believes that it happened that way. After a while, you may even start to wonder if maybe it was you who misremembered. You begin to question your sanity. If you point out the inconsistency of his recollection, he calls you crazy and other names not worthy of anyone. Of course, everything was and is your fault—from his point of view.

He believes that you are responsible for his moods and his mistakes, every one of them. He cheats on you. Or even if he doesn't, you feel cheated and dirty. He makes you feel worthless, inept. It is also possible that he mistreats you physically. You are bereft that you have given everything to this man who doesn't love you. *If I try harder, maybe he will love me,* you think.

But he won't. He can't.

That he won't or can't is one of the most important lessons you must learn, the reality you must face. You can't change him. He doesn't *want* to change. Why should he? He prefers to keep things the way they are. Your husband certainly isn't perfect, but he is not capable of self-criticism. The fact that you are unhappy does not bother him at all. It just gives him power. He feeds on it. You are in denial if you believe otherwise.

Like most abused women, it is likely that you are afraid of what your husband will do if you try to leave him. But you deserve better than this. We all deserve love for being who we are. You need to know that you are good enough just as you are. There are many good men—better men than he—who would appreciate you for who you are and the love you can offer. And what would be the worst that could happen to you if you left your husband and didn't meet a good man? Your situation would improve. You'd have nobody denigrating or hurting you. There are much worse things than being alone.

When I told my husband that I wanted a divorce, he screamed at me that I was going to hell. I told him that I was already there. And that was the truth.

## ABUSE DEFINED

*"Do not arouse the wrath of the great and powerful Oz.*
—FRANK L. BAUM

Most couples have disagreements from time to time. On occasion, one partner may cross the line and say things that he or she does not mean only to apologize profusely afterward. If the apology is made with sincerity and the offense not repeated, the couple can restore the relationship. In a healthy relationship, both partners value the needs of their partner as well as their own. They make compromises when necessary, and there are mutual respect and trust.

Unhealthy relationships are different. Abusers do not apologize sincerely after a disagreement or crossing a line. They do not value their partners' needs as much as their own. They do not compromise.

If you feel diminished or disempowered in any way by your partner on a regular basis, this is a sign you should not ignore that he is an abuser.

Not all abusers show the same traits. However, any combination of the traits listed below is a confirmation that you are dealing with an abusive person who needs to dominate, control, and manipulate you. If you are married to an abuser, he may:

- Have an explosive temper, which is frequently unpredictable and often for no apparent reason.
- Be extremely jealous of you and others.
- Mask his insecurity with an air of bravado.
- Check your cell phone log, text messages, and email, and read your old and current correspondence without your permission.
- Frequently put you down, be judgmental and hypercritical of you, perhaps raising one of his eyebrows or rolling his eyes in a show of contempt when you speak.
- Keep you up all night or wake you up to continue his verbal attacks on you.
- Be very controlling, telling you what you can and can't do.
- Isolate you from your friends and family, demanding that you spend all your time with him.
- Be possessive and suspicious, requiring you to explain every minute of your day, and disclose who you saw and what you discussed.
- Have mood swings and blame his bad moods on you.
- Make false accusations.
- Refuse to accept personal responsibility for his behavior, mistakes, or problems, shifting blame to others or you.

- Hold you responsible for his negative feelings and sense of well-being.
- Be abusive to you when he drinks or takes drugs, and then blame his drug of choice for the abuse. (Note that if he chooses to get high, he is choosing to abuse you.)
- Break your possessions or throw or strike objects.
- Blame you for his loss of self-control.
- Deny you access to money or financial information, taking your paychecks and withholding bill payments.
- Belittle or criticize you in front of your children.
- Believe in rigid stereotypical gender roles. He expects you to serve and obey him. He thinks that women are inferior and less intelligent than men.
- Let you know that he believes that you are inferior and defective.
- Expect you to be perfect and to fulfill all his needs. He also blames you for not living up to his unrealistic expectations.
- Start sex while you are still sleeping. He demands sex when you are ill or exhausted and shows no concern about whether you want to have sex. He forces you to have sex or hurts you or makes you perform any unwanted activity. (Note that being forced to have sex is rape, even if the perpetrator is your husband.)
- Either threaten you or threaten to hurt himself to manipulate you.
- Restrain you, hurt you, or disrespect you physically in various ways.
- Show no concern for your happiness and well-being.

## GASLIGHTING

*"Gaslighting is a form of psychological abuse in which false information is presented with the intent of making a victim doubt his or her own memory, perception, and sanity. It may simply be the denial by an abuser that previous abusive incidents ever occurred, or it could be the staging of bizarre events by the abuser with the intention of disorienting the victim. It is a way to manipulate the thoughts and behavior of the victim."*
—WIKIPEDIA

The form of abuse known as *gaslighting* is more common than one might think. You might not even recognize the extent to which it has been happening to you until long after your divorce is final and the fog in your mind clears. If like me, you wanted to assume the best about your husband, you may have charitably attributed a pattern of lies to either his faulty memory or yours. It is very destabilizing when someone intentionally deceives you, as you begin to doubt what you know is true. It makes you lose perspective and trust in yourself, which is what your partner wants. Nobody wants to believe that the man they married is manipulative and a liar.

My ex-husband threw coffee in my face on more than one occasion. It wasn't piping hot, fortunately, so it did not burn me. Although those incidents didn't leave physical marks on me, they were signs of utter contempt for me and did a lot of damage. I can only imagine what waterboarding would feel like, but I would guess this is very close. He later denied that he ever did such a thing while looking directly into my eyes, saying that he threw the coffee at the wall and not at me. I found his gaslighting to be as scary as the incident itself.

My ex-husband had lied many times before, and I always made some excuse for him, such as thinking that he or I was misremembering a situation and that something hadn't been done on purpose. He had reinvented the past on many occasions, always to put himself in a better light, and I had at times questioned my memory of events to give him the benefit of the doubt. But our daughter had seen him throw coffee in my face on one of those occasions, so she confronted him when she overheard him denying it. Even so, he refused to change his story, as he was incapable of admitting to having done something that was not in agreement with his grandiose self-concept.

The truth was that my ex-husband was a habitual liar and I had been making excuses for him to protect his self-esteem and our marriage. I also must have been subconsciously making excuses to protect myself. I didn't want to face the fact that I had married a pathological liar with no moral compass. The coffee incidents finally removed the blindfold from my eyes.

## NARCISSISM AND PSYCHOPATHY

If you have experienced extensive emotional abuse and your abuser lacks empathy, you are probably dealing with a narcissist or a psychopath, someone born without a conscience. Telltale signs include an exaggerated sense of entitlement and exploitation of others, but the primary sign is a lack of empathy. This man is a predator. The most important things to him are his self-esteem, looking good, and maintaining power and control over his victim—you.

If he is a narcissist, in the clinical sense, one or more of the following personality characteristics may apply to your husband.

- A grandiose self-image
- A sense of entitlement
- A lack of empathy
- Self-centeredness

If he has the antisocial personality of a psychopath, your husband's personality may be characterized by the following behaviors.

- Impulsive thrill-seeking
- Selfishness
- Callousness
- Lack of personal affect
- Superficial charm
- Remorselessness[1]

A very good fictional example of a man who displays narcissistic and psychopathic traits is James Bond. Disagreeable, erratic, highly deceitful, selfish, callous, and exploitative, his personality makes for good spy movies, but not for good husbands. I believe that the reason some women are attracted to this type of man in the first place is that they do not feel they have permission to take care of their own needs; initially, they are attracted to him because he knows how to take care of himself very well. They live vicariously through their mates until they realize that their husbands' self-centered behavior is destructive and hurtful to them. Sadly, they are often in the thrall of this bad boy behavior until after they become pregnant or have had children with these men, which makes it more difficult to disengage from the relationships.

## PHYSICAL ABUSE

Although emotional and psychological abuse can be just as damaging, physical abuse is much harder to excuse. If you have been slapped, kicked, punched, pushed, or choked, then your husband is a very dangerous man, and you must get out of the house and the marriage as soon as possible. Others may be aware of your situation because they have seen bruises or wounds on your body, or your husband may be deliberately hurting you in ways that enable him to avoid detection. He may be physically intimidating, shoving you or grabbing things out of your hand, or standing too close to you in a threatening manner while screaming and spitting in your face.

My ex-husband frequently invaded my space and followed me from room to room, not giving me any personal time or a moment's peace. He would pound on the bathroom door to make me unlock it, even if I was in the middle of using the toilet, while there were other bathrooms in the house that he could have easily used instead. He would insist that he needed to talk to me while I was using the bathroom or that he needed something that was in there. He wasn't ever willing to wait, even when I told him that I would be right out.

Those kinds of behaviors and boundary violations are degrading. It requires considerable time to heal the emotional wounds of this sort of treatment. After I had moved to a different house by myself, it took several months for me to stop being jumpy and hyper vigilant if I heard an unexpected noise at home. My startle response was very high, even in a public place such as a movie theater. It was embarrassing. I had been in such severe agitation and distress that I suffered from post-traumatic stress disorder.

In retrospect, I should have let my husband break down the bathroom door and then called the police with the physical evidence, which would have been the proof of abuse that I needed. I just didn't want to escalate a volatile situation while our children were present in the house. I also didn't value myself enough yet to refuse to be treated in such a barbaric manner. I chose to accept unacceptable behavior to avoid conflict, and that is on me.

## HE IS DEEPLY WOUNDED AND THEREFORE VERY DANGEROUS

In *The Wizard of Oz and Other Narcissists,* social worker Eleanor D. Payson explains the personality of narcissists and why change is so difficult for them. If your husband is a wounded narcissist, he treats you the way he does because he has low self-esteem that he covers up by putting you down to make himself feel better. He is projecting on you what he unconsciously feels about himself: that he is either worthless or inadequate and unlovable.[2] A man who is comfortable in his skin knows that he is going to make mistakes from time to time, and owns them. He makes amends and moves on to something else. A narcissist, by comparison, is unable to admit that he makes mistakes because admitting that he made a mistake means acknowledging that he is flawed. He is not able to see his problems, much less take responsibility for them.[3]

There is nothing you can do for your abusive husband or change about yourself that can make him happy. It is not possible. Also, it is not your responsibility to make anyone else happy. Each of us is responsible for our happiness and our feelings.

It is not necessary for you to understand this man or to even empathize with him. He does not have the capability reciprocally to empathize with you. Yours is what Payson terms a *one-way relationship.* Stop making excuses for his behavior. It's time to realize that there is only one thing that you can do: Get out of this marriage and save your life. He is inflicting insidious damage on you.

There is at least a four times higher rate of personality disorders among abusive men than among the general population, around 80 percent vs. 15–20 percent. So, if your husband is abusive, this is a sign that he is likely to be mentally ill and out of control.

Leaving him is a compassionate thing to do for him as well because it will prevent him from continuing his abuse of you and your children, which he would never want to do if he were well mentally. If you don't get out now, the abuse could escalate, and it is unlikely to get any better.

Here are some dreadful statistics of which you need to be aware.

- Women account for 85 percent of the victims of domestic violence in the United States.[4]
- More than one in three American women experience domestic violence in their lifetimes.[5]
- Their domestic partners killed 30 percent of female homicide victims in 2000.[6]
- Domestic violence affects women regardless of race or level of income, although black women and women with lower annual incomes are at greater risk of violence.[7]

Many women, including me, project good qualities onto their spouses that their spouses just don't have. This is wishful thinking, just a fantasy. We don't want to admit to ourselves that the person we thought we married has nothing to do with the man we are being abused by now. Even if you once loved your husband or still do, if he bullies and demeans you it is a sign that he does not love you. This is not your fault—he is incapable of love. He can't love you because he does not love himself. If he did love you, he wouldn't treat you as he does.

## PSEUDO SORRY: WORKS NOT WORDS

*"I have always thought the actions of men the best interpreters of their thoughts."*
—JOHN LOCKE

Your husband is not sorry for the things he does if he convinces you to stay with him and then continues to abuse you. He is not sorry if he makes excuses for what he does, if he fails to admit that what he is doing is abusive, and if he fails to accept responsibility for the abuse. He is not sorry if he blames you for his actions. He must agree to admit all the details of the abuse to a professional counselor if he is serious about saving your marriage and making real change in himself. If he is not willing to get ongoing counseling with a psychotherapist or even to admit to his abuse of you, he is never going to change.

And he won't need to change if you stay with him, either. There will be no motivation for him to do so. Unless he takes responsibility for the nature of his actions and their effect on you and your family, and unless he is willing to do whatever is necessary to change and make amends, he is not genuinely repentant for what he has done. Any apology he gives you is false and intended to fool you into maintaining the status quo unless it is backed up by a change in his behavior. Your husband is not genuinely sorry unless he makes an effort to be completely and consistently honest with you and treats you with respect as an equal partner in your marriage from now on.

If your husband acts as though he has remorse for a brief time and then reverts to his same old destructive patterns of behavior, it is time for you to acknowledge the fact that he is not sorry. It is not what he says that counts; it is what he does. Through his actions, he is showing you exactly who he is. This evidence is what you need to believe, not his words.

As difficult as acknowledging who he is may be, recognition of this is a positive step. Although he may be incapable of change, you are! You can change your life starting today.

## ENOUGH ABOUT HIM

*"The most difficult thing is the decision to act, the rest is merely tenacity."*
—AMEILIA EARHART

Now that you are clear on who and what you are dealing with, it is time to concentrate on you and what you deserve and want for your own life. If based on the preceding descriptions you have identified that you are in an abusive marriage, you must get a divorce. The abuse will not stop until you leave him for good. You will have to overcome any fears you have of what might happen when you leave so that you and your children can begin to live in peace and be happy. You can only build a better future by taking action. This is important to you and them.

Now is not the time for you to worry about what your husband wants or needs, or to wonder if he can survive without you. He is a born survivor, and he can take care of himself very well, thank you. My ex-husband was quick to find a replacement for me so that his needs would be taken care of. Love had nothing to do with it. He didn't skip a beat.

Let go of hope for what could have been and acknowledge the sad reality of what was. A good marriage with this man just wasn't ever going to happen with you or anyone else, either. Staying with him is dangerous. It's time for you to move on.

The power of love is not about power at all.

CHAPTER TWO

# THE TRUTH ABOUT YOU

## MIRROR, MIRROR

*"Owning our story can be hard but not nearly as difficult as spending our lives running from it."*
—BRÉNE BROWN

We are good daughters, sisters, friends, and mothers. We are good colleagues, homemakers, leaders, teachers, and neighbors. People may admire us or be envious of our apparently perfect lives. Even so, we are deeply ashamed of our failure at home to provide a stable, happy family for our children, our failure to make our husbands happy, and our failure to get them to stop abusing us. *If only we could be perfect, to get things right,* we think, *he would stop.* We dream of having someone appreciate us for who we are, of being appreciated by those who are supposed to love us the most.

It takes a while for us to realize that we can't change our husbands or make them happy no matter what we do. Once we've had this realization, we arrive at a fork in the road. We can turn left and give up and become numb. Or we can turn right and decide to fight for our very lives. Fighting is what I finally did when I realized that either I would have to get out or I would end up in an early grave. Until then, I was sleepwalking through life. When it got bad enough, it was a wake-up call.

My therapist called my ex-husband a joy killer. The energy vampire I married sucked me dry like one of the Dementors in the Harry Potter novels, foul creatures who drain peace, hope, and happiness from anyone near them.

Is that what your partner is like, too?

If you don't think you deserve better, please look at your children and then ask yourself: Does the mother of my children deserve to be treated like this? Does anyone? As I was, someone may have brainwashed you into thinking that you don't deserve to be treated with dignity, respect, or love. You must no longer be willing to accept the big, fat lie that your needs, wishes, and desires aren't important.

Many women who are married to abusive men, if not most, were either abused or neglected in their families of origin. But this is not always the case, as many abusive men are simply clever and charming; often they do not reveal their true colors until after their weddings. Psychologically speaking, women tend to be attracted to men who they think will enable them to revisit and possibly heal the unfinished emotional business of their childhoods.

Both of my parents were alcoholics, and I have many unhappy childhood memories. My father had a cruel streak as well as an explosive temper. He would sometimes get violent for no apparent reason when he came home from a stressful day at work, so I was always on edge. His long train commute home from work and excessive drinking didn't help matters. Like most women in the 1950s and 1960s, my mother didn't work, so he had money worries. I was a lightning rod for most of the physical abuse in our household, which was unpredictable and mostly unprovoked, although sometimes my sisters also experienced it.

My mother, who did not protect us from the abuse, was a depressed alcoholic who would frequently be sleeping off a bender in her bed when I got home from school, even as a young child. When I did get her attention, it wasn't safe, so I frequently hid in my room, studying, and stayed out of trouble. I did not realize until I was an adult that my mother wasn't rejecting me; she just wasn't able to cope with her depression and was oblivious to my pain and basic needs. It wasn't personal.

My father had transferred his overwhelming rage from a difficult childhood of his own, his combat experiences as a very young man in World War II, and his stressful job on to me. It was too much for him to manage on his own. He needed a scapegoat who couldn't fight back.

Neither of my parents had good role models of how to be a good parent, and they could not give me what they had never received themselves. Back in those days therapy was rare. They had no support to heal their pain. Now I can feel compassion for them. I understand they didn't know how to take care of me or to show me that they loved me while they were still alive.

My wounding as a child made me very vulnerable to a predator. I wanted so badly to have a relationship—to give and to receive love—that I overlooked the warning signs that were there while I was dating the man I married. My father had never noticed me unless it was to criticize or punish me. This treatment resulted in my being susceptible to marrying the kind of man that I did who criticized me mercilessly.

My husband was raised a Catholic, had never been married, and was educated and charming, although self-absorbed. To me, he looked like a good candidate for a husband. I took the chance to marry him. I thought I could make it work and make him love me by being a good and loving wife. That never happened, of course, no matter how hard that I tried.

I am not sure what your circumstances are, but it is quite possible that you did not value yourself enough to think that you had other options than to marry your husband, or that there was a good man out there somewhere you could meet who would want you and treat you with love and respect. There are such men, but you will have to learn to love yourself first before you are ready for a healthy relationship. Please treat yourself with compassion and do what you need to do to heal so that you can make better choices in the future.

In *Not Under Bondage,* domestic abuse expert Barbara Roberts, an evangelical Christian, does a good job of enumerating the reasons why women don't leave an abuser, which include trying to save her marriage, her life, and protect her children. She wisely states that submission is not consent. Here are some of the reasons she mentions.[1]

- Lack of identification of the problem
- Illness and lack of energy
- The children
- Belief in commitment to the marriage
- The relationship had some good parts
- Compassion for the spouse
- Traumatic attachment
- Shame
- Terror
- Disbelief or bad advice from others
- Lack of support from others
- Condemnation from others and self
- Fear of being able to cope on one's own
- A housing crisis
- Living in hope

For most of us, deciding to divorce is difficult enough without having to deal with our relatives, our friends, our communities, and our churches making us feel guilty about it. I finally came to the point where I decided to stop defending myself to others. I don't need to defend my life or my existence or my life decisions to anyone. I do the best that I can, praying for guidance from God, and that is enough. If you are going to be happy, you will need to do the same. The fact that you are here, alive right now, is all the proof that you need that you are valued, you are supposed to be here, and you have a divine purpose.

Show yourself some compassion and understanding for why you didn't leave your husband before now. You are leaving now, and that is enough. Don't expect support from others, or that they will know what to say even if they do want to be supportive. Many people do not want to take sides, especially if you have acted as if everything was fine before, and your husband presents himself as an upstanding, reasonable, and nice person in public.

Well-meaning friends and relatives may ask you thoughtless and hurtful questions, such as: Why didn't you leave him sooner? Why did you marry him in the first place? What did you do to make him angry? Why don't you try harder to make the marriage work? Or, why don't you just forgive him? Some may blame or judge you. Some may not believe that you are telling the truth about the abuse or your partner.

Other people will make hurtful comments when they are trying to be supportive because they don't understand what you have been through or how you feel about it. When others judge you to have brought this upon yourself, or expect you to "try harder" or to continue to tolerate the marriage and the abuse, my recommendation is that you not respond at all. Simply state that you are getting a divorce from an abusive spouse. You owe no one any additional explanation. If someone presses you for more details, firmly state that you are getting counseling from a professional. Then change the subject or walk away.

Visit Barbara Roberts' website, www.notunderbondage.com, if you would like to read more suggested responses to hurtful questions or comments.

If you do go to her website or read her book, which I think are helpful resources, please know that I do not agree with Roberts' opinion that you do not ever have to forgive your abuser. For the sake of your happiness, personal growth, and peace of mind, I think that it is very necessary—once the divorce is behind you and he can no longer abuse you—for you to forgive him. You will need to release him to release yourself. Keeping anger in your heart for years will block your happiness and make you a bitter person, vulnerable to disease. You will remain tied to him energetically if you don't forgive and release him and yourself at the appropriate time.

The whole point of going through the divorce is to be happy and at peace with yourself. Right now, you need to use your healthy anger in productive ways to help you get through this. Staying angry after the anger has served its purpose is not good for you at all. You forgive to set yourself free. Forgiveness does not mean tolerating abuse or forgetting that it happened to you.

It was too difficult for me to do alone, so I had to give my inability to forgive in prayer repeatedly over a long period to Archangel Michael for transformation into love. I finally admitted to myself, after much soul searching, that my ex-husband was an unbalanced individual who was doing what he thought he needed to do from a place of fear, and that it was tragic that he was unwilling to get help to deal with his problems. It eventually made me feel a lot of sadness and compassion for him. Although he is much too dangerous to for me to communicate with or be around, I felt lighter and at peace after forgiving him. I have concluded that what he feels or thinks about the divorce, or me, is none of my business. Today I want nothing in my heart except love.

## ALREADY JUSTIFIED

Throughout this book, I am going to offer you tools to help you get started down the path of recovering or building healthy self-esteem. For me, improving my self-regard has been and will remain a lifelong project. I have had to work through a lot of damage that occurred over five decades. I am still a work in progress. We all are.

Please do not blame yourself for what has happened. It is not your fault. Many women feel ashamed or responsible for the abuse that their husbands have perpetrated on them, partly because of having been brainwashed by their abusers. Do not buy into negative messages any longer. One thing you need to look at is why you tolerate it—not to judge yourself, but to understand it so that you can change the quality of your current and future relationships. Make the decision not to tolerate abusiveness any longer.

If you have engaged in the dynamic of verbal abuse with your husband, you may have become defensive, justifying yourself and your needs at every turn. I sometimes used to engage in arguments with my abuser to defend myself and became emotional in the way that I reacted. On occasions, I said things that I regretted later, even if they were in fact true. It doesn't matter. It was degrading to both of us to engage in attacking each other. It is hard to treat someone with respect who is degrading and condemning you.

Do not try to justify yourself any longer; you do not owe that to anybody. In God's eyes, we all have equal value. In your marriage, you gave your power to a cruel Wizard of Oz, a man hiding the truth that he is mentally and emotionally disturbed behind a curtain. He is not God. He has no right to judge you or anyone else. You must take your power back from him if you are going to have a happy and meaningful life.

Your future happiness is up to you and no one else.

Going through a divorce is hard enough, but divorcing an abuser is incredibly difficult. The process is going to change you as a person, and this is something that you need to embrace. You must change if you are going to avoid repeating this pattern of submission to unacceptable behavior, the negation of your needs, people pleasing, an inability to say no or to protect your boundaries, and so on.

Start saying no to requests for help when you don't have the time or desire to participate. Do not give an explanation or an excuse. Just say "I can't help you, sorry" or "I am not able to help, but thank you for thinking of me."

When somebody asks you for help with a project, try to remember that they usually want to dump something on you that they don't want to do themselves. Don't let anyone "volunteer" you without your consent, which people will try to do if they know you have been an easy mark in the past. Just say no. If someone presses you for a reason, do not explain, just say "I can't, but thank you."

Practice makes perfect. You will be going through a divorce for many months, and you need to marshal your resources for yourself and your children, instead of squandering them on other people's needs. The divorce is a wake-up call letting you know that you need to make some changes in yourself if you are going to be happy.

You must let yourself feel your feelings to heal. Have a good cry. Forgive yourself for any mistakes that you have made, and recognize that God loves you. Finding a few peaceful moments to meditate and pray every day may seem difficult, but it is essential that you try to do so every day to become calm and centered. It will give you strength.

## THE WALLS WHISPER

*"It is not what you do for your children, but what you have taught them to do for themselves, that will make them successful human beings."*
—ANN LANDERS

Even if you think that your children are too young to know, it is likely that they are aware of most of what is going on at home, which is not a safe place for them to be. Even if they are not abused personally, they are adversely affected when they witness or hear abuse or disrespect of their mother. If you continue to be abused as they get older, they will be at increased risk for emotional problems, such as anxiety and depression, as well as behavioral and academic problems. Although it is true that some children from abusive homes show no apparent symptoms of psychological distress, abuse affects how they view the world, their boundaries with themselves and others, and what is acceptable behavior with loved ones.

The good news is that children are resilient, and that love combined with direction and therapy can heal their wounds. Most children can overcome the effects of being in an abusive home through professional counseling, a loving family, and community support. The best gift that you can give them as their mother is to set boundaries as to what is acceptable behavior and model for them how people who love each other should treat one another.

Remember, you are sending them a message every day that you stay in an abusive marriage that it is OK for your husband to treat you the way he does. Do you want your son to grow up to be just like Dad? Or for your daughter to marry a man just like her father?

I didn't find out until long after the divorce that my husband had used physical violence against my daughter when I wasn't home to protect her. He yanked her by her hair and dragged her. My daughter finally told me about these incidents when she was in her mid-twenties. I was shocked. She told me that she felt angry that I hadn't protected her from the physical abuse.

My ex-husband was careful to make sure that I wasn't around when he abused her. If I had known, I believe that I would have left him a lot sooner than I did. I did not ask my children if he had been physical with them when I wasn't around, a grievous failure on my part. I think that I was too caught up in my pain to notice, and it brought me a lot of sorrow and grief to find that out later.

If you are abused, it is quite possible that your husband is also abusing your children when you are not around to see it, and they are too afraid to tell you.

## MOTHER KNOWS BEST

*"Start by doing what's necessary, then do what's possible, and suddenly you are doing the impossible."*
—SAINT FRANCIS OF ASSISI

I thought for a long time that I needed to sacrifice my happiness for my children. But what I modeled was a poor example to my daughter of what to look for in a husband and to my son of how to be a good one.

I tell my daughter now that happiness is a choice and it is her responsibility to make sure that she has a fulfilling and happy life. That responsibility belongs to nobody else but her. My son also knows how I feel about this issue, and I feel it is important that I show him by example.

I had hoped that my being a good wife and mother would make me happy. But it wasn't enough. I wanted a relationship based on mutual respect and love, where man and wife loved and took care of each other. I wanted to be able to state my needs and safely to disagree if I needed to. None of my needs was being met, and I was treated with contempt. I was very sad and hurt, turning my feelings inward, where they turned into depression and overeating. I came to believe that my needs and I meant nothing. This belief is common among domestically abused women. I was suffering from the martyr syndrome, and it was about time that I got down from the cross.

When you do not face the reality of your situation and do something to change it, you will continue to suffer. I stayed in denial of what was happening for way too long and so my suffering continued unnecessarily for years. It was up to me to end the suffering. Nobody else was going to do it for me.

Please don't stick your head in the sand and hope for things to get better in your own home. If you have already tried therapy and your husband is not willing to go with you, you must accept that he is not going to change. He may try to intimidate you by telling you how much money you are wasting unnecessarily, insisting that everything is fine, or claiming that you are crazy and defective. You need to face the reality of what you are dealing with and make the decision to stay or to leave.

One technique you may find helpful to make this decision is to get out a piece of paper and a pen, and write the following in two columns: A) the benefits of staying, and B) the benefits of leaving. If your husband is abusing you, there will never be a situation where the benefits of staying outweigh the benefits of leaving, even if you must struggle for a few years after you leave. Writing it down on paper will help you see this for yourself.

## SCRIPTURE STIGMA

*"You are not what others think you are. You are what God knows you are."*
—SHANNON L. ALDER

I thought God wanted me to sacrifice my life and stay married to a man who didn't deserve me out of a perverted sense of loyalty, as well as my Catholic sensibility. But this is not at all what God wants. As Neale Donald Walsch states so beautifully in his book *What God Wants,* God wants nothing because God already has and is everything that God ever could want. He is everything, and in everything, including you, so he doesn't need you to suffer. God wants us to be happy. God's will for you is your will for you. He asserts: "God cares for you by giving you the power to care for yourself. Each human being can create his or her own reality."[2]

I believe that the Bible was divinely inspired. However, I do not take its meaning literally. Whether you do or don't, if you are a religious Christian you may feel you need a spiritual justification for leaving your husband because you took vows in church when you got married.

My feelings of guilt when I was contemplating divorce were partly due to my upbringing and the strong emphasis on tradition in the Catholic Church. Like other people, I believe that a married couple who are not getting along have an obligation to try counseling to save their marriage, especially if there are children involved. But I also believe that a woman subjected to domestic abuse has the right—and the obligation—to leave her marriage as soon as she can. Your pastor or priest has a moral obligation to support you when you are the victim of domestic abuse. If your pastor tries to "stay neutral," the pastor is condoning the abuse you have endured by not holding your husband and abuser accountable—and you may need to point this out.

Nobody has walked in your shoes or suffered what you have had to endure. Some well-meaning people in your spiritual community may simplistically quote passages from the Bible or canon law to try to convince you that you are in the wrong for deciding to get a divorce from your abusive husband. Out of ignorance, they may say that even after your divorce you will remain married in the sight of God and that divorce is an unpardonable sin. Or someone might tell you that divorce is only allowed in the case of adultery. Those kinds of remarks can be very painful to hear and may leave you feeling isolated.

Many Christians believe that marriage has four purposes: to satisfy social needs for companionship, to satisfy sexual desire, to rear children, and to facilitate the divine plan for human redemption. It is important for you to recognize and grasp deep down that if you are in an abusive relationship, you do not have a true marriage. Continuing to tolerate abuse prevents your spouse from suffering the consequences of his actions and from "seeing the light." In fact, if the dynamic of abuse continues, it is going to be very difficult, if not impossible, for either of you to be filled with Spirit and at peace. This is not God's plan for either of you.

In a real marriage, both spouses share equal responsibility within the family, and it is up to the couple to decide who is responsible for which tasks or duties in the home, based on competency and preference. Decisions should be made mutually and cooperatively rather than on the basis of what is traditionally men's work or women's work. In Ephesians 5:33, the Apostle Paul calls on husbands and wives to be subject to each other out of reverence for Christ. And in Galatians 3:28, he says "There is neither Jew nor Greek, there is neither bond nor free, there is *neither male nor female*: for you are all *one* in Christ Jesus."

Your husband has violated your marriage by demeaning you and dishonoring you. With his abuse, he is treating you as having less worth than he does or none. You do not have a real marriage in God's eyes. My belief is that God hates violence more than he hates divorce.

Now, after years of counseling, I am aware that my low self-esteem, established firmly in childhood, allowed me to be vulnerable to accepting marital abuse in the first place because it was a familiar pattern to me. I also believed some flawed messages about what and who God is from my religious upbringing as a Roman Catholic, although it did give me a strong moral compass. The closer I feel to God, the more I can discern how much He loves me. God made us all in His image and did not make mistakes.

In 1 John 4:7–8, it is written: "Beloved, let us love one another: for love is of God, and everyone that loveth is born of God and knoweth God. He that loveth not knoweth not God; for God is love." I believe that if any woman stays in an abusive marriage, it is an abandonment of herself and a perversion of what God wants for her. I know this to be true in my heart of hearts.

While you are going through your divorce, it will be important for you to establish a personal connection with God yourself through reading, contemplation, prayer, and meditation. One of the gifts of divorce is the opportunity you are given to question everything, including your most closely held and cherished beliefs. Please do not fear this process. It is necessary for your personal spiritual growth. You can trust your discernment, for in Romans 12:2, it is written: "And be not conformed to this world: but be ye transformed by the renewing of your mind, that ye may prove what *is* that good, and acceptable, and perfect, will of God."

God is calling you to himself directly. How wonderful. No intermediaries are necessary for this to occur. It does not necessarily mean that you will change or sever your connection with your church. Questioning your beliefs may deepen your faith. The most important thing of all is that you have a more profound personal relationship with God.

The support system at your church can be a lifesaver for you, and some churches have divorce recovery support groups. Please check the website www.divorcecare.org to find a support group in your area. Personally, I had stopped going to church for a long time, but I now attend Mass again on occasion and get a lot more out of it.

My intention here is to encourage you to think for yourself, which is what God wants you to do. You may disagree with me on some of my points, and that is fine with me. I am glad that you are thinking about them. Do not live your life as others would have you do. They have no right to hold you under bondage. Live your life according to your convictions. Other people are not God and have no right to judge you. Talk to God directly and remember that God wants you to be at peace, not to remain in hell to please some judgmental, interfering person who doesn't have to live in hell with you. Stop being a people pleaser.

## TAKE THE WHEEL

*"The moment you are old enough to take the wheel, responsibility lies with you."*
—J.K. ROWLING

For years I mistakenly thought that God had abandoned me because my husband made me feel worthless. In fact, I had abandoned myself. Doing nothing and staying in a bad marriage is a passive choice, but a choice nonetheless. It has nothing to do with God's will.

Fear creates obstacles that we need to overcome. You may have a fear of violence, fear of recriminations, fear of ostracism or judgment by others, fear of being alone, or fear of having to stand on your own two feet. You will need to be brave and trust in yourself and in God to give you the tools you need to overcome your fears and reclaim your life.

When you are in a traumatic situation or feel depleted or scared, the most important thing that you can do is to take one day at a time. Sometimes I took things minute by minute to get through the day during my divorce. You may feel completely overwhelmed if you try to do more than that.

Take at least one positive action on your behalf every day, and do not underestimate your abilities. Who you are right now is good enough to sustain you through this crisis. You can do anything with God's help. God is more powerful than the abusive man you married. And you are, too. You just may not see this yet.

You likely have been deeply wounded by the abuse in your home. Now you need to gear up for battle in the legal system. You need to renew your energy, focus, plan, and heal to prepare for it. In Part Two, I will introduce you to strategies that can help you build your strength physically, mentally, emotionally, and spiritually, so you can do everything you need to do to be successful in navigating through the divorce and having a happy and productive life.

# PART TWO

# THE GREATEST LOVE OF ALL—TAKING CARE OF YOURSELF

*"You, as much as anybody in the entire Universe, deserve your love and affection."*
—BUDDHA

CHAPTER THREE

# BODY

## FEEL YOUR FEELINGS

*"The wound is the crack in which the light gets in."*
—RUMI

Although you know that you need to make changes, you may feel paralyzed by fear. You may be very afraid of your husband and want to leave him, but also of the prospect of getting a divorce and then being alone, paying the bills, and facing the uncertainty of your future.

Deep down you already know what you need to do. But you will need to summon up some courage to do it. Being brave doesn't mean that we are not afraid. It means that we know we are strong enough to feel our fear and still do the right thing anyway.

For a while, I thought that I felt angry because I was getting a divorce. It wasn't until after the divorce was final that I realized I had some very deep fears to deal with if I was ever going to be happy. I felt broken, unlovable, and afraid of my loneliness. I had felt lonely while married, but now I was a divorced woman in my mid-fifties who was overweight from having eaten my way through a bad marriage and divorce. What I had feared most all my life was being alone, and that fear is exactly what it was time to face.

We must face our biggest fears, as they have lessons to teach us. It is also important to allow yourself to experience your negative feelings, to feel sad and angry. I am not talking about wallowing in self-pity indefinitely, but fully feeling and then releasing your emotions. If you don't, they will hang around you like a dark cloud, eventually festering and turning into depression or a physical disease. Emotions are energy in motion.

A while ago, I spoke with my therapist about this issue. I had become angry at some things that my ex-husband had done out of vindictiveness two years after our divorce was final. I didn't want to feel angry anymore. I wanted not to feel anything at all so that it wouldn't bother me. My therapist told me that I was being unrealistic. He said I should go ahead and get angry. To rebuild my self-esteem, it was vital to honor all my feelings, the "good" ones and the "bad" ones. By going ahead and allowing myself to get angry, I would be able to release those feelings and get over the anger much more quickly than if I tried to pretend that I was not angry.

This advice has proven to be very helpful to me during the past several years. I discovered that my feelings belong to me and are my own business. I stopped giving my ex-husband the satisfaction of knowing when he got to me. And I realized that it had not been safe for me to feel or express my emotions in childhood or my marriage, so I had to remind myself that I was now safe and it was OK for me to feel them.

It is empowering to feel your feelings and then calmly make a conscious decision as to how you are going to respond to them. You will make better decisions when you realize that you have a choice of how you are going to react or even whether you will react at all. It helps to remember that feelings are not permanent. We need to embrace all those feelings, as they inform us if we are truly listening to ourselves.

Once you have separated, you can expect your husband to push your buttons emotionally. Divorce is a complicated and stressful process, made worse by the dynamic of abuse. He probably will make threats and invent unrealistic demands to try to convince you that you will lose everything if you leave him. How should you deal with that? The one thing that you can do that will help you the most is to ignore your husband as much as you can and try to stay out of his presence. Do not engage him by responding to negative emails or phone calls.

You can also practice spiritual aikido and dodge the negative energy, which will have no place else to go but back to its sender. Visualize a spiritual wall of protection around you whenever he is near, or he pops into your mind. Glinda, the good witch in *The Wizard of Oz,* had a beautiful white bubble around her. You could slowly breathe deeply in and out during stressful moments and visualize yourself in a similar bubble. Personally, I visualize a golden bubble of protection that is the Holy Spirit around me.

When it comes to matters related to your children's welfare, it will be better to respond through a third party whenever possible. For the rest of the time, don't engage him at all and just direct him to have his attorney contact your attorney. Figuratively plant flowers in your life to crowd out the poisonous weeds of his negativity until they die out.

If you want to deal with your divorce effectively, feel and then release your emotions about it as quickly as you can and make sure that prayer, deep breathing, and meditation become part of your daily practice. Even spending a few minutes engaged in one of these practices each day will pay huge dividends in your ability to stay grounded and calm.

During this period, seek out friends and activities that give you positive energy and nurture and affirm you. Avoid negative people. Visualize a happier life, and trust that it will soon come to pass.

Also, make lists. Stress affects short-term memory for many people, so it will make you less likely to forget important chores and obligations if you make a list and refer to it daily. Knowing you have a list you can rely on can be an anxiety reducer.

## HARNESS YOUR ANGER

*"Bitterness is like cancer. It eats upon the host. But anger is like fire. It burns it all clean."*
—MAYA ANGELOU

Anger that remains unexpressed or is dealt with ineffectively turns inward and transforms into depression or bitterness. If you ignore what your body is trying to tell you it can make you sick. Yes, you have good reason to be angry—infuriated by your husband for his atrocious behavior and outraged at the situation that you find yourself in. In time, you will forgive him and move on to be truly happy, but that effort needs to take place *after* the divorce process is final or else you might inadvertently allow your husband to continue to abuse you or to take advantage of you in the divorce settlement at great cost to you and your children. Before forgiveness must come the appropriate use of your anger.

Right now, you will have to put your armor on and fight for yourself, because your husband is going to come after you now with everything he's got—ruthlessly, vindictively, and relentlessly. That's what you should expect. If he stooped low enough to verbally or physically abuse his wife and the mother of his children, he is capable of a lot worse if he feels that he is not in control. Wounded animals are much more dangerous when they feel threatened.

Protect yourself by giving yourself permission to get and stay angry for a good long while. You must. You are going to need your righteous anger to propel you forward to act. Do not make excuses for your husband's behavior or harbor false hope that he is going to suddenly change his temperament and behave like a gentleman during the divorce. *Anger* is not a dirty word. It is a message from your body that you need to stand up for yourself. It is time for you to value your well-being, opinion, and feelings more than those of others. Channel your healthy, justifiable anger into productive action and use its energy to move in a new direction.

Use your anger to stand up for yourself in a constructive manner. It is part of the human condition, a sign that something is very wrong and needs correction. I am not talking about taking reactive, vindictive, or destructive actions. Those types of responses could be dangerous for you if your husband is a violent person. Rather, use your anger to take actions that help you to protect and defend you and your children. Anger wakes us up and gives us necessary strength.

The physical symptoms of anger include feeling hot in the neck and face, perspiring, clenching the jaw, shaking or trembling, dizziness, headache, stomachache, and rapid heart rate. When I got angry with my husband, it would overwhelm me. My tongue would feel thick, and my brain would freeze so that I could barely speak, much less defend myself in argument, after years of accumulated anger. Both my face and neck would turn bright red, and I would feel a pit in my stomach as if I had been sucker punched. I was afraid of my anger, so I tried to suppress it.

If your anger issues are unresolved and chronic, you may feel anxiety, muscle tension and pain, nausea, heart palpitations, tightness in the chest, tingling, problems with concentration and memory, and fatigue. You may repress your anger and feel hopelessness or depressed. You may suppress the feelings in your body and just feel numb and detached. You may resort to drugs, alcohol, overeating, or some other compulsive behavior, such as excessive spending or gambling, to try to help you forget your feelings.

It may be necessary for you to find a psychiatrist to get medication to help you deal with some of these symptoms; however, you also need a therapist to guide you on how to deal with the root of your anger and teach you how to process your feelings in a healthy manner. Before you consent to take any medication, ask about the side effects and whether the drug is addictive. Be sure always to follow dosage instructions and contact your doctor immediately if you experience side effects or find yourself craving more medication than was prescribed.

If your anger and anxiety go unresolved for too long, your immune system may become compromised, and you will be at heightened risk for stroke, high blood pressure, colds and flu, gastrointestinal problems, coronary heart disease, and even heart attacks, chronic sleep disorders, and serious memory loss. Those are just the physical risks. There are also emotional, mental health, and spiritual risks to consider.

After my divorce, when I was physically safe from abuse, I finally realized just how bad the abuse I had endured was. Until then, I had been so numb that I wasn't even aware that I was suffering from post-traumatic stress syndrome (PTSD). It took a very long while to heal, but I could finally feel alive again without all that anger and pain.

## LISTEN TO YOUR BODY TALK

*"The true warrior is not immune to fear. She fights in spite of it."*
—FRANCESCA LIA BLOCK

Many abused women develop eating disorders, chronic anxiety and depression, gynecological problems, and other physical and emotional problems, as well as drug and alcohol addiction. If you don't think that you have any problems related to the abuse in your marriage, you need to see a therapist and find out why you are in denial. You can't cure that of which you are not aware. If you are abused, whether physically or verbally, your body is in distress. Constant exposure to fear and violence is linked to a weakened immune response, premature aging, and learned helplessness, a state of mind in which you think that everything is so bad that there is nothing you can do but give up and remain a victim, feeling trapped and hopeless.

Violence is not just physical; it can take the form of constant verbal attacks on you that instill fear or compromise your well-being. Throughout this, your body is talking to you by giving you the gift of anger, depression, anxiety, fear, and other signs. I believe that God speaks to you through your gut instinct and other physical and emotional messages that you feel in your body.

We all were much more intuitive as children. But we usually lose the precious gift to trust ourselves and others as we get older. We tend to ignore important messages that our bodies tell us, like the signal to stop eating when we are full. More importantly, we are the only species on this planet that ignores the sense of danger that we feel when we encounter someone who intends us harm. We dismiss our sense of self-preservation if we are afraid of being viewed as impolite or ridiculous by a predator when we really should be protecting ourselves.

Pay attention to what your body is telling you. If you have a sick feeling in your gut or your heart races with fear or dread whenever your husband opens the door and walks in, something is wrong. If you feel bad physically on a frequent basis when he is around, or you are getting sick with one illness after another, your body is speaking volumes to you. You may even save your life by acting upon your instincts. A 2014 Violence Policy Center study reveals that over thirteen times as many women were murdered that year by a man they knew (1,388 victims) as were killed by men who were strangers (107 victims).[1] According to an article by Robert Preidt in the *U.S. National Library of Medicine* (January 28, 2016), more American women are killed by someone they know in states with high rates of gun ownership.[2]

Don't believe everything that you think. Believe your body talk instead. You are not helpless, even if you think you are. You simply have been brainwashed to be compliant for a very long time by a very sick man. Your body knows the truth and is trying to get your attention. Trust your gut feelings, as they are important. You need to get out of there, and your body is telling you to do just that if you will only listen.

## GOOD EATS

*"I choose to make the rest of my life the best of my life."*
—LOUISE HAY

Pay attention to what you eat and drink, especially while you are under stress. If you deprive your brain of good nutrition, it will not function when it is crucial for you to have your wits about you. Your decision-making will be greatly improved during this crucial time if you watch your diet. It is also an act of self-love.

You deserve to be healthy, and there is no time like the present to start good habits. Here are a few guidelines to follow.

- Drink at least eight glasses of water every day
- Take a multivitamin
- Cut down or eliminate processed foods, desserts, sugar, and artificial sweeteners, which will only make you crave more carbohydrates and sugars. Also, cut back or eliminate white foods, such as potatoes, white bread, pasta, or any other foods with a high glycemic index, as they contribute to obesity, diabetes, and poor cardiovascular health. Too many carbs can cause you to feel fatigued later in the day
- Eat a lot of fresh produce—try to ingest a rainbow of colors every day
- Stop buying soda, processed snacks, or desserts at the grocery store to save money so you can spend more on nutritious fresh fruits and vegetables
- Avoid caffeine after two in the afternoon so that you will be able to fall asleep at a reasonable hour

One thing most women are concerned about is aging, and inflammation is a main contributor to the aging process. Chronic inflammation leads to strokes and heart attacks, and there is evidence that it may cause some kinds of cancer. To reduce it, drink plenty of water and incorporate foods into your diet such as: extravirgin olive oil, walnuts, broccoli, fatty fish, grass-fed beef, grapes, cranberries, cocoa, red wine, and tea. Drink cocoa with skim or low-fat milk to reduce the saturated fat content. Sugar in the form of high-fructose corn syrup, as is found in many processed foods and soft drinks, contributes to obesity and is also very hard for your liver to metabolize. Chronic consumption of this ingredient elevates uric acid, which is damaging to your kidneys and causes inflammation.

It is also important that you floss your teeth daily to avoid inflammation in the mouth, as it can lead to periodontal disease and is linked to heart attacks.[3]

Mindful eating is going to make a huge difference in the way you feel physically and the way that you feel emotionally about yourself. The battle will be won in the grocery store and the kitchen. Shop the perimeter of the grocery store, since that is where the healthy foods are. You need to maintain your strength while you are going through this stressful ordeal, so be kind to yourself and eat well. This means consuming lean meats, fish, and plenty of fruits and vegetables.

You may not feel up to cooking, so adapt and learn some tasty short cuts. For example, to avoid cooking, you could buy a cooked rotisserie chicken at the grocery store and throw together a salad. This will take less time and cost less money than eating out. Use the leftover chicken to make chicken salad, and have soup and sandwiches the next evening. Or use it in a cheese quesadilla, white bean chili recipe, or a chicken casserole recipe with cheese and cream of whatever Campbell's soup.

Keep it simple. Learn to cook more and love leftovers. They are your friends. You have a lot going on right now and need to preserve energy and time. Do a Google search for fast and easy healthy recipes. Toss a beef roast in your crockpot on low with a few ingredients before you leave for work in the morning.

You want your children to have a good diet, and they will learn by your example. Put well-balanced meals on the table to ensure that they eat healthy most of the time. In doing so, you may find that you lose a little weight if that has been a problem for you in the past. It is fine to have pizza or to eat out occasionally, just not all the time. There is no lasting comfort in comfort food because it makes you fat. You will feel better about yourself if you take care of your body and if you are a good role model for your children.

The smell of home cooking sends a message to your children that they are loved and cared for. You already know that homemade meals are much healthier for your family and less expensive than relying on fast food.

If you don't know how to cook, now is as good a time to start as any. Cooking will distract you and keep your mind off your troubles. It will also save you money and help you stay on a budget. You can find all kinds of information and easy how-to videos on cooking websites and YouTube. After the divorce, you may also want to go to cooking classes to meet other people as well as learn useful skills. Some local high schools offer very affordable evening classes during the winter months for parents on a wide range of topics, including meal preparation, or you can find classes taught by local chefs held at private homes.

Before you go to the grocery store on Saturday, decide which recipes you plan to use during the week, make a list, and buy the ingredients you will need. Encourage your children to participate in menu planning and in trying new things. You can plan it so that you only need to cook three or four nights a week and then eat leftovers the rest of the week. Also, encourage your children to help you cook. If they are old enough, they can peel and dice veggies, set the table, and do the dishes. Chores are good for children. They need to learn how to cook so that they can become independent and healthy adults. Doing these things together as a family will also help bring you together.

Do not allow phone use or eat in front of the TV during dinner. There is no communication or real connection while everyone is staring blankly at a screen. You may find out some very important information about what is going on in your children's lives if you show them that you care by asking open-ended and nonjudgmental questions at the dinner table. They need to feel safe, valued, and loved during this difficult time of transformation—as do you.

# MOVE IT

*"Take care of your body. It's the only place where you have to live."*
—Jim Rohn

Exercise helps to reduce stress by releasing chemicals that increase our sense of well-being. Aim to exercise three or four days a week for at least half an hour. This regimen will help you to be alert and give you the stamina you need while you are in this stressful situation of getting a divorce. It will also improve your memory and mood. Also, taking the time to exercise is an act of self-care that will improve your self-esteem.

Go for walks in nature and pay attention to the sights, smells, and sounds around you. Breathe the fresh air. Notice the birds, squirrels, and other animals that cross your path. You need some time alone to process your thoughts, ground yourself, and reconnect with your spirit. The natural environment is the perfect place to unwind and think.

My mother did not take care of herself, and neither did I for most of my marriage. I didn't know how to, partly because I didn't have a good role model. Neither did she, so I am not blaming her. Once I became an adult, it became my responsibility to learn how to do this. It is your responsibility to love and take care of yourself. This approach is often a lot harder than it sounds. Especially if you have an abusive and controlling husband, who demands that you put yourself last. Now that you are divorcing, choose not to do that. If you must get up an hour earlier in the morning to create time for your workout, get up. It may surprise you that you feel much better, stronger, clearer, and more energized when you do.

Exercise will help you reconnect with your body. When I have been unable to stop a negative eating pattern, focusing on exercise has helped to get me back on track with better habits, such as eating more healthy foods and drinking more water. It has a ripple effect on all my other behaviors. Please do keep in mind that maintaining a healthy body weight is 30 percent exercise and 70 percent eating habits. Make both a priority. Make *you* a priority.

Yoga is another wonderful form of exercise for reducing stress and bringing you into present-moment awareness. On a regular basis, you need to be able to set aside your problems temporarily so that you have time to heal and recover. You will focus more on your breathing and how conscious control of your breath helps you to regain your balance and some modicum of peace when you are doing yoga. You also will become more flexible and stronger. There are several side benefits to yoga as well. For example, you may start paying more attention to how the food you eat affects your body and become a more mindful eater. It may give you a real boost of confidence as well as a heightened self-awareness and a more positive attitude.

Qigong, a practice of aligning breath, movement, and awareness with origins in China, can also help you to reduce stress and get back in touch with your body as well.

You could take Zumba or a dance class to get moving. The music will lift your mood so that you forget about yourself and your troubles for an hour. It will also help you to firm up, which is great for your self-esteem. I try to go to Zumba classes three times a week. I look utterly ridiculous jiggling to rap and pop Latino music, but that is the music the much younger instructors prefer to play. It is good for my health and keeps me humble.

# THE M AND MS: MASSAGE AND MEDICATION

*"Nothing is so healing as the human touch."*
—BOBBY FISCHER

Massage therapy will help you to relax and reconnect with your body. The caring touch of another person in a safe space is healing. Research suggests that massage reduces high blood pressure and may boost immunity, as several studies have found there are dramatic decreases in the stress hormone cortisol after massage sessions. Massage may help you to avoid getting a cold or other illness while you are under stress. It creates chemical changes that reduce pain and stress throughout the body by reducing the brain chemical substance P that is related to pain. People with fibromyalgia, a form of muscle pain, showed less substance P in their saliva and reported a reduction of pain in a TRI study after a month of twice-weekly massages.

Try to get weekly massages, but even every other week would do you a lot of good. Just being touched and treated with care regularly by someone who is safe is therapeutic.

Many massage therapists are spiritual, which is one reason why they feel called to the profession. I have been going to the same massage therapist for many years; she is a real healer with an intuitive sense of touch. I do not have to tell her where my body hurts or is sore. She senses it. Deep tissue massage can help to release the emotional pain that is unprocessed and held in the body. Through therapeutic massage I have been able to let go of a lot of very old emotional pain from childhood, some I didn't know I was still carrying around. These stuck emotions probably would have turned into a disease if I didn't get them out of my body.

If you try one massage therapist and that person is not a good fit for you, try someone else. There are also therapeutic massage devices that you can buy to help you relax so that you can get a decent night's rest.

Be sure to drink plenty of water after getting a massage, as a massage usually causes a lot of toxins to release, and you need to flush them out of your body. Try taking a relaxing bath afterward with Epsom salts as well to draw out toxins and reduce inflammation.

If you can't sleep or if you become depressed, see a psychologist or therapist for counseling. See a psychiatrist if you believe you need a prescription. You are going through a lot of emotions and are under a lot of stress. If you haven't had a physical in a long time, please schedule a complete checkup with your medical doctor. Make sure that you ask about the side effects of any medication prescribed to you before you agree to take it, and consistently follow the instructions your doctor gives you for taking the medication.

In most cases with an antidepressant or sleep medication, you will need to avoid drinking alcohol completely. It is a good idea for you to avoid or at least limit alcohol right now anyhow, as it is a depressant. Where possible, try some of the natural ways to reduce stress that I outline in this book instead of taking a drink.

You do not need to compound your problems by becoming an alcoholic. You need to be fully present for yourself and your children. If you are already an alcoholic or believe you are heading down that path, go to an Alcoholics Anonymous meeting as soon as possible.

If you suffer any side effects from a prescription medication, stop taking it and call your doctor immediately to discuss it. If your doctor is unresponsive to your concerns, go to a different doctor right away. Always listen to your body and respect its messages to you.

If you are perimenopausal or menopausal, your hormones may be wreaking havoc with your emotions and affecting your ability to get uninterrupted sleep. Christiane Northrup's book *The Wisdom of Menopause* explains how to deal with the changes in your body and how they are a wake-up call for the next phase of your life. I started going to a female doctor who specializes in bioidentical hormones when my male gynecologist told me that I would just have to live with the hot flashes and night sweats. I seriously doubted that he would put up with waking up soaking wet every night, so I found his remark patronizing and dismissive. I found immediate relief under my new physician's care. She also solved my inability to fall asleep at night. Making small changes that she suggested, such as taking magnesium and melatonin right before bedtime, solved my problem naturally.

Check with your doctor to make sure that anything you take is appropriate. Your doctor should review the current list of medications and supplements you take to advise you properly.

## JUST BREATHE

*"If you want to conquer the anxiety of life, live in the moment, live in the breath."*
—AMIT RAY

The hardest thing to do if you are depressed or stressed about your marriage and your life is, well, anything. You may become so depressed and lethargic that you forget to eat or oversleep. You may have barely enough energy to get through the day. That's when you need to breathe. The best thing that you can do for yourself during this time is to breathe deeply and often.

The miracles of life and healing both start with the breath. Your breath will help you to be more alert and to think more clearly and calmly during moments of stress if you will remember to stop and breathe first before you respond, instead of reacting impulsively. I have noticed that at times of stress and anxiety I sometimes stop breathing altogether. Also, that breathing calms me down—when I remember to do it.

Learning how to breathe properly takes practice and mindfulness. It will calm you and keep you grounded if you will take the time to slowly breathe deeply into your gut several times a day, noticing where in your body you are tense, and deliberately relaxing those areas. It will also bring your awareness back to the present moment, which is where you must stay focused if you are going to get through your divorce successfully. Mindful breathing can also help you to control your negative emotions and reduce insomnia.

Remember that you still need to feel your feelings, including anger. Deep breathing will allow you to remain in control when you're angry and decide what your exact responses are going to be. Being able to stay in control of yourself is to be able to respond rationally and strategically instead of abruptly and reactively, which may not be in your best interest.

Breathe deeply into your lower abdomen, not shallowly into your upper chest. Count to four, breathing slowly in through your nose and down into your lower abdomen. Hold for a count of two, and then breathe out slowly through your mouth for a count of four. Do this from five to ten times, until you are relaxed. Repeat often throughout the day, every day, as needed.

If you are agitated or anxious, another breathing technique you could try is to close off your right nostril with your right thumb while you put your right middle or index finger on your forehead to stabilize your hand. Breathe in solely through your left nostril to a count of four, hold for a count of two, and then release your right thumb and close off your left nostril with your right ring finger and little finger, and breathe out through your right nostril to a count of four. Repeat this process for up to ten minutes. If you are left-handed, it's OK to use your left hand to open and close your nostrils. Use the hand that makes you feel more comfortable.

If you are groggy, have low energy, or feel more depressed during the daytime, use the opposite pattern of nostril breathing. Close off your left nostril and breathe in through your right. Exhale through your left nostril. Keep the same counts of four in, two held, and four out.

If you want balance, concentration, and mental clarity, try alternate nostril breathing, where you breathe in and out the same nostril and then switch sides. Keep the same counts of four in, two held, and four out.

*Caution:* If you begin to feel lightheaded, stop immediately and go back to your normal breathing pattern. If you have recently had surgery, ask your doctor if deep breathing is OK to do.

Breathing is one of the most important things you can do for yourself while you are going through your divorce because your breath is the source of your life force. It is good for your soul. In Genesis 2:7, it is written: "And the Lord God formed man of the dust of the ground, and breathed into his nostrils the breath of life, and man became a living soul." Rabbi Rami Shapiro told a small group in a meeting that I attended that when you die God kisses you on the mouth and takes your breath back. So, breathe in and be mindful. Every breath is a gift.

## WATER WELLNESS

*"The cure for anything is salt water: sweat, tears, or the sea."*
—Isak Dinesen

Be sure to drink eight to ten glasses of water a day, each day. Most of us do not drink enough water. Beside the air that we breathe, water is the most important thing we put into our bodies. It helps to regulate our physical functions and carries vital elements such as oxygen, hormones, and chemical messengers to all the parts of the body. It is necessary for the breakdown and absorption of nutrients as well as to remove toxins from the body. Symptoms of dehydration are frequently misdiagnosed. These include a lack of energy and physical pain, especially in the joints. Water deficiency plays a role in many health disorders, including Alzheimer's disease and inflammation, according to Dian Buchman, author of *The Complete Book of Water Healing*.[4]

On average, the adult human body is about 57 percent water. Yours was as high as about 75 percent water when you were born, decreasing in water content with age. It can be as low as 45 percent in an obese person. Thirst is frequently mistaken for hunger.

A good plan is to pace your water consumption so that you drink it at intervals throughout the day. Aim to drink a glass of water before breakfast, another before going to work, one at mid-morning, another at lunch, another at midday, one in the afternoon before leaving work, another at dinner, and the last in the evening about an hour before bedtime. Note that if you drink too close to bedtime, you may need to make an extra trip to the bathroom in the middle of the night.

It may take a while for you to be able to build up to eight glasses daily, so increase your water consumption gradually. Remember, coffee, tea, and soda do not offer the same benefits as pure water.

One unanticipated side benefit of starting to drink so much water was that I had to get up out of my chair at work to go to the restroom more often. I sometimes would sit for hours, forgetting to get up and stretch and becoming stiff and sore because I was not paying attention to my body. I was so absorbed in work that I was living only in my head. Drinking water got me out of my head and back into reconnecting with my body.

Take long baths if you can. Baths have been used for centuries to relax, heal, and detoxify the body. Epsom salt baths are helpful after exercise or a massage to reduce swelling and remove toxins. Baking soda can be used to relieve itching and for rashes. Turmeric soothes arthritic joints, beer helps with psoriasis and other skin conditions, and seaweed has been used for centuries to reduce the appearance of cellulite. I frequently meditate and pray while I soak, or just reflect on the day. Listening to relaxing music while in the tub will help soothe your frayed nerves as well as improve your mood.

## THE NOSE KNOWS

*"Nothing can beat the smell of dew and flowers and the odor that comes out when the sun goes down."*
—ETHEL WATERS

Natural scents can be calming and healing. Aromatherapy uses essential oils extracted from the flowers, bark, stems, leaves, or roots of plants as a form of alternative medicine to enhance well-being. It is important to use pure essential oils, as synthetic oils offer little positive effect. The inhaled aroma from these essential oils sends messages to the brain that enhance mental and emotional well-being. Some also have therapeutic physical benefits when applied topically in a carrier oil, such as coconut oil, jojoba oil, almond oil, or grapeseed oil.

Different oils may reduce muscle tension, improve mood, and promote relaxation and calmness. Lavender, ylang ylang, chamomile, and clary sage oils, for example, are used to soothe anxiety and stress. They affect your mood because the olfactory bulb, which analyzes smells and is part of the limbic system, is connected with the regions of your brain that handle both memory and emotion. Note that odors can trigger vivid memories, so it is important to seek out scents that calm and soothe you.

You can find many essential oil diffusers online, electrical devices that spread the aroma of essential oils throughout a room, usually in a fine water mist. You can also use the oils with a humidifier by sprinkling a few drops of the oil on a tissue and holding it in front of the escaping steam. Do not put the oil directly into the humidifier, as it will just float on top of the water instead of being dispersed in the air with the water vapor.

*Caution:* If you are or suspect that you may be pregnant, or you are breastfeeding, seek professional guidance before using essential oils. If you are concerned about skin sensitivity, do a small test with a tiny drop of oil on your skin. A good rule of thumb is to start with a little before you use a lot. Always follow the directions provided by the manufacturer.

Exposure to the scents of trees, flowers, and the soil whenever you're outdoors is also therapeutic. While going for walks and working in the garden, be sure to breathe the wonderful smells of nature, which will calm and heal you. Exposure to natural scents will help you appreciate being alive. There is something reassuring in knowing that miracles of nature are happening all around you and you are part of a bigger plan. The roses are just as beautiful and the sunset just as magnificent even if you have troubles.

Take off your shoes and feel the earth beneath your feet. It will keep you grounded.

Spend a few dollars every other week on flowers. The benefits to your mood and emotional well-being of having beauty and pleasant scents in the home are immense. Consider their purchase money well spent, even if you are on a tight budget.

## DREAM WEAVER

*"Little girls who dream become women with vision."*
—AUTHOR UNKNOWN

If you are to get through this highly stressful period of your life successfully, it is important for you to get quality sleep on a consistent basis. A lack of sleep can contribute to obesity, impaired immune function, diabetes, and depression.[5] It can also decrease your ability to be optimistic and sociable, negatively affecting emotional intelligence and the ability to think constructively.[6] At night, not only do our bodies eliminate toxins and other metabolic wastes that have built up during our waking hours, but our brains also process and consolidate new information and memories, make creative connections, solve problems, and remember how to perform tasks.[7] Sleep is the critical way that our minds save our memories and cement everything we have learned in our long-term memory banks so that it can be remembered and utilized.

You must get enough sleep to be able to think critically and have the energy during the day that you need to function. If you don't get enough sleep during the divorce, you will be much more likely to make unnecessary mistakes.

The best way to protect your sleep is to maintain a regular sleep schedule, exercise regularly, limit caffeine and alcohol intake, eliminate noise and light, and turn off the television, cell phone, and other electronic devices for at least an hour before bedtime. Try not to eat for three hours before bedtime, even if it means rescheduling dinner for an earlier time. Avoid engaging in conversations with your husband that might be likely to escalate into arguments as these will affect your peace of mind.

Take a bath right before bedtime, read, pray, or meditate. Wind down. Try using a white noise machine to sleep if you can't eliminate noise completely from your environment.

Make sure that the temperature in the room is comfortable and that the room is dark.

I found that I slept better if I laid out my children's clothing, as well as mine, for the next day before going to bed. I also made their lunches the night before so that I wouldn't have to worry about those in the morning. Do as much as you can at night so that you can lay your head on the pillow with fewer worries. May you sleep with the angels.

CHAPTER FOUR

# MIND

*"Forever is composed of nows."*
—EMILY DICKINSON

Your presence is a gift. So long as you are breathing, you have a unique purpose and contribution to make to your children, your family, and the world. Your husband has tried to convince you that you are worthless to maintain control over you and feel better about himself. What he is doing is wrong and damaging to you both. Remember that your children need you and that you deserve love and respect, as we all do.

Stop believing the nasty things your husband says. He is very likely suffering from mental illness, or he wouldn't have treated you so poorly. Would you believe everything that any other mentally ill person told you? The fact that he is ill does not excuse or condone what he has done. But it does mean that you must remove yourself and your children from the toxic and potentially dangerous situation of sharing a home with him. Brainwashing is a powerful tool that most abusers use to keep their victims powerless.

If you have already separated from your husband or you are in the middle of divorce proceedings, do not let down your guard. Stay focused on what is going on right now so that you can make good decisions about what to do next. If the focus of your attention is on the past and what he's done to you, then you are spending your time unproductively. Refocus your attention on your children and what you need to do right now to get out of a bad situation.

Limit your grieving to from twenty minutes to a half hour while you are in the bath at night after your children are in bed. I used to call this time my "pity party" time. It was something I looked forward to for release after a stressful day so that I would not mentally and emotionally check out while I was with my children. Yes, you have regret and sadness, and you will need to do a lot of grieving over the marriage that you should have had, the husband that you should have had, and not what you did have. But the best time for mourning and regrets is *after* you get out of the situation and through the divorce.

Right now, you need to concentrate on more important things during most your day: your children, your job, your self-care, and preparing for the divorce. Do not berate yourself for what you did or said, or for what you failed to do or say, as self-criticism is unproductive and won't change anything anyway. It will only keep you stuck in the past. If you resist what has happened to you in the past, then you are resisting what is going on right now in your life. And whatever you resist persists, to paraphrase psychologist Carl Jung.

Acceptance is the key to the possibility of change. Accept that nobody is perfect. Accept that you have always done the best that you could under very difficult circumstances. Accept that you are in an unhealthy situation. Acceptance is the door that opens to the path of change.

Concentrate on what you are doing right now. Accepting your current reality can give you the power to change it. The present moment is the only moment in which we can act or make a difference. Take life one moment at a time so that you do not get emotionally overwhelmed or feel discouraged.

Stay fully present for your children as well as for you. Their childhoods will disappear before your eyes while you are wallowing in self-pity and regret over the past. Enjoy your time with them. The most important gifts you can give your children are your time, your attention, and your love. These have infinitely more value than high-tech games, fancy clothes, or expensive vacations. If your husband can give your children those things after the divorce and you cannot afford them yet, don't worry. What they need from you is your presence and undivided attention. They need you to create and maintain the loving relationship with them that they and you deserve.

If you worry about the future, you may become paralyzed with fear. Worry can keep you from making progress in doing the things that you need to do right now. If you do what you need to do in each moment as the moment presents itself, the future will take care of itself. Plan for the future, but keep focusing your attention on what you are doing today.

Do you feel afraid? If so, what do you fear? If your fear is for your safety or the safety of your children, then your body and mind are telling you to take immediate action. If you feel fearful about the future, bring your attention back to the present. Instead of worrying, pray for guidance, right thinking, and a good outcome for you and your children, then plan carefully and act. Working on a plan and having a good plan in place will reduce your anxiety.

Focusing on the present moment and what you need to do right now will give you the clarity you need to make better decisions regarding your divorce and the future life you want for your family.

# EGO AND SELF: PRIDE AND JOY

*"I believe that each of us comes from the Creator trailing wisps of glory."*
—MAYA ANGELOU

In *The Power of Now,* Eckhart Tolle encourages us to learn from a past mistake, but says that it is a mistake to "dwell on it mentally so that self-criticism, remorse, or guilt come up."[1] That unproductive dwelling on the past makes it part of your sense of self which always will be linked to a false sense of identity. You are not your past or what has happened to you, so don't let the past define who you are. You are not a failure or a screw-up, or incompetent or stupid.

You are a spiritual being living in a human form, with human limitations. If you expect yourself to be perfect, you are holding yourself to a higher standard than the rest of humanity. The fact that your husband expected perfection from you, as most abusive men do of their wives, was unrealistic, cruel, and unloving. He certainly was not perfect himself, far from it. He did not expect perfection of himself, only from you. You must learn to let that go and forgive yourself if you are ever going to be happy.

Your ego is an inner force that motivates your actions, your responses to experiences, and your reactions to others, sometimes without your conscious awareness. It is closely tied to your concept of self, your awareness of being unique and separate from other people. After I had begun therapy, my therapist told me that my self-identity had disappeared. Any sense of who I was didn't exist anymore because the identity of my toxic spouse had consumed it. My ex-husband viewed me as an extension of himself. I only existed to serve his needs and wants, to cater to his moods, and make him happy. He felt that it was my duty to serve him and the children and believed that any needs or preferences of mine weren't important. When I did assert myself on occasion, he treated me with contempt and condescension, including name-calling in front of the children. There is no wonder why I felt so depressed!

Our culture still celebrates the idea of wives and mothers as entirely self-sacrificing individuals who "get" to live through their husbands and children. In this paradigm, a woman's identity disappears, and she suppresses her needs and desires. If she has hobbies or a life outside the home, she may be considered selfish rather than admirable for practicing excellent self-care.

Men give themselves permission all the time to work late out of ambition, to play tennis or golf, and have drinks after work with their friends. Nobody judges them or even thinks twice about this behavior, including their wives. More women than ever work outside the home in addition to raising their children and running their households without receiving much help from their spouses. There is an implicit understanding that women have the main responsibility for children and home. If a husband "helps," he receives praise for his "generosity."

Of course, a double standard is not acceptable. Men and women should be equal partners, while most men prefer to keep things the way that they are. Why wouldn't they? If we want this to change, it is up to us. Women will have to insist on equality in the home as well as in the boardroom if we are going to get it.

Why did I put up with name-calling and being berated by my husband for so long? Why do you? I know that neglect and abuse in my childhood caused me to have low self-esteem, so I did not initially have the strength or the will to stand up to my husband and walk out early on. I was also deeply ashamed to have such an unhappy and unloving marriage. I thought that it must be me, that it proved something was wrong with me. Because I made the mistake of confiding in my ex-husband that both of my parents were alcoholics and that my father had abused me, he told me that I was defective, calling me "damaged goods" within earshot of our two children. He used that intimate confidence against me repeatedly to tear me down as if my childhood was my fault. It didn't matter to him that I didn't drink or that I was a loving and attentive mother.

Women customarily take on blame or responsibility that does not belong to them. I think this goes back for generations and is ingrained in our culture. A part of us—the ego—worries about appearances, wants to fit in, believes we need to be the center of attention, competes with others, and consumes itself with issues related to our importance, pride, and gratification. The ego causes us to value others' opinions of us more than our own. A wounded ego, whether it's inflated or deflated, is dangerous. Your husband's wounded ego is largely responsible for the suffering he has caused you. Because of my wounded ego, I was embarrassed to admit to people that I had a failed marriage. Our egos can ruin our lives if we let them run our lives.

It is very important that you not let your ego make decisions regarding your divorce.

## KNOW THYSELF

*"Whatever is in me is stronger than what is out there to defeat me."*
—CAROLYN MYSS

After years of marriage, I didn't know who I was anymore. I had become disconnected from myself. Perhaps you are too. It is important to get to know yourself again, authentically.

Start paying attention to what gives you joy and keep a list of those things. Is it going for a walk in the morning? Is it listening to a certain type of music? Is it being out in nature, smelling the aroma of flowers? Is it cooking with your children? What truly makes you happy? Add to this list regularly. Let your feelings be your compass.

Pay attention to what makes you afraid, fearful, or sad. What are the triggers that make you angry? Start a second list where you track the negatives in your life, the things that prevent you from being happy and your true thoughts and feelings about your situation.

Do you blame yourself for the abuse in your home? Do you avoid conflicts and disagreements at all costs? How does that manifest in your body? Do you have headaches, nausea, or a racing heartbeat? Are you afraid? Do you avoid friends and family to hide the abuse? How does that make you feel? How do you feel about yourself most of the time? How does your partner make you feel? Do you feel trapped? Hopeless? How long have you felt this way? How did you feel before you met your spouse?

Start journal writing, especially when you get up in the morning. Set a timer for ten or fifteen minutes and just start writing stream of consciousness. Allow yourself to write about subjects you would rather avoid. Those are the subjects you probably need to write about the most. Use a prompt like, "What I don't want to write about is . . ." If you don't want anyone to read what you've written, you can always tear it up right after you write it.

Or begin by writing a question to your higher self, such as: "What would you have me know right now?" or "What do I need to focus on today?" Doing this will give you a lot of clarity. Your higher self is the authentic core of your being that is connected deeply to Spirit. It is the quiet voice of your conscience, inner wisdom, creativity, and love. You can access its guidance through journaling, prayer, and meditation. This is particularly important while you are planning your future. Your higher self can help you make good choices for your children and yourself.

Build your self-esteem by making a list of your best qualities. Also, make a list of your faults and try to improve as a person every day. It is not necessary or helpful to dwell on individual mistakes that you have made. Forgive yourself now for having made them, and then leave them in the past. I am talking about working on habitual weaknesses, such as having a short temper, being jealous, too self-critical, unkind, or a gossip. Every one of us has something on which to work. Work on your faults one at a time if you want to make progress. This work will keep you humble.

Tell yourself again how wonderful you are. You are lovable even though you are a work in progress. The fact that you are willing to look at yourself and improve is admirable. Accept your humanity. Accept who you are right now, the good and the bad. Embrace all of who you are.

## THOUGHT WEEDING

*"Change your thoughts and you change your world."*
—NORMAN VINCENT PEALE

Thoughts are things, and they have great power because our lives reflect how we think.

Each one of us is responsible for our thoughts and actions. If you pay attention to what you are thinking and weed out negative and self-defeating thoughts, you will change your life. If you think you will succeed, and then because of this thought you take the necessary steps to do so, you will be much more likely to succeed. Similarly, if you think you are going to fail, you probably will. You will be less likely to try to succeed. You may even sabotage yourself subconsciously so that you do fail.

Our innermost thoughts manifest through our choices and actions. Pay attention to your thoughts and actively reject the ones that are not helpful.

Awareness is key. Question your habitual thoughts, especially those that are negative, judgmental, or limiting. When you examine them, I believe you will see that your parents, teachers, and husband, and even your friends, plant most thoughts of this type in your mind.

Like most people, I didn't think about the fact that I alone was responsible for my thoughts until I started reading books on spirituality. Now I recognize that it is up to me to pay attention to what I am thinking and guard my mind. Negative thoughts and doubts are going to pop up from time to time, so I need to be vigilant and root out the ones that do not serve me.

*Scientific American* magazine ran an article a couple of years ago that discussed how repetitive thoughts carve deep grooves in the neural pathways of the brain, and how we cannot remove them with willpower alone. We can, however, replace negative thoughts by the repetition of positive thoughts or ideas that replace and override them. Repeating positive affirmations is a method that helps to restructure the brain's neural connections.[2] Even if the practice seems corny or awkward to you, there is a biochemical basis why it works.

Repeating positive affirmations right before you drift off to sleep can help seed them in the garden of your subconscious mind, where they need to take hold for lasting change to take place. Personally, I have found it even more helpful to write out the affirmations I am working with long hand on a notepad several times each night.

Pick up a copy of *You Can Heal Your Life* by Louise Hay, which teaches the process of working with affirmations. Then make index cards of affirmations devised to counteract your most frequent negative thoughts and keep them on your night table. Several favorite affirmations from her book are: "I am enough," "I am valuable," and "I love and forgive myself."[3]

Hay wisely states not to resist a negative thought when it occurs. Just to ask the question, "Where did that come from?" The thought may have come from childhood if you were abused verbally back then, or it may have come from your spouse or another person.

I am not advocating the use of falsely positive or dishonest affirmations, like "My marriage is perfect." I am talking about affirmations regarding your self-worth and self-love.

Catastrophic thoughts or negative generalizations you may have, such as "My life is over," "I am worthless," "I can't ever do anything right," or "Nobody will ever love me," are mental tapes that have been looping through your brain for years, maybe decades, and yes, they can be replaced with effort by more positive and loving thoughts.

Weeding negative thoughts and planting positive thoughts in your mind to replace them requires months of applied repetition, not days, but it does work. So, do it. Value yourself enough to do that which is necessary to become strong enough to get through your divorce with a reasonable settlement. Taking responsibility for your thoughts will enable you to have a more fulfilling and happy life, which is the life that God planned for you. You must do this if you are going to be happy and productive. To change your experience, change your thoughts.

In *Question Your Thinking, Change the World,* Byron Katie offers us a series of four questions to ask ourselves and think deeply about if we have a stressful or negative thought.[4]

1. Is it true?
2. Can you absolutely know that it's true?
3. How do you react when you believe that thought?
4. Who would you be without the thought?

I have found that Question 4, "Who would you be?" can be particularly liberating. I wish I had known years ago that I don't have to believe everything I think and that I can choose to disagree with an unproductive thought and disregard it. It is my responsibility to weed it out.

For most of my life, I believed that I was powerless and a victim, and unworthy of taking care of my own needs, love, or happiness. I was wrong. Now I know that I can change my thoughts and my actions. And that is enough. When I need help, I pray for the Holy Spirit to help me eliminate or outright remove my negative, judgmental, and limiting thought patterns.

You become what you believe, and the thoughts and words that you tell yourself (which you base on what other people told you) will become your destiny unless you decide to change them. You get to choose what you think, and the most important opinion about you in the world is your own. What other people think of you is their business, not yours.

Focus on what you think is right for your life and your children. Don't allow yourself to marinate in negative thought patterns that limit your potential and give you nothing in return but unhappiness and missed opportunities for joy and success.

All of us live in our minds and are responsible for our thoughts. Weed your garden every day so that it stays beautiful.

## TURN OFF

*"All television is educational television. The question is: What is it teaching?"*
—NICHOLAS JOHNSON

Watching too much television may be one of the ways you avoid dealing with your problems. It helps to numb pain, plus watching it may mean you are less likely to have to engage in conversation with your husband, who is not safe. But be careful. The side effects of television can be very harmful. If you do not discriminate and limit what you watch, you could pollute your mind with negative images and messages, and interfere with your ability to think clearly. You need all your critical thinking faculties working well right now to get through your divorce.

Read this list of some of the side effects of television.

- A lot of the violence on television, behavior that is often portrayed to be enjoyable and acceptable, can make viewers less sensitive and increase aggression, contributing to anti-social behavior. Sports events can also get viewers riled up.
- Watching violence or stressful situations on television can trigger stress responses in viewers' bodies. That is why your heart beats faster, or you find yourself sitting on the edge of your seat when you are watching an action movie or violent film. Your subconscious mind experiences the violence on television as real.
- Television gives viewers an inaccurate view of reality. Brain activity switches during television watching from the left side of the brain, which is responsible for logical and critical thought, to the right side of the brain, which reacts emotionally and is highly suggestible. For advertisers, this is the perfect state in which to seduce you into desiring and purchasing unnecessary items that they will try to convince you are necessary to feel good about yourself.
- Sensitive issues, such as sex and substance abuse, are often handled in an inflammatory way or give the wrong message. Programs often glorify sex and portray women as sex objects. Increased promiscuity can be a result. Some shows normalize excessive drinking and drug use.
- Many people become obese from mindlessly consuming large amounts of unhealthy snacks and soft drinks while

watching television. A sedentary lifestyle from excessive television watching contributes to obesity as well.

- Family members are less likely to communicate and spend quality time with each other if they glue their eyes to the TV set. They are also less likely to read books, resulting in reduced literacy and critical thinking.
- Some news programs report excessively on violence and death around the world. They replay the same scenes of horror over and over, which can contribute to viewers' sense of hopelessness, depression, anxiety, and despair.
- According to many research studies, television hampers the development and function of areas of the brain that are in control of moral judgment and attention.[5] Excessive viewing leads to problems with concentration and distractibility—even ADHD as frequent scene changes desensitize the ability to concentrate attention for any length of time. Parts of the brain responsible for logical thought tune out during television viewing. Brain waves in the low alpha range, a hypnotic brain state associated with suggestibility, are induced within just a few minutes of watching television. Brain activity is so low because the brain is passively engaged. This is unlike the alpha state in meditation, which beneficially promotes relaxation and insight. Unfocused daydreaming and the inability to concentrate can result from watching too much television.

You are responsible for protecting your mind and the minds of your children by limiting what you allow in television viewing content and exposure. Try to limit television viewing to one hour on weekdays and up to two hours each day on the weekend nights, which is the equivalent of one movie each weekend night. Monitor the content and screen out violent programs or shows that contain sexual content. Try instead to watch uplifting family shows, like *Nature, Masterpiece Theatre,* family comedies, or programs on the Discovery Channel.

It is also important for you and your children to avoid watching television or computer activity at least ninety minutes before bedtime so that you can easily fall asleep. Children under the age of six should not watch television at all as their developing brains are too malleable. Research has linked excessive television viewing to a higher incidence of dementia later in life, so it is important to instill good habits in your children early in life.

Reading for at least an hour a day, exercising, and meditation can counteract some of the side effects of television viewing. Learning a language or how to play a musical instrument also engage the brain and can also help to reverse these negative effects. When you do watch television after the children are in bed, choose a family oriented sitcom or a funny movie. Smiling and laughter could help you feel better by releasing good chemicals such as serotonin and other endorphins in your body. The distraction may lift your spirits.

## PICK YOUR POISON

*"If you don't heal the wounds of your childhood, you bleed into the future."*

—OPRAH WINFREY

People sometimes medicate themselves with gambling, sex, drugs, alcohol, or food to numb the unmanageable pain of trauma.

Substance abuse with alcohol and drugs is a disease that is chronic, progressive, and potentially fatal, and can lead to other diseases, according to Tian Dayton in *Trauma and Addiction.*[6]

The National Institute on Drug Abuse found that the largest risk factors for addiction are an untreated childhood mental disorder, including PTSD, hanging around other people who use drugs, sensation seeking, and self-medication.[7] Substance abuse creates additional wounds and trauma for family members, which can easily result in another generation of addicts.

You must do everything that you possibly can to break this cycle. If you have an alcohol or drug addiction, you have an obligation to your children and yourself to get counseling, check yourself into an inpatient program, and join a support group such as a twelve-step program to keep you sober. You cannot do this on your own. Admit you need help and get it immediately. You must get well first before you attempt to take care of children on your own.

People are much more dangerous to themselves and others while under the influence of drugs or alcohol. They are out of control, and any tendency toward violence and abuse becomes more pronounced. If you are married to an alcoholic or a drug addict, immediately leave with the children for your safety. My father's alcoholic rages were terrifying, as the lessening of inhibitions from his drinking made him prone to inappropriate behavior, cruelty, and violence. An abusive man who is also an addict is extremely dangerous.

According to an article on the website Recovery Connection.com, changes in the brain chemistry of certain neurotransmitters related to substance use create the cravings, the increasing tolerance (which leads to even more powerful cravings), and the withdrawal symptoms associated with the cycle of addiction. The process of thought and decision-making is severely compromised by these chemicals, leading to denial, minimization of the problem, and justification by the addict.[8]

If you are a drug addict or an alcoholic, substance abuse treatment, self-help groups, and counseling will help you to avoid relapses. Willpower alone is usually unsuccessful. You will still have a very good chance of getting custody if you can show thorough documentation of your husband's abuse and your efforts to stay clean.

Food is often used in an addictive manner. I consoled myself with food when I was bored, lonely, sad, angry, or anxious. Because I became an emotional eater, I put on a lot of weight during my marriage. I know now that I also subconsciously used my weight as a shield to make myself sexually unattractive to my husband, as I no longer wanted him to touch me. The problem with this approach was that I was abusing my own body. I ended up with acid reflux, high blood pressure, and plantar fasciitis in my feet. Emotional eating took a toll on my health and possibly years off my life expectancy.

When your abuse has reached the point where it is no longer bearable, you may become numb and disconnected from your body. It may be necessary for you to wait until after your divorce to deal in earnest with a weight problem if you have one. Please show yourself some compassion if you cannot deal with it right now. That said, it may be very helpful to do something about it now. It may give you comfort to have control over something in your life when everything else feels out of control. Becoming more conscious of healthy eating may improve your self-esteem, which in turn may help you to cope more effectively with the divorce.

I am not advocating crash dieting, but developing healthy eating habits and treating your body with love. Restricting your calories to an unreasonable amount will not help you to be at your best when you need to be strong, alert, and decisive. If you eat too much or eat the wrong things, the important thing is to forgive yourself for not being perfect and simply do your best to get right back on course in taking care of your body. "The challenge is not to be perfect, it's to be whole," as Jane Fonda says.[9] And healthy. One thing that has helped me is to be more aware of what I eat every day and track it on the free app My Fitness Pal. There are plenty of other apps and websites that can help you with nutrition and healthy recipes.

If you do want to take control of emotional overeating, portion control is as important as what you eat, so buy an inexpensive scale and use it. It helps to use measuring cups to see how many calories you consume. Eating on small plates increases satisfaction. Have greens take up half the plate, and low-glycemic carbs and lean protein a quarter of the plate each.

Please avoid fad diets that are not well-balanced meals. Your body is stressed out enough as it is. If you want to join a weight loss program, stay with nutritious and safe programs, such as Weight Watchers or Jenny Craig. You may also want to check out local meetings of Overeaters Anonymous to deal with compulsive overeating. If you suffer from bulimia, please seek immediate medical attention.

Avoid taking diet pills, as most of them haven't been proven effective, many have unwanted side effects, and some may be downright dangerous. They aren't subject to the same rigorous standards as prescription drugs. Just because they are sold over the counter doesn't mean that they work or that they won't be harmful to you. Some of them have hidden ingredients or contaminants, so there is an unwarranted risk in taking them. Many of them can result in high blood pressure, increased heart rate, irregular heartbeat, heart attack, stroke, or death. If you think you must take diet pills, ask your doctor for a prescription. Prescription diet pills are likely to be safer and more effective than over-the-counter diet aids.

Pay attention to your body's signals. Sometimes your body is just trying to tell you that you are thirsty, and you are confusing thirst with hunger. It is always good to drink a glass of water first to see if that is what is motivating you to suddenly steer towards the refrigerator. Ask your body what it wants or needs, and ask yourself what you are feeling now. And ask these questions to yourself out loud.

- Am I bored?
- Am I upset?
- Am I lonely?

Breathe deeply in and out and wait for the answer. It will come. Sometimes you will be shocked to hear you tell yourself that what you need is comfort, companionship, or something constructive to do. Breathing deeply and focusing on your breath will help you to reconnect with your body and your life. Go for a walk.

Try to stay in your body while you are eating. Many of us check out mentally while we are mindlessly stuffing comfort foods into our mouths. For example, we are unaware of what or how much we are consuming, or how quickly, while watching television. So, it is not as if we are enjoying our food. Compulsive eating is just a crutch, an escape mechanism, which is adding another problem to the many problems you already have.

A really good book to read on the emotionally charged issue of eating as compensation for feeling bad is *Women, Food, and God* by Geneen Roth, which provides many helpful insights into why we overeat and what we can do about it. Her eating guidelines are:[10]

- Eat when you are hungry.
- Eat sitting down in a calm environment. This does not include eating in the car.
- Eat without distractions. Distractions include radio, television, newspapers books, intense or anxiety-producing conversations, or music.
- Eat what your body wants.

- Eat until you are satisfied.
- Eat (with the intention of being) in full view of others.
- Eat with gusto and pleasure.

These guidelines are very helpful, but you still need to eat a balanced diet and not consume too many calories. You must burn the calories that you take in or you will gain weight. The only way to know whether you are eating too much is to track your calorie count every day.

Remember, the comfort in high-fat comfort food doesn't last, but the fat does.

## BREAKING BAD

*"A change in bad habits leads to a change in life."*
—JENNY CRAIG

The odds are high that you have developed some very negative habits along the way to deal with the stress and shame of the abuse in your home. Some women drown their sorrows in food or alcohol, others numb themselves in front of the television or complain endlessly to friends without making any effort to change their situation. Willpower alone is not going to work to change these habits. Create a plan to achieve a realistic goal and focus on the progress that you make. It takes time, but you can do it if you want to do it.

Do not wait until the divorce is over to take control of your habits and your life. Learn how to change habits effectively so that you do not get overwhelmed. Life does not stop just because you are going through a divorce. Seeing success in self-control in small things will help to restore your confidence so that you can take back your power in the big ones.

You can do it! Here are some tips:

- **Take on one good habit or tackle one bad habit at a time.** Focus on only establishing or changing that one habit; and be consistent. It normally takes an average of sixty-six days to perform a task automatically, according to a 2009 study in *European Journal of Social Psychology.*[11] Many sources say that it takes thirty days to change a habit, but a habit has not changed until it becomes automatic. Don't start trying to change another bad habit until you know for sure that you have permanently changed the first one.
- **Be realistic about what you can do and focus on your progress.** Do not set yourself up for failure. Unrealistic expectations will only make you feel worse. Start with a small goal that you are certain to meet, and then increase it once you think you can do more. The top cause of procrastination is self-criticism so do not expect yourself to be perfect. Instead, set realistic goals.
- **Plan for how to reach your goal.** Write your goal down and refer to it often. Plan to include your new good habit in your busy schedule. Block out time on your calendar for the days each week that you want to perform your new habit until it becomes second nature to you. Set electronic phone alerts for it. If you want to add meditation to your daily routine, for example, practice it at the same time every day when you are least likely to be disturbed. Create a schedule for exercising and make sure that you have a change of clothes packed in the morning before you leave for work if you are going to the gym straight from work. Plan and prepare for success.
- **Figure out what your triggers or obstacles are and replace them with other activities.** If you get a strong urge to eat fattening foods, eat some grapes or a handful of almonds instead, or breathe deeply, have a drink of

water, call a friend, pray, or go for a walk. Don't buy food you want to avoid in the first place. It doesn't belong in your house.

- **Get a support system if you need one.** Call a friend. There also are support systems online that you can lean on, such as Weight Watchers.
- **Stay positive.** If you mess up, you are only human, so just try and try again. Be kind to yourself and don't give up. Learn to forgive yourself immediately. Treat yourself with compassion. You have been through a lot, and you deserve it.
- **Keep your goals secret from your husband.** If you are still living with your husband, he may try to sabotage you if you let him know what you are doing. Avoid sharing your plans to change any habit. Just do it. If he offers you dessert when you are trying to lose weight, say that you are not hungry and thank him for the offer. If you resist and express anger or disappointment that he is tempting or sabotaging you, his behavior will continue and may even escalate. It will be more peaceful if you avoid unnecessary arguments.
- **Focus only on what is within your control.** Take pride in your efforts and do not focus on the results. Let go of what is not in your control. It may mean that your goal takes longer to reach than you thought it would, but if you are trying and doing everything that you can, that is all that you can ask of yourself.
- **Repeat new behavior until it becomes automatic behavior.** I initially put sticky notes on the medicine cabinet in my bathroom to remind myself to take my vitamins and supplements, repeat affirmations, and meditate every day. Now I don't need to even think about

doing them anymore. They are among the first things I do in the morning.

- **Reward yourself for making this change, just not with food.** Decide before you tackle the habit what your reward is going to be. Little rewards, like a hot soak in the tub with a new magazine or a pedicure at a day spa can boost your self-esteem. And they work.

Try to eat healthily, get enough rest, exercise, and get some exposure to the sun every day if you can. You can't take care of anybody else if you don't take care of yourself first. Your husband or ex-husband may try to make you feel guilty for taking care of yourself to push your buttons. There is nothing wrong with your taking care of yourself, so don't feel guilty about it because someone else has an agenda. Your body is a gift from God, and you need to take care of it.

## EDUCATE THYSELF

*"All of life is a constant education."*
—ELEANOR ROOSEVELT

It is helpful to read books to help you to understand yourself and your relationships, and how you were susceptible to being abused so that you can avoid it in the future. Self-help books such as *Codependent No More* by Melody Beatty, *Ten Things to Do When Your Life Falls Apart* by Daphne Rose Kingma, and *Shame and Guilt: Masters of Disguise* by Jane Middleton-Moz were books that I found especially helpful. There are many more books listed in the Resources section at the back of this book.

If you start reading a book and the advice doesn't resonate with you, put it down and pick up another. Don't waste your time reading something that doesn't help you. Try another book. I promise you will find something that works for you.

If you have a limited budget, try your local library or local used bookstores. You can also find articles and blogs online on a variety of topics that will be helpful during your transition through the divorce.

Of course, you can read a lot of self-help books, but they won't help you unless you implement some of the ideas they discuss in your daily life. To make the process of change easier, I recommend that you read only one self-help book at a time, take notes, and implement the ideas that resonate with you over a period of months.

Reading books will give you more self-awareness, but you still must do the work to change. Journaling and self-reflection at the end of the day are very important when implementing changes. Refer to your notes. Hold yourself accountable if you want to change the way you react in situations that tend to repeat themselves in your life.

## CHAPTER FIVE

## SOUL

# LOVE THE ONE YOU'RE WITH–YOU

*"Do you want to meet the love of your life? Look in the mirror."*
—BYRON KATIE

Take care of your appearance. Dress nicely and put on makeup. Give yourself a manicure. Use moisturizer. It will make you feel better. I wasn't always good at doing this, but I always felt better when I did. This tip is not about vanity. It is about self-love. Action frequently precedes thought, so if you make a habit of treating yourself well even if you don't feel like doing it, the habit will spark the feelings over time of self-worth and love that you deserve. It may take a while, but it will happen. You are worth it.

Giving yourself permission to love and care for yourself means that your children, who watch everything that you do, will be able to give themselves permission to love and care for themselves as well. Do it to be an example for them until you are healthy enough to feel that you should do this for yourself and no other reason.

Placing value on your happiness and well-being will help you to reduce depression and anxiety. I found little rituals of self-care very calming while I was going through my divorce. These are physical affirmations to yourself and the world that you expect to be cared for and you deserve it. Wish for yourself what you would wish for others.

## EVERYTHING IS ENERGY

*"If you want to find the secrets of the universe, think in terms of energy, frequency, and vibration."*
—NIKOLAS TESLA

You are an electromagnetic being whose thoughts and emotions affect the energy flow within and around you, shaping your experiences. You feel a lightness of being when you are happy and hopeful, and you feel a heaviness and slowness when you are sad or depressed. If you start the day in a bad mood, it is more likely that something negative will happen that day.

Also, your perception of events is influenced by your thoughts and feelings, so that you may even view something that happens more negatively than is warranted when you are in a bad mood. If you expect bad things to happen, they do. As you know, this is a *self-fulfilling prophecy.*

Why does this happen? Your ability to step back from a situation, to be resilient, and not to take things personally is impaired when you're having a bad day. By contrast, a positive outlook enables you to bounce back more quickly from setbacks and to problem solve to get around roadblocks in your path more easily and quickly. Although it is not possible for most people just to think themselves into a better mood, if you embrace the belief that the universe is working in your favor and look for evidence that supports this belief, you may soon feel more positive.

Being repeatedly abused by someone you love changes your view of the world. It makes it easier to believe the world is an unfriendly and unsafe place because in your experience you have evidence that this belief is true. Your husband is unkind and unloving. Your home is unsafe. You may believe you are powerless to leave. Such a belief couldn't be further from the truth.

Your self-image may be damaged to the point where you may feel that you are unworthy, unlovable, incapable, and helpless. You may have been brainwashed to the point where you have internalized some of the negative comments that your abuser made. If so, these remarks are now affecting how you think and feel about yourself.

Becoming aware that your thoughts and emotions affect your energy will help you to be vigilant about the thoughts you allow your mind to believe are true. Remember not to believe everything that you think, or that someone unsafe tells you that you should.

We all have automatic thoughts that affect our emotions. Question any negative automatic thoughts that you have about yourself and your options in life whenever they pop up. Spend time around positive and supportive people. Look for proof that the world outside your home is a friendly and safe place. It can be. Improve your perceptions, and you improve your world.

## THE SEVEN CHAKRAS

*"We live as ripples of energy in the vast ocean of energy."*
—DEEPAK CHOPRA

An invisible web of energy ties every living being and every inanimate form on Earth together. Discoveries made by particle researchers in the field of quantum physics over roughly the last century confirm the presence and properties of this intricate web. In *The Divine Matrix,* Gregg Braden discusses experiments that show our connection to a field or matrix of energy that connects us to everything. This field appears to be intelligent and responds to our emotions.[1]

There are many references in the both the Old and New Testaments affirming that God is light. The Nicene Creed, 325 c.e., refers to Jesus as "Light from Light, True God from True God."[2] The Kabbalah, a form of Jewish mysticism, views light as God's first manifestation of Himself in the universe. The biblical book of Genesis says that creation emanated from God and dispelled primordial darkness. The implication is that light is the first and fundamental essence, and all life, truth, and goodness proceed from it.

The light of God is always available to you if you reach for its love and protection. Energy healers have learned to work with this light on behalf of their clients. We can also work with our personal energy using a combination of breath and intention.

You might think that the brain would generate the strongest electromagnetic field in the human body. "'The heart generates the body's most powerful and most extensive electromagnetic field," according to an article in *Institute of Noetic Sciences*. Its amplification is sixty times greater than that of the brain, and can be detected several feet away from the body."[3]

The human body has many energy centers. Of these, seven major centers of energy, called *chakras* in the ancient language of Sanskrit from India, are located next to a hormonal gland. They are cone-shaped and radiate and receive energy, like radio transmitters. Each is correlated with a color of light, and with different levels of consciousness related to our existence. These colors are visible to certain sensitive people, but most of us cannot see them.

Working up the body from the tailbone to the top of the head, the seven major chakras are:

1. **The root chakra.** A spinning red disk of light located at the base of the spine that keeps us connected with the Earth's energy and correlates to physical safety, the will to live, self-judgment, and endurance.
2. **The sacral chakra.** A spinning orange disk of light located in the lower abdomen associated with emotions, sexuality, sensuality, and creativity.
3. **The solar plexus chakra.** A spinning yellow disk of light at the solar plexus connected to self-control, personal will, the body's energy, and personal power.
4. **The heart chakra.** A spinning green disk of light in the area of the heart, linked to compassion, love, forgiveness, and identity.
5. **The throat chakra.** A spinning light blue disk of light in the area of the Adam's apple, connected to personal expression, intuition, and authentic communication.
6. **The third eye chakra.** A spinning indigo blue disk of light in between the eyes associated with clairvoyance, ability to be in charge, and perception.
7. **The crown chakra.** A spinning violet or purple disk of light at the crown of the head connected to the higher self, divine guidance, and knowingness.

## CLEARING YOUR CHAKRAS

Fear-based thoughts will cause the chakras to become "dirty" and to shrink. Your chakras are also affected by other people's negative energy. It is, therefore, a good practice to clear your chakras at the end of every day to remove negative energy and influences. To clear them, sit quietly with your eyes closed and breathe deeply. Focus on each chakra, in turn, starting with the root chakra, and visualize it rotating in a clockwise motion. Imagine yourself breathing bright light into it in its corresponding color, cleaning and filling it up. For example, imagine yourself breathing bright red light into your root chakra.

While you are breathing in colored light, ask the following questions.

- To clean and restore your root chakra, pay attention to any fear or insecurity that you are experiencing. Ask: Do I feel safe?
- To clean and restore your sacral chakra, bring your focus to your body and emotions. Ask: What am I feeling right now?
- To clean and restore your solar plexus chakra, consider what you have the power to choose or change today. Ask: Have I set boundaries with others?
- To clean and restore your heart chakra, open your heart to give and receive love. Ask: Have I loved myself as well as others today?
- To clean and clear your throat chakra, consider whether you are behaving authentically with others. Ask: Am I being truthful?
- To clean and restore your third eye chakra, desire an outcome. Ask: Am I paying close attention to what is going on around me?

To heal your crown chakra, let go of control of the outcome to God or the universe. Ask: Am I spending at least a few minutes every day in prayer or meditation?

## CUTTING YOUR ENERGETIC LINK TO YOUR HUSBAND

Your energy field (aka your *aura* or *etheric body)* extends a few inches out and all around your physical body. It is in immediate contact with the unified energy field that resembles a web of light. Because of this, you can sense another person's mood without that person having said a word to you about it. There are cords of light that attach you to your loved ones and other people with whom you have contact during the day. To someone who can perceive the human aura, the cords that connect a woman and her abuser appear unhealthy, heavy, and dark.

In moments of weakness when you are blaming yourself for things that have occurred or when you are feeling depressed or worried, you may make yourself vulnerable to attachments from people (think of them as energy "vampires") who would like to drain you, including your husband. Because he is a mentally and emotionally wounded person, it is quite likely that he will "dump" toxicity on you energetically—psychically—even after the divorce. Your abuser also may be draining you of your life force through the etheric cords that connect you. By learning how to remove the etheric cords that connect you and your husband (or anyone else in your life), you can free yourself of any residual effects of that unhealthy relationship, reduce his energy drain on your life force, and initiate healing of wounds to your chakra. Repeat this process as often as necessary to maintain your well-being.

To cut these psychic cords with your husband, visualize yourself surrounded by a bubble of white or golden light representing spiritual protection, and then breathe deeply in and out several times.

Then visualize yourself gently pulling out the toxic, negative cords in your solar plexus that connect you with your husband. Use your hand to do a karate chop in front of your solar plexus to break these cords if it makes your visualization more effective.

Finally, see any holes left from the pulled cords being filled and healed with divine white or golden light.

If you would like angelic support in this process, ask Archangel Michael to help you remove cords of negative attachments from your aura. Most will be attached to the solar plexus. However, some of the cords may also be attached to your back (behind the heart) and the back of your head. Know that when you ask, help will be given. But you must ask.

After completing this process, remind yourself that you are safe, loved, and protected. Give thanks.

Repeat the process as often as necessary to break the connection and change an unhealthy pattern of thought and feeling. Once you have removed the energy cords, your energy level will improve, and you will feel lighter and more positive about your future.

At any time, you can close your eyes, breathe, and imagine yourself pulling your own energy back into and around your body.

This is a good technique to do if you've been interacting with a lot of people on a busy day, if you've just had a meeting with your lawyer or a mediator, or if you had an icky interaction with your ex-husband when he came to pick up your kids for visitation. You can also clear your energy field by showering with lemon glycerin soap or by spritzing a mist of lemon water around you. Using a water diffuser with pure (not synthetic) lemon essential oil in it will also do the trick.

I recommend that you visit a Reiki healer or a Reconnective healing practitioner if you feel drained or emotionally weakened during and after the divorce. Clarity, intuition, resilience, and decision-making are all affected by whether your energetic state is high or low. It is important for you to maintain an optimistic perspective and the feeling that you have a right to claim what you deserve. Maintaining a connection to your higher self and Spirit may be difficult, if not impossible if your chakras are not clear and you are attached to negative energy. It is like looking out a car windshield that is extremely dirty. What you see is distorted, if you can see at all. If you try to "drive" in this state, you may have an "accident."

The exercises I have given you are like a spiritual window cleaner. It is your responsibility to take steps to ensure that you keep your energy field clean and open.

## MEDITATION

*"If you just sit and observe, you will see how restless your mind is. If you try to calm it, it only makes it worse, but over time it does calm, and when it does, there's room to hear more subtle things—that's when your intuition starts to blossom."*

—STEVEN JOBS

Meditation will help you cope better with your day if you do it first thing in the morning. It can also help you to unwind and shake off the residual impact of the day in the evening.

Spend five or ten minutes in the morning and evening breathing deeply and meditating by focusing on the movement of your breath. Or meditate at another time, if that is easier. When you are upset, it will probably be the last thing that you want to do, but that, in fact, is an excellent time to meditate. The times when you least want to do it are usually when you most need it because it can help you to calm down and think more clearly. It is also beneficial to meditate when you are feeling physically ill as it promotes healing.

There are a lot of self-help books on the topic of meditation, as well as many meditation groups that you can join to receive instruction and support. You may enjoy going to a meditation group, if you have the time, for the social connection with positive people. But what you need most is to sit down and do it regularly.

Some people have the misperception that meditation involves non-thought, which is just not possible. It is not necessary to eliminate your thoughts during meditation to benefit from the practice. You will have thoughts! Thoughts naturally come and go. The idea is to breathe in deeply and pay attention to your breath. When thoughts arise, acknowledge them, and label them as worrying, regretting, or planning thoughts, and do not attach to them. Just observe them and let them go on their way without allowing yourself to get pulled into the storyline.

The goal is to stay focused on your breath and stay centered in the present moment, which brings peace. If a thought lingers, simply go back to concentrating on your breathing. Focus on what your body is feeling and let go of any tightness.

The Desert Fathers tradition included the Jesus Prayer, a method of repetitive prayer to help with contemplation. The formula was to repeat "Lord, Jesus Christ, Son of God" on the in-breath, and "Have mercy on me, a sinner" on the out-breath.[4] The repetition is not only comforting; it helps to release unsettling, negative, and obsessive thoughts—a form of mental activity known in Buddhism as the *monkey mind.*

Some repetitive phrases are known as *mantras.* They are instruments of thought that are helpful for dealing with mind chatter. *"Om Shanti Om,"* is a popular mantra often employed by yoga practitioners. Shanti means "peace" in Sanskrit.

The difference between mantra meditation and centering prayer is that centering prayer is not an exercise in focusing attention on something, such as a mantra; rather it is concerned with the intention to consent to the presence and action of God in your life during the time of prayer.[5]

According to Cistercian monk Father Thomas Keating in his book *Intimacy with God: An Introduction to Centering Prayer,* whatever makes a connection to God most accessible to you is what you should do. You may initially feel frustrated, and your mind may not be able to grasp God, but you can learn to be at home in the cloud of unknowing.

Meditation in the ancient tradition of the Kabbalah uses repetition of the many Hebrew names of God to enhance awareness and connect to the divine presence. Repetition is used to crowd out unwelcome thoughts, attain peace, and bring about positive changes in life. The aim of Kabbalah meditation is to make the practitioners carriers of the light of God.[6]

It may take some experimentation to find what works to calm the monkey mind in your meditation, but your peace of mind is more important than anything else. For convenience and out of the tradition of my faith, which is Catholicism, I use masculine pronouns to identify God, but many other people either don't think that God has a gender or that God encompasses both genders. My personal belief is that God is beyond knowing and description.

When you meditate, find a quiet space. Turn off the ringer on your phone and lock the door if you must, so that you won't be disturbed. Sit with good posture, in a comfortable chair with both feet on the floor and your hands gently resting on your thighs close to your knees with your palms face up. If there is not much privacy in your home, use the bathroom as your meditation room.

Close your eyes and imagine that you are surrounded and infused by white light, then breathe. You could try counting to four when you breathe in and when you breathe out, pausing for two counts in between. Imagine that you are breathing in the light of God and breathing out negative energy, unproductive thoughts, and limiting beliefs.

You may also want to concentrate on a phrase or word as you breathe in and out. Try *love, peace,* or *Abba* ("father" in Aramaic and Hebrew). If a thought comes, acknowledge it and be patient, and bring your focus gently back to your breath.

Come back again to your breath or your word every time you notice that your mind has wandered.

Answers may not come during your meditations, but instead over the next several days or weeks. At some point during the day you may get an idea or sense of "knowing," or you'll get a message in your dreams. You may want to write a question and put it under your pillow before you go to sleep.

Keep a pen and paper by your bed to write down your dream as soon as you wake up so that it is not forgotten. You may get divine guidance that you will not be able to remember later

if you don't write it down right away. Write down as many details as you can, and you will be more likely to figure out their meaning.

Dream messages are usually symbolic and archetypal, as well as personal. The meaning of your dream symbols may differ markedly from a dream interpretation book, so you will have to interpret the messages yourself. They are just for you in language that you can understand. As many dream messages are in metaphor, it may take you a little while to figure out what the messages mean for you. Fortunate coincidences may start to happen. You may meet someone who can help you. Be sure to ask for help if that is the case. There is a reason why that person is showing up in your life right now. Accept help that is offered. Always say thank you, as gratitude is a magnet that draws more good things to you.

## PRAYER POWER

*"Some things have to be believed to be seen."*
—MADELEINE L'ENGLE

In her audio program *The Power of Prayer,* medical intuitive Carolyn Myss says that the role of prayer is mainly for personal transformation, truth, insight, illumination, and the inner journey. According to Myss, prayer can be a petition, such as for health, protection, or guidance, but it should not be used to ask for unnecessary material things.[7] She is deeply influenced by Saint Teresa of Avila, who wrote her renowned treatise *The Interior Castle* in 1577 as a practical blueprint for an intimate relationship with God.

You may pray for God to remind you of what is important. Or pray with humbleness for God to give you the ability to see clearly, to see the truth in yourself and others, and to give you the strength, protection, and guidance to do what you need to do. You may also use prayer for the examination of conscience so that you can be a better person, one willing to make the sacrifice to change for the better so that you can be of service to others. That is the way to peace and true joy.

Prayer helps us establish a deeper connection with God and transformation of the self. It does not change other people. You have no control over anyone else. Only yourself. So, pray to adhere to right thought and right action. As you change for the better, so will your outer circumstances. Be a work in progress with God's help. Pray for the grace of faith. Pray for world peace.

During my divorce, I mostly prayed when I was extremely upset and unable to hear the voice of God or my intuition. I didn't have the tools to connect with God in a meaningful way. After praying for guidance, I stumbled upon helpful books and people.

To have a direct contact with God, you will need to be calm and receptive, listening in the stillness of your inner being so that you can feel at peace and loved because you are. Your role in praying is to have faith that God hears every one of your prayers. Pray and then let go. Trust in a power higher than yourself.

You may get the answers to your prayers in different forms, such as an urging, a knowing, a dream, a serendipitous contact with the right person, a book or video, or a conversation. Sometimes no answer is the answer. It may not be the answer that you want, but it may be the one that you will receive. Be receptive and pay attention. It is still up to you to take the right action based upon the guidance you receive.

Pray and have faith. When combined with correct action, prayer changes outcomes.

Remember, you can't just hope or pray for change. You have to be the initiator of change.

A good motto is: Pray and prepare, then act.

## COMMUNITY

*"From a practical standpoint, we must have certainty not in the Creator and His ability to protect and care for us, but in the efficacy of the tools that He has provided for us."*
—PHILIP S. BERG

You may need more than meditation and prayer to get you through difficult times. A sense of community with other members of your religious community and your spiritual counselor—whether that is a pastor, minister, rabbi, imam, or meditation teacher—could help you to stay grounded and feel a sense of belonging that you don't have at home.

Feel free to stay at your current church or temple if it feels satisfying to you. If not, try other churches. Go for a walk with God in a park and appreciate the wildlife. Be open to trying different things until you feel as though your soul's needs are being met.

If you believe that things in your life are hopeless and you will fail, you are right. If you believe that no matter what happens, you will survive and thrive, you are right.

Your beliefs are a prayer, so what do you *choose* to believe?

## SACRED SIGNS

*"Look deep into nature, and then you will understand everything better."*
—ALBERT EINSTEIN

I recommend that you read *Animal Speak* by Ted Andrews to learn how to recognize and interpret signs from the animal world. I received a crucial omen soon after my divorce when I thought all the risks were finally over. A large red-tailed hawk flew into the middle of my front yard, which faced a very busy street, and perched on my lawn for a long time. I just happened to look out the window and noticed that it had remained there, turning its head from side to side, keenly observing its surroundings with great interest, unperturbed by the noise of the traffic. It was odd that it did not fly off, so much so, in fact, that its presence seemed surreal. I recognized at that moment that it was a divine sign that something urgently needed my attention and I wasn't yet seeing the whole picture.

According to Andrews, the hawk is the messenger bird, meaning we should pay attention whenever it shows up.

We often get sacred signs from the animal kingdom or in our dreams when we most need them. As it turned out, on the day the hawk landed on my lawn I had received an email from my ex-husband demanding that I sign quit claim deeds related to the divorce and mail them to him right away. If I had done so without protecting myself first, it would have potentially ruined my credit. I would have had no recourse other to pay his mortgage payments if he didn't pay them himself. Essentially, I would have become his financial hostage.

I thank God and that red-tailed hawk for giving me the gift of reminding me to check the implications of my ex-husband's demand carefully. Apparently, my lawyer had overlooked this issue while preparing my divorce decree. Thankfully, I received a warning from a bird of prey, a messenger from heaven.

Pay attention to what is going on around you. You may get useful signs in unexpected ways. I got this message from nature because I noticed that it was there. Receiving it was not an unusual occurrence, and I am not more special than anyone else. Signs are all around you, too, which you will see if you pay attention. The more time you spend in nature, being alert, the more likely you are to get guidance like this.

## MUSIC MAGIC

*"The only thing better than singing is more singing."*
—ELLA FITZGERALD

Listening to music can be healing when we are in pain, especially classical music, folk music, pop, or soft rock. There is some indication that music affects levels of oxytocin and can trigger the release of endorphins, a natural opiate. An article entitled "Music on the Brain," published in *Time,* described the research of Robert Zatorre, a neuroscientist at McGill University in Montreal. In studies with PET scanners, he has shown that the parts of the brain involved in processing emotion light up with activity when a subject hears music.[8] Also, listening to the right kind of music can lower your blood pressure.[9]

It is important during this difficult time in your life for you to avoid listening to music that saddens you or that sounds loud and aggressive, which could cause your body to release stress chemicals, such as cortisol. Your brain already has been flooded with cortisol because of the stress and fear you've experienced in your marriage and possibly in court or mediation. Cortisol and other stress-related hormones can decrease the size of the hippocampus in the brain, which has a significant negative effect on learning and short-term memory.[10]

Fortunately, these effects also can be significantly reversed if you take care of yourself during and after the divorce if you minimize your exposure to additional stress and actively do whatever you can to activate your relaxation response, such as with meditation or the right kind of music.

Since ancient times, people have understood that music has healing properties. Neurological music therapy now has given an explanation why. Because positive mood affects the capacity for memory, it is important for you to listen to positive music in the car or wherever else possible.[11]

The fact that certain music heals makes sense considering that everything is in a state of vibration, including us. Everything is sound vibrating at different frequencies. There are an upper limit and a lower limit to the frequency of sounds that the human ear can hear. Some other animals hear sounds that we cannot at higher frequencies, such as dogs and cats, or at lower frequencies, such as elephants. From subatomic particles moving around the nucleus of an atom to planets in distant galaxies that are rotating around their stars, everything is in motion, vibrating at a particular speed. You could say everything is making music.

When we are happy, we feel lighter, and our level of vibration is faster. When we are depressed, we feel heavy, and our vibration is slower. It is necessary for you to tune out the negative messages you receive from your husband and from some music, especially songs containing lyrics that degrade or objectify women, as these may trigger traumatic memories and symptoms of PTSD. If you hear a song with offensive lyrics on the radio, change the station immediately or turn it off. Remember that everything you choose to listen to affects your perception of the world.

Tibetan priests and Christian monks have practiced chanting for many hundreds of years because it is sacred and spiritual. This practice has many health benefits for the body, mind, and spirit, including lifting depression and lethargy and giving one a profound sense of peace. Humming, or self-created sound is particularly soothing to the central nervous system.[12]

Humming for five minutes can help you lower your breath rate from fifteen to seventeen shallow breaths a minute to as little as four to six full breaths per minute. Slowing down the pace and deepening the breath will lower your blood pressure and heart rate, increase your levels of neurochemicals and hormones, such as melatonin and pain-relieving endorphins, and reduce the levels of stress-related hormones in your body. It's fun, fast and easy.

Sit comfortably with your eyes closed and let your jaw, facial muscles, and shoulders relax. Take a slow deep breath into your belly and then make an *Mmm* sound while you exhale with your lips gently closed. Repeat for up to fifteen minutes.

It is a good idea to sit quietly for a few minutes after you are done and pay attention to how peaceful you feel.

If you like that, also try the sound of *Ahhh,* which is great to do when you are tense.

Making your own music never felt so good, and you don't even have to be able to keep a tune to do it. I sure can't.

## IN THE BEGINNING WAS THE WORD

*"No matter how difficult and painful it may be, nothing sounds as good to the soul as the truth."*
—MARTHA BECK

It is extremely important that you pay attention to the words you speak. What you say out loud has even more power than thoughts that you have not verbalized.

Pay attention to how you talk about yourself. Sometimes we don't even realize the negative way in which we talk about ourselves to other people. We say things like: "I could never do that," "I'm not that smart," or "I'll never have . . ." Words are so powerful that you can convey a self-defining image through repetition that becomes a self-fulfilling prophecy. Never limit yourself. It's bad enough that other people have done that to you. When you catch yourself starting to say something self-deprecating or self-limiting, please stop. Reframe the ideas in a way that is truthful yet positive and encouraging.

Start talking about yourself positively. I am not talking about bragging or being arrogant. Say instead, "I can do that," "I can learn how," or "I will work to have what I want". Then do it.

Other people, including your children, lose respect for you if you put yourself down in front of them. They even may begin to feel superior to you because of it. Some women automatically say, "Excuse me," when someone else bumps into them. This is a form of submission. If you accidentally bump into someone else, it's certainly appropriate to say "Excuse me," but do not apologize when there is nothing to apologize for. Stop apologizing for your existence. You have a right to be here, as much as anyone else on this planet. Have enough belief in yourself not to put yourself down in front of anyone.

If you make a mistake, apologize for it sincerely, make amends, but only apologize once. You have no control over whether the other person will forgive you. Do not keep apologizing, as it only keeps you powerless and stuck in the mistake. Forgive yourself, make any necessary changes to avoid making that mistake again, and move on. Remember, the other person makes mistakes, too. Do your best and keep trying. If the other person keeps bringing up the mistake, ask them what is bothering them, as you have already apologized. If they don't accept your apology, let go of the matter. You may need to let them go if they are unwilling to forgive.

All your spoken words are important, as they "speak" to your integrity, so keep your promises, tell the truth, and avoid negativity and gossip. Silence is better than speaking without thinking. It will help you to become a better listener.

Avoid exaggeration and white lies. If some of your friends encourage any of these tendencies, it may be time to find new friends.

It is imperative that you not make promises to your children that you may be unable to keep. The best course is to make as few promises as possible. Say "I'll try, but I can't promise", which is more honest. Trust is hard earned and easily lost.

Treat yourself with respect by not allowing others to mistreat or disrespect you in their words also. Your outer circumstances change when you change the words that you use when you talk to yourself as well as to others and insist upon being spoken to respectfully.

You are not selfish for taking care of yourself. You take better care of others if you are at your best. You also provide a positive example when you set boundaries with your children regarding how they talk to you. Your insistence shows them how they will be able to take good care of themselves as adults.

There is tremendous power in the word *no*. Use it to set boundaries and to stop letting other people treat you like a doormat. If you don't give yourself permission to do this, what do you think that your children will do when they find themselves in a similar situation? Say yes to a good life and to taking care of yourself with your vocabulary.

## SELF ESTEEM IS AN INSIDE JOB

*"I find that when we really love and accept and approve of ourselves exactly as we are, then everything in life works."*
—LOUISE HAY

I know that I would never have married my ex-husband, much less stayed with him for so many years, if I had better self-esteem. Having had your self-esteem badly eroded by an abusive marriage, and possibly by abuse in your childhood as well, it is important to remember that what happened to you does not define you. It neither defines who you are now nor does it define your capacity for joy and love in the future. What your parents or husband did to you, and what they didn't give you that you needed, is not your fault. Those events do not make you unworthy of love and respect. Your soul is whole and untouched by human events.

Abuse is a pattern of behavior that can travel from one generation to the next unless we decide to break the cycle. It does not define you if you decide to change the way that you look at it. The past can be used like decayed mulch to fertilize a garden of compassion. You must change how you look at yourself and increase your self-esteem to avoid having similar experiences in your other relationships. The way to improve your self-esteem is to accept and love yourself just as you are right now. Your self-acceptance will also help your children to feel more secure. They pattern their self-esteem after yours.

There are two components of self-esteem: competence and relationships. In each of us, there is a balance between the need to feel competent and the need to feel lovable. A feeling of being unworthy or having a negative self-view could cause you to place more emphasis on your weaknesses than on your strengths. If you do, over time you will be more likely to remember comments that tend to validate your negative self-view. You may even discount or disagree with compliments or appreciative remarks because they don't validate your low opinion of yourself. This is how you might create a false reality through self-limiting beliefs.

By contrast, a person with high self-esteem focuses on her strengths, not her weaknesses, and still believes that she is lovable, despite her imperfections. Having imperfections is what makes us truly human. If you had very critical parents as well as a critical spouse, you will have to actively work to change your self-talk when you make a mistake. Look at every mistake as an opportunity to learn. Forgive yourself for it immediately. Apologize for it if appropriate. Learn from the mistake so that you do not repeat it.

That's it. Don't dwell on a mistake or denigrate yourself by saying things like "I never do anything right," "I'm such a klutz," or "I'm so stupid," that would allow your old negative thought patterns to take over. You must choose not to believe everything that you think, especially when it diminishes you. When a negative thought appears, recognize it for what it is. It is not a helpful thought, so purposefully stop to tell yourself that you don't have to be perfect since the rest of humanity isn't. After this, distract yourself with something positive or by repeating affirmations. Then give the mistake over to God.

My therapist, Jerry Campbell, told me that self-esteem is dynamic and therefore subject to change. It can diminish if you fail to succeed at goals, have setbacks, make mistakes, or take actions that are not in line with your intrinsic values. But your self-esteem also improves when you accomplish something difficult, do something for someone else, have compassion for yourself and others, or set appropriate boundaries with someone who is trying to violate them. Isn't that great?

Self-esteem that is based exclusively on appearance, approval from others, academics, sports, or other accomplishments is subject to big up and down swings from feeling worthy to feeling worthless because it is based on transient outer-generated sources of happiness. A more effective strategy to maintain self-esteem long term comes from having compassion for yourself and others, and setting goals like being connected and supportive to others. According to an article in *Scientific American Mind,* this is a more effective strategy to maintain self-esteem long term.[13] The authors of the article describe a technique called self-distancing. If you try to see yourself from the perspective of a third-party observer, the proverbial "fly on the wall," during emotional situations, the mental distance it gives you will serve as a buffer to assist you in more rapid recovery from your negative feelings.

Although it is difficult to improve self-esteem, it is not impossible. It takes time and effort. I had used positive affirmations to help bolster my esteem without much success until I saw a Wayne Dyer video in which he mentioned two very important things to do while using affirmations. First, you must say them with emotion—as if you believe them to be true now, not in some future time, but in the present. Second, you must visualize what it would be like if what you were affirming was already true, and then act as if it were already true. When I applied Dyer's two tips, affirmations had more of an impact on my psyche.

Have faith. Your mind is a powerful tool that you have been given to create what you want in this life. This method of assuming what you want to create already exists is very effective. Assume that your prayers and affirmation have already been answered and give thanks. That is demonstrating faith.

A third, spiritual step added to the first two given by Dyer could make your affirmations even more powerful self-esteem boosters for you. Express gratitude to God for what you have already received and for what you are now receiving each day. God's grace can be a constant source of esteem.

I was doing these things and still having issues with my progress, so I suspected that I had a subconscious block. I found a wonderful exercise to remove blocks in *Tantra for the West* by Marc Allen. Here's how it works.[14]

On one sheet of paper, write your affirmation over and over. For example: "I love and accept myself exactly as I am now."

Write "Thank you" of another sheet of paper that you put side by side with the first page. On this page, write down whatever pops into your mind that disagrees with your affirmation each time you write the affirmation. Use this technique to identify your blockages.

After you know what your blocks are, allow yourself to be thankful for the insight, and then go back and write your affirmation ten to twenty times more to counteract the formerly subconscious blockages to it.

Use this technique daily until you get to the core of your resistance and then create an affirmation to counteract it so that you can release it once and for all.

Check in with yourself periodically throughout the day. Ask: How am I feeling? What is the emotion? Why? What caused it?

Notice how often you are self-critical and tell yourself to stop doing that to yourself when it happens. Stop exaggerating your flaws and start giving yourself more credit and praise. Treat yourself as you would a good friend who is not perfect, but has many fine qualities.

Make a list of your positive qualities. From this list, create five or six affirmations that you can repeat out loud and with conviction whenever a negative thought about yourself arises.

Our spoken words reverberate with power and are self-realizing. What you say about yourself to yourself and others matters. So, watch your words as well as your thoughts.

## GREAT FULL

*"Gratitude makes sense of our past, brings peace for today, and creates a vision for tomorrow."*
—MELODY BEATTIE

Keep a gratitude journal and writing implement on your nightstand. As a practice, every morning when you wake up write five things in it for which you are thankful. Your list might include things such as, "I am grateful for my children," "I am grateful for my health," "I am grateful for my job," and "I am grateful for my friends who support me." We always have things to be grateful for. They can be simple things. Doing this will set the tone for the day.

Even in this time of crisis, maintaining a perspective of gratitude will make your life a lot easier. It will help to ease the pain and is a great practice to maintain throughout your life. You may want to discuss the fact that you are actively practicing gratitude with your children and ask them to do the same thing. It will make a great discussion over the dinner table every night if each of you describes something for which you are grateful.

A complementary process is to do something thoughtful or generous for someone else every day who may not be as lucky as you are. This could be as simple as holding the door open for someone or giving a dollar to a homeless person and telling that individual that you hope his or her luck changes. It will make all of you feel better to help someone, and it will make that person feel better, too. It is empowering and raises our self-esteem when we realize that what we do and say matters to other people.

I was affected by the commencement speech that actor Denzel Washington gave at Dillard University in 2015, in which he told the graduates to put their slippers under the bed at night so that they would have to get on their knees to retrieve them the next morning. He said that this would be a good time to give thanks to God. "Say thank you in advance for what is already yours. . . . True desire in the heart for anything good is God's proof to you sent beforehand that it is already yours. When you get it, reach back; pull someone else up. Each one, teach one. Don't just aspire to make a living, aspire to make a difference."[15]

Hearing this, I started putting my slippers under the bed at night shortly after that, and have maintained this beautiful practice ever since.

CHAPTER SIX

# IT TAKES A VILLIAGE

## HELP, I NEED SOMEBODY

*"Friendship is a wildly underrated medication."*
—ANNA DEAVERE SMITH

After my mother passed away in 1994, I suffered from sleepless nights and depression. I got counseling for the first time and went to a psychiatrist, who prescribed Ambien, a sedative, for insomnia and Zoloft, a mood stabilizer, for depression. Despite taking medication, I remained unable to sleep and talked with my psychiatrist repeatedly about it over a period of many months, but he was dismissive of my request to switch medications. I should have changed my psychiatrist when he wasn't responsive, but I viewed him as the expert.

It also didn't help that my husband kept waking me up in the middle of the night, night after night, to yell at me. I don't remember now why he was yelling. The fact that he chose to wake me from a sound sleep to berate me was abusive and cruel, especially since I had a full-time job and got no help from him in taking care of our two children or running the household.

It was then that I was misdiagnosed with bipolar disorder. Many years later my diagnosis was changed to PTSD by my current psychiatrist, whom I have seen since 1997.

I went for about six months without sleeping soundly, partly because my husband interrupted my sleep and partly due to my grief over my mother's death. It was extremely difficult under these circumstances to function at work and be at my best for my children. Although he had done it once before, I completely snapped one morning after he screamed at me and threw a cup of coffee directly into my face. I had a complete nervous breakdown and ended up in a psychiatric hospital. While I was there, I was injected with a massive dose of Depakote to break the psychosis. I still remember having difficulty lifting my feet when I tried to walk. I shuffled my feet as if they were glued to the floor, like the Chief in *One Flew Over the Cuckoo's Nest* by Ken Kesey.

It was painful for me to be institutionalized. I felt ashamed and like a failure. But I was determined to quickly recover as I had two young children to take care of, an unreliable husband, clients to service, and bills to pay. Twelve days after my breakdown, on Good Thursday, the hospital released me. I went back to work the following Monday, right after Easter. It was extremely difficult for me to put back together my Humpty Dumpty self, but I was in survival mode.

My husband resumed yelling at me to make home-cooked meals every night for dinner shortly after I returned home. He wanted things to go right back to the way they were before my hospitalization. The fact that I was in such a weakened state and needed time to recover was of no consequence to him. Being a narcissist, he was incapable of empathy. I did what I could to take care of the family, but from then on, I cut back on making elaborate meals and ordered takeout more often.

The lack of compassion my husband showed me with his continued demands and criticism during this period in my life was the worst abuse of a human being that I could imagine from someone who was supposed to love me. At the time, I was in no position to leave him.

I have not had another breakdown since, and believe that if I had not been so badly traumatized by my husband it would never have happened in the first place. If I had taken responsibility to leave him many years earlier, before the abuse got so bad, I am certain that I could have avoided falling apart. So that is on me. The reason that I am telling you this very personal story is so that you will take responsibility for your own life, and so that you know that you can survive almost anything. I did, and I am not any better or stronger than you are.

I continued to see my therapist and waited to file for divorce for over a year after the breakdown, as my children were both still young. Frankly, I was afraid that he would try to get custody even though he had not been involved in their care up to that point. This was a reasonable fear, as my husband did threaten to try to get sole custody once I did file for divorce, shouting that I was this crazy and irresponsible person. He followed me from room to room, screaming, and refused to leave the house or to stop sleeping in the master bedroom when I filed.

Unfortunately, you can't make a spouse leave the house just because you have filed for divorce. If your spouse escalates the abuse because you have filed for divorce, which is quite likely to happen, you can have him removed for your safety and that of your children. I then made the mistake of dropping the divorce petition due to my husband's refusal to move out and waiting thirteen years to refile it because the attorney I had at the time told me that I had no other option than to stay in the house with him. That decision cost me thirteen years of my life.

If your husband doesn't move out, there *are* other options, like leaving with the children and getting a cheap apartment, staying with friends or family, or going to a shelter. Please do not sacrifice your life for the sake of your children. It is a mistake and not the selfless act that you think it is at all. They suffer, knowing that you are in pain, and they learn some very bad lessons if you stay and accept mistreatment. It is not just what they see and hear. They also know what you feel. From my misguided choice, my children learned that I did not respect myself, as I was willing to continue to be abused. In allowing myself to remain a victim, I showed them that I had not accepted responsibility for my life.

Your husband will not change unless he wants to change. If he is unwilling to go to counseling or if he tells you that the troubles in your marriage and your unhappiness with his behavior are your problems, not his, he is right. These are *your* problems. You will have to decide what are you going to do about it.

Whatever you do, if you do decide to leave your home, make sure that you take the children with you or you could lose custody of them to your husband. The courts may consider your leaving them behind to be abandonment, either a sign that you are an unfit mother willing to leave them in danger or that you are lying about the domestic abuse. Your children are not safe in your husband's care, so you shouldn't ever leave them with him. Period.

Your husband may refuse to leave and try to intimidate you to leave without the children once he knows you have filed for divorce. Do not let him force you to leave the house without them under any circumstances. Call the police if you must. There are plenty of resources listed at the back of this book and online to help you. To access these, you just need to ask for help.

If you are concerned about your husband disappearing with the children, you must act first, and quickly take them to a safe place or shelter. Don't tip him off that you have plans to leave.

If he has shown himself capable of abusing you, then he is capable of almost anything.

## LEAN ON ME

*"Friends and good manners will carry you where money won't go."*
—MARGARET WALKER

Lean on me, just not on everyone. Do not, for example, confide in your husband's relatives. Blood is thicker than water, and they won't believe you, anyway. Or they will believe you and then still repeat what you said to your husband, which might prove to be dangerous.

Some of your relatives may not be safe, either—particularly if they have enjoyed decent relationships with your husband—so don't be surprised if a few of them judge you.

Some of your well-meaning friends, people you have confided in, might act unfriendly toward your husband out of loyalty to you, unintentionally tipping him off, which may also be unsafe. It is best to confide only in friends who don't see or interact with your husband. Confide mostly in your therapist.

If you have one or two friends with common sense and discretion, it's OK to confide in them on occasion. But do not overdo it if you want to keep them as your friends. Remember that other people have their own problems and yours might be too heavy a burden for them. You need to be considerate of them so that they do not come to dread your phone calls or visits.

Do your best to avoid being around people who say hurtful things or bring you down while you are going through this difficult time. At least limit your contact with them. Don't confide in them at all to avoid more emotional damage. You need to be around people who are nonjudgmental, supportive, and discreet. It is up to you to protect yourself.

If you work outside the home, remember that in most situations it is best not to confide that you are having marital problems. Restrain yourself from telling your coworkers, even if they are friends, or your boss. It is not considered professional to share details of your marriage or to bring personal issues to work. If you have a falling out with your coworkers, they might tell other colleagues your secrets, or even your boss, out of spite. Even if you don't, spilling the beans on juicy gossip is hard for most people to resist. So, don't tempt them. It is bad enough that your marriage is ending, you don't want to risk creating financial problems, too. You need to keep your job. To do so means continuing to get good reviews at work.

Sometimes it is hard to avoid letting people you see every day know you are going through a divorce, but you are under no obligation to share any of the details. One exception with the "no sharing in the workplace rule" is if you are suffering from physical abuse. In this case, you will need to tell your boss and give him or her a copy of a legal restraining order, if you get one. It is not necessary for you to go into detail other than to say that you are in physical danger.

Your best friend, besides your dog, is a good therapist who does more than just listen. My therapist tells me what I need to do to take care of myself, recommends books for me to read, and tells me the truth. You need a truth teller on your side, someone who is unbiased and gives you feedback. If your therapist is passive and doesn't give you good advice, get another one.

I would not recommend that you choose a priest or a pastor for your therapist. For one, Catholic priests have never been married. For another, most professional clergy do not have degrees or formal training in psychology or personal relationships, although there are some exceptions. Ultimately, you are going to have to make your own decisions, since you are the one who will live with the results. A professional point of view and advice will be very helpful to you in this regard.

You will need to work on self-esteem issues if you are married to an abusive man, as he no doubt has eroded your sense of self-worth over a long period. Therapy is helpful, but make a change either in your therapist or in the method you are using if you get stuck. Personally, I found group therapy unhelpful to me, as the participants in my support group stayed mired in the same drama of the past without making any visible progress from one week to the next. I felt as though I was a hamster on a wheel. Maybe group therapy helps others, but it didn't help me to listen to other people's problems. I needed to work on my own. It may help you, but if it doesn't, try something else.

I found cognitive therapy to be extremely helpful. Reading positive books, whether to do with faith or spirituality, as well as saying affirmations and trying just to live centered in the present were tools I tried to practice every day. When I did, they were very effective.

If you can't afford to pay for a therapist, free counselors are available. You can find a lot of free resources for divorce, abuse, and depression counseling online—just don't search for them from your home computer if your husband is still living with you. It could escalate the violence against you if your husband discovers your search history. Fly under the radar. Use a computer at work, a computer that belongs to a trusted friend or relative, or a computer at the public library to do your research.

If your spouse is physically abusing you, the abuse could escalate at any time. You need to act fast to get out before it does. According to the National Network to End Domestic Violence, over two million people call a domestic violence hot line every year to get advice, escape a crisis at home, or to help someone they think may be a victim. There are trained professionals there ready to help you get to safety. Please see the Resources section at the back of this book for helpful websites and hotlines.

Whatever you do, do not confront your husband or escalate the argument. Walk away. Run away. Pack a bag or grab a premade go-bag (see page 134 for details) and leave the house. When you are in danger and being threatened, it is not the time to prove that you are right in an argument by standing up to your husband or fighting back. Your safety and the safety of your children are the only things that matter. A little later, we will discuss an action plan to safely help you get out as soon as possible with your children.

Studies show that access to domestic shelter services leads to a 60–70 percent reduction in the incidence and severity of women being assaulted again during the three to twelve months follow-up period compared to women who did not have such access.[1] In fact, using shelter services leads to a greater reduction in being assaulted again than does either court protection (a restraining order, for example) or law enforcement protection, or even moving to a different location.[2]

As many as 60 percent of abusers are alcoholics. If you married one, please see the Resources section for information. If anyone at an Al-Anon meeting advocates that you do an intervention with an alcoholic spouse to help him reform, however, do not take this advice. You are dealing with a dangerous man with seriously impaired judgment and should avoid confrontation at all costs. Your husband may behave perfectly fine in front of witnesses, but the odds are extremely high that he will use the first opportunity alone with you to punish you for humiliating him in this way.

Most alcoholics, even those in recovery, are oblivious to the pain that they inflict on others. If there are children involved, it is vitally important to protect them from your spouse. It is just as much your responsibility as that of your husband to keep your children safe and protected. If you can't do that when he is around, then get out and get your children out now. I am for saving marriages and families, if possible, but we must protect our children first. It is our primary duty to protect those least able to protect themselves. You have a choice to make. Your children don't. They have no power, no say, and no place to go. It is up to you to protect them.

If you think that you might have a problem with alcohol or drugs, then there is a very high chance that you do. Get help immediately and do not make any major decisions until you are clean and sober and are sure that you will remain that way.

An important thing to remember while you are in crisis is to trust your gut. Not all the advice that you receive, no matter how well meaning, is going to be helpful in your specific situation. That includes some of the advice in this book. You must start listening to messages from your inner wisdom. Pray for guidance. Believing in yourself and listening to your intuition, which is your God-given internal guidance system, will help you navigate the war zone you are in more effectively than anything else possibly could.

## THE BEST LAID PLANS

*"Plan your work for today and every day, then work your plan."*
—MARGARET THATCHER

Try to plan. But remember that life happens, sometimes taking you places you may not want to go. My plan was to marry a good man and raise a family with him, with plenty of happy memories and love. That is not what I got, but I clung to my dream for three decades, thinking that I would be able to change him if only I tried harder. Sometimes it is less harmful just to cut your losses. The truth hurts, but it is still the truth. The sooner that you accept that what is happening *is* happening, the sooner you can exchange it for a better reality.

Do you know the song made famous by Kenny Rogers, "The Gambler"?

*You've got to know when to hold 'em*
*Know when to fold 'em*
*Know when to walk away*
*And know when to run*

If your husband is abusive to you, it is time to run! And don't ever look back.

I give a lot of advice on a variety of topics in this book, and you may not have the time or ability to take advantage of all the things offered here. The most important thing is your safety and the safety of your children. If that means you must leave with only the clothes on your back, then that's what you have to do. The smartest thing to do if you are in a war zone is to get out of the range of fire. Be careful and ready to act at a moment's notice. Plan your departure and do the things that you need to do when he is not around. You don't want to raise his suspicions.

## GIMME SHELTER

*"In skating over thin ice, our safety is in our speed."*
—RALPH WALDO EMERSON

Most abusers won't leave and will try to intimidate you to stay. Leave anyhow. If you are fearful for your life, you need to get out of there now. Stay with family or friends, rent a new place, or stay temporarily in a battered women's shelter.

It will be safer not to discuss your plans with anyone (including family or friends) who might tell your abuser where you are—even accidentally. An estimated 1.3 million women are victims of physical assault by an intimate partner every year.[3] Ninety-four percent of the more than 1,600 women who were murdered by men in 2013 knew their killer.[4] Leaving an abusive relationship can put a woman in real danger. Her abuser may decide to stalk the woman and injure or kill her, so it is important to be vigilant after you escape your abuser and get to the shelter. The address of these shelters is not public information.

You can find a domestic abuse shelter through your local police, social workers, or the toll-free National Domestic Violence Hotline: 1(800) 799-7233, which is completely anonymous and confidential. The Salvation Army provides confidential emergency and transitional shelters where women and their children can stay, as well as assistance with steps toward independent living and recovery (see Resources).

If you are truly afraid for your life, do not go to your workplace, favorite hangouts, school, or visit friends or family, in case he decides to hunt you down. You must also change the school your children attend so that he cannot track them down and then take them and disappear. Or follow them back to the shelter.

Your local shelter can offer you emergency housing, legal advice for obtaining a restraining order against your abuser, counseling to help you deal with your suffering, and job training to help you become independent and self-supporting.

## PREPARE, PRACTICE, PROTECT

*"The formula for success is simple: Practice and concentration then more practice and concentration."*
—BABE DIDRIKSON ZAHARIAS

Although you can request the police to be present while you leave, it is more likely that you will need to leave in a hurry, so plan your escape now. Don't wait.

Another abusive or violent episode may occur before you leave. If you become afraid for your safety, there are some things you can do to minimize the damage.

When your husband is present, you should:

- Stay away from the kitchen, where there are sharp objects.
- Try to get to a room with a door or window that you can use if you need to escape.
- Avoid small spaces, such as closets or bathrooms, where he can corner you.
- Keep guns, knives, and other sharp objects locked away or not easily accessible.
- Avoid wearing any jewelry or clothing, such as necklaces and scarves, he can use to choke you.
- Keep your cell phone with you as much as possible. Store 911 as well as the number for the local domestic shelter (look it up now), into your automatic dial contact list so that you can make a call in an emergency.

If your spouse attacks you, call the police immediately and make a note of the dispatcher's name. Get the name and badge number of the officer who takes your report when the police arrive. In the meantime, if violence is unavoidable, curl up into a ball in a corner and protect your face by holding your arms up and interlacing your fingers in front of it.

Inform a neighbor of your situation and see if you can run to her the next time you need help. Or ask a trusted friend—someone your husband doesn't know—if you can go to her house temporarily. The individuals you ask for help will need to be willing to help. You shouldn't wait until the next incident happens to find out that you picked the wrong person. Some people won't want to get involved.

It is a bad idea to use the home of a next-door neighbor, close family member, or mutual friend for emergency shelter, as your husband will be able to find you there.

If you are injured, get medical help, and make sure that your injuries are well documented. You can use photographs and medical reports as legal evidence in court during your divorce and in a custody battle. Have pictures taken of your bruises or any other injuries that were inflicted on you.

Whatever else you do, remember not to leave the children alone with your husband. Give your children instructions on how to get help the next time he becomes violent. If they are old enough, make sure to teach them a code word or signal from you indicating that they should get to safety at a preplanned location, then call 911 and give your address and phone number to the police. Practice how to get out of the house safely with them.

Tell your children never to interfere in any violence between you and your husband. Explain that they can help you by first staying safe themselves and then calling the police.

Be sure to remind your children that they are not to blame for the violence, and neither are you. Make sure they know that your husband could become violent if they tell him of your plans to leave.

A good idea is to always back your car into the driveway and keep the driver's door unlocked just in case you need to escape in a hurry. Make sure your car always has gas in the tank and that you keep a spare ignition key hidden inside the car in case you don't have time to grab your key chain before leaving—or in case your husband takes away your keys.

Pack a bag with the things that you will need if you have to get out quickly. It should contain cash, your driver's license, your credit cards, your checkbooks, a list of your assets and debts, a set of clothes for you and the children, toys, court papers, your passport, birth certificates, marriage certificate, social security cards, medical records, medicines, insurance information, immunization records, welfare documents, immigration papers, and other legal documents. It is very important for you to have copies of court papers in your possession to prove to the police that your spouse is violating a court restraining order if you summon them. Put your go-bag in a very safe place or give it to a trusted friend or relative to hold for you.

A list of important phone numbers such as friends, relatives, doctors, and schools will also be needed. You should also collect information on resources now, including your local battered women's shelter, before you need them. When you leave, if you have time to grab jewelry, pictures, and other items of value, do so, but leave them behind if staying longer jeopardizes your safety or that of your children. Remember, these are just things.

Begin to keep a journal of any verbal or physical abuse, recording dates, threats, and events. Make sure that you hide it well from your spouse.

If your husband is not abusing you in front of the children, I believe it is necessary for you to tell them the truth about what is happening before they hear a different version of events from him. It is likely that he will lie to hurt you and protect his image in their eyes. The truth will eventually come out, and your kids are going to eventually lose faith in the parent who has told them lies. Things will become difficult for you in the meantime if he turns the children against you. He is a master manipulator and could keep them under his spell for many precious years that you don't want to lose with them.

Tell them what Daddy did and why it was wrong or why it makes you afraid in a sentence or two, instead of labeling him. A lot of detail is not necessary and should be avoided to minimize damage to their psyches.

Don't tell them that "Daddy is a bad person," tell them "Daddy has done bad and scary things, and I don't feel safe living with him anymore." Tell them that you also don't feel safe leaving them alone with him anymore.

If you must file for a restraining order or an emergency protective order, you can obtain one from a local court without a lawyer. You will need to fill out paperwork, and the order, issued by the judge based on the information in the complaint, forbids the abuser from coming within a certain distance of the victim. It may also make other restrictions, such as forbidding him to place phone calls or send emails to you.

The laws vary from state to state, but typically an emergency order remains in effect until a hearing takes place—usually within ten days—at which time both sides are invited to present evidence. The judge then decides whether to grant a final order, which may last up to a year.

Even if you don't think that your husband is physically violent, if he has been verbally or emotionally abusive I recommend that you obtain a protective order before informing him that you plan to divorce him. He is not stable if he is abusive and the realization that he is losing control over you could tip him over the edge. If you must call the police, they could potentially release the children to their father unless you have this type of court order in hand. It will protect you and the children from him until the judge schedules a hearing.

Enroll the people you interact with in your children's school and your workplace in helping to keep your family safe. Give a copy of your restraining order to the principal of your children's school and the daycare center, as well as your new phone number. Be sure that they know not to give your phone number to anyone who asks. Insist that all the necessary staff members are informed. Also, let the people who take care of your children know who is permitted to pick them up and show them a picture of your husband. Make sure that they know it is unsafe to release your children to him or to anyone else you haven't authorized.

If your children's caregivers ask for details, you only need to tell them that you are in danger, and so are the children. The rest of the story is none of their business. Set a boundary if they press you for more information. You want them on your side, so just say politely that it is too painful an issue for you to discuss and that you are worried for your children's safety. Period. If you have moved, make sure that they know not to give your new address out to anyone.

Make sure that your employer, neighbors, and friends know that you have a restraining order. If they have never met your husband, show them a picture of him.

Most states have laws that call for an arrest if the police find probable cause that a restraining order has been violated, even for driving past the victim's house. Unfortunately, there is widespread hesitation among police to enforce restraining orders so many are not upheld. In 2005, the Supreme Court ruled in Gonzalez vs. Little Rock that the police could not be held liable for violence that ensued due to the lack of enforcement of a restraining order.[5]

If your husband violates a restraining order, call the police immediately. Write down the names of the police officers, and the date and time that they came out in response to your call. You will need this information when you go to trial.

If your husband violates the restraining order more than once and has threatened physical violence or has been violent, make sure the police know this fact when they come out. This behavior is *stalking*. The laws against stalking are not always enforced effectively by law enforcement officials, especially if the stalker is considered a "pillar of the community."

You may ask to get the restraining order moved from family court to criminal court and have your husband prosecuted for felony stalking. You may need to get aggressive and insistent about this to ensure that he is prosecuted. Stand up for yourself and don't let someone else decide that your abuser gets a free pass. It may mean life or death for you and for your children.

The illusion of protection can be worse than not having it at all. If you fear for your safety, the best recourse is to leave home immediately for a domestic violence shelter.

Once you are in a safe house, you should contact your state's division of social services or child support enforcement office. You do not need to hire an attorney for a child support order, but you will need to hire an attorney for your separation and divorce. Do not use the same attorney that your spouse is using (see "He Will Not Be Fair" on page 161).

You may want to contact the local Legal Aid Society, which you can locate at the Legal Services Corporation website, to find a free or reduced-rate attorney in your area (see Resources). The National Domestic Abuse Hotline can also give you a referral.

If you are having trouble feeding your children or need clothes, contact your local Salvation Army and Food Bank (see Resources). They can also help you with getting on a food assistance program. If you do not have a job, visit the unemployment benefits website for resources or to apply for benefits (see Resources). The Salvation Army also provides skill set evaluations, educational and skill supplementation, interview and job placement assistance.

Head Start and many local churches offer child care services. Contact the Social Services Department in your area to find out what is available (see Resources).

Do not be embarrassed about asking for help. These services are available to families in need for a reason. Once you get on your feet, pay it forward by giving back to your community. But you can't do that unless and until you become self-sufficient. There is no reason to suffer without food, clothes, or shelter in a country as wealthy as the United States.

If you are not in immediate danger, check online for help in getting a job, acquiring job skills, or taking college courses at your local community college while you are preparing to get out. Having a sense of independence will help improve your self-esteem, and your efforts to become independent will provide a good example for your children.

Before you separate from your husband, set up a bank account in your name alone. Have the statements from this bank account sent to a post office box instead of to your home address. If you can do so, remove half of the jointly held funds and placed them in your personal account for safe keeping, to prevent your husband from draining the accounts and leaving you without any funds to pay bills. Do not drain the joint account yourself, however, and leave your husband without funds, as that would be unethical.

Disclose what you have done with money in your first meeting with your lawyer. Attorneys have a difference of opinion as to whether a woman should move funds to her private account before she files for divorce. In my opinion, an abusive situation warrants taking this step. An abuser will do whatever it takes to be punitive and maintain control, and that means that it is highly likely that he will drain the household accounts as soon as he becomes aware that his wife plans to divorce him.

Although your attorney can ask the judge in your case to issue a temporary order to freeze your jointly held bank accounts, such measures take time. You need to have funds for your day-to-day living expenses and to pay your attorney and court expenses in the meantime.

As discussed elsewhere, your husband will likely use delaying tactics and may even take you back to court frequently, as mine did. If you have no access to funds, you may be forced to drop your divorce action or to accept an unfair settlement.

The husband of one woman I know closed all their shared bank accounts shortly after she filed for divorce so that she had absolutely nothing on which to live. She had three minor children to feed and had to find ways to live without funds until she received her next paycheck. The judge is going to look at that kind of behavior with disapproval if this couple's case goes to trial, but it didn't make it easy for her family.

If you don't think that your abuser will do this to you, you are mistaken. It happens all the time when people are splitting up.

Keep at least a month's worth of living expenses in hard cash in a safe place outside your home, to be used only in an emergency.

You should also try to get a restraining order that protects your marital assets when you file for divorce. This kind of order will prevent your husband from clearing out your banking and investment accounts. Make sure that the bank and any brokerage firms involved have a copy of this order as soon as possible.

It is probably a good idea for you to put important documents and cash, as well as your fine jewelry, in a safe deposit box of your own at a bank and to take a complete inventory of what is in a joint bank box you may hold with your spouse. If you have a joint bank box, inform the bank that both signatures are required to open the joint box once you initiate divorce proceedings. Get the name of the person you talk with at the bank and write it down, making sure that person is aware that you are documenting the conversation. This step will help you to prevent negligence on the bank's part as the staff will not be able to claim ignorance.

If you have a home safe, change the code on the lock. If your husband has a key to the safe, change the lock or purchase a new safe that he doesn't have access to—after removing the contents from the old safe that belong to you.

Expect your husband to take or destroy any documents that you leave in the home, where they are unprotected. There is no safe place there to hide things. Do not expect him to do anything less than to try to hurt you. His actions may include pawning or selling your jewelry.

You may want to lock your laptop computer in your car hidden from view or leave it at work if there is anything on it that you don't want him to see related to your finances.

Change your passwords for online access to bank or brokerage accounts, credit card companies, utility companies, and other online stores where you have stored your credit card information for convenience, such as Amazon, PayPal, and eBay. Also, change the access codes for any ATM cards or credit cards that you have. Make sure that the list of your new passwords for these cards and accounts is in a secure location outside of the home.

# COPE WITH WHAT IS

*"Life is not what it is supposed to be. It is what it is. The way you cope with it is what makes the difference."*
—VIRGINIA SATIR

If you are married to someone who has been physically abusive in the past, you need to accept that filing for divorce is going to make him prone to escalating the violence. And you need to prepare for this possibility in advance. As an abuser, your husband is capable of anything—and you already know he wants to hurt you, so don't be caught off guard. Remember who and with what you are dealing.

Once your husband has left home, there are precautions you need to take.

- Change the locks on your doors and put locks on the windows. Replace wooden doors with steel or metal doors. If you can afford it, install a security system and a motion-sensitive lighting system around the perimeter of the building.
- Continue to keep your cell phone with you always. Install a phone line in a room that you can lock from the inside.
- Change to an unlisted phone number and make sure you have caller ID and the ability to block unwanted callers on your phones.
- Use an answering machine to screen your calls. Have your calls screened at work by the receptionist, if possible.
- Get a post office box for your mail so that your husband cannot open and read it.
- Open new accounts at a different bank, and bank in a different location than before.

- Do not talk on your cell phone when you are walking to or from your car or garage at work, or anywhere else. Your husband could sneak up behind you.
- Pay close attention to your surroundings and wear a police whistle around your neck and carry a bottle of pepper spray in your purse.
- Take a self-defense course.
- Reschedule any regular appointments that your husband may be aware of for a different time on a different day.
- Change your route to work, and take the children to school by new routes.
- It will be much safer if your children change schools so that your husband cannot kidnap them. Most kidnappers are parents. Abusers often act out of retaliation against their ex-wives. You cannot be too careful; change schools more than once if necessary.
- Even if you aren't worried about your ex-husband disappearing with the children, you should keep recent pictures of your children, along with records of their heights, weights, coloring, scars, and other noticeable markings. Pictures and records should be updated once a year. A good resource is the National Center for Missing and Exploited Children (see the Resources section).
- If you are worried that your husband may kill you and you are still living in the family home, relocate immediately. Nothing is worth risking your life or the lives of your children.
- It may be necessary for you to change your work hours or your place of employment. Do whatever you must do.
- Frequent different stores and gas stations, and join a different church.

- Try not to go to lunch or dinner alone, and avoid going to familiar places by yourself at night. Darkness could give your abuser cover to sneak up on you.
- Plan an escape route from home in case your husband breaks in, and teach this route to the children. Continue to keep a go-bag packed with the important items mentioned in "Prepare, Practice, Protect" (see page 1346) in case you must leave in a hurry.

Be sure always to keep any court orders and emergency phone numbers with you.

# PART THREE

# TAKING CARE OF BUSINESS

*"You must do the things you think you cannot do."*
—ELEANOR ROOSEVELT

CHAPTER SEVEN

# PREPARING FOR BATTLE

## STRATEGY OR TRAGEDY: IT IS ALL UP TO YOU

*"Never give up, for that is just the place and time that the tide will turn."*
—HARRIET BEECHER STOWE

Take charge of your defense, because as soon as you announce your intention to divorce him your abuser is going to attack you from all sides. Nobody else is going to defend you quite as well as you can. Remember to document dates, places, and times of verbal or physical abuse in a journal that you keep well-hidden if you're still living with your abuser. Don't forget to take pictures of any bruises, and make sure that these images are well hidden. Put a date on every printed photo. Download them from your smartphone and store them elsewhere in the cloud in case he checks your photo files on your phone. These photographs will be evidence in court.

If your husband gets violent, call the police and have them take the pictures of your bruises. Documentation will help you during the divorce, as you may have trouble reconstructing episodes from memory. High levels of stress negatively affect short-term memory. Keeping a journal that you can produce in court may help you win sole custody of your children, whom you need to protect.

You have no choice, but to hide these items, as your husband will have no problem destroying evidence. Do not assume that he doesn't snoop when you are not there; the odds are very high that he does. You are probably dealing with a very suspicious and paranoid person. Your husband may have started snooping right after you got married.

My husband felt it was his right to go through calendars, journals, or anything else of mine that he pleased. I had assumed that he respected my privacy as I had respected his, so I was shocked when I found out that he hadn't. He demanded that I throw out my calendars, which had important dates on them. I had thought that it was safe to leave them under a stack of papers in the bottom drawer of my desk, which was naive of me.

The most important thing that you can do when you are preparing for a divorce is to get informed, pay attention, and anticipate outcomes. My attorney may have been more intelligent than I was, and he certainly was more knowledgeable than I was about legal matters, but that was irrelevant when it came to my protection. I had to do that myself by thinking ahead about possible outcomes and how to avoid the negative ones. You will need to do the same.

You may have an attorney who cares about you, but who may miss things because of his or her workload, so you need to participate actively in the process of looking out for yourself. Your attorney will not be able to anticipate your husband's likely moves and countermoves as well as you do because you know his character, patterns, and idiosyncrasies. Take responsibility for protecting your interests.

Do as much research as you can about your finances and then decide what you want to achieve in the divorce settlement. Make a list of belongings and assets you would like to receive in the settlement as well as an appropriate amount you will need to receive for alimony and child support if that is relevant. We will discuss these issues in more detail in the next few chapters.

Take care of your health and stay focused. Negotiating a divorce is a marathon, not a sprint. As best you can, avoid letting your husband inflict any new damage on you. Anticipate his likely actions. He still may surprise you, so you must keep paying attention. For motivation, keep the end in mind that you will be much better off when you have put this all behind you. Fantasize about a divorce party, even if you don't plan to have one. I fantasized about a pretend funeral with a ceremony to bury my bad memories.

## FINANCIAL COUNSEL

*"Don't follow any advice, no matter how good, until you feel as deeply in your spirit as you think in your mind that the counsel is wise."*
—JOAN RIVERS

If you and your husband have investment accounts, enlist a financial advisor to help you in determining which securities to ask for in the settlement. To make sure that the advice you get is in your best interest, do not use the same person your husband uses. Have your advisor prepare a financial plan for you to see what kind of shape you are in and when you might be able to retire. If there are annuities involved, you will need to have him/her explain the features and benefits, internal expenses, penalty period, and riders to determine whether you want to retain any of those assets after the divorce.

If you don't understand all the terminology on your financial statements, which many people don't, ask your advisor to explain things to you in simple language. If he or she is not clear or becomes impatient, it's time to get a new advisor! Finance is not rocket science, but you need to fully understand all the investments to be able to decide what you want in the divorce. Ask a lot of questions. Do some research yourself online and don't believe everything Suze Orman tells you. Life is more complicated than a byline, and so are investments. You need thoughtful advice.

Keep in mind that your attorney specializes in law, not investments, even if he offers an opinion. Your brother or neighbor is probably not an expert on investments, either. I recommend that you take charge of your own affairs and keep your financial information private. If you get unsolicited offers to help, say thank you and decline. It's none of their business. You don't want friends or family members asking you for a loan because they now think that you can afford to give them one.

While we are on this topic, don't ever loan money to family or friends. It is very unlikely that they will ever repay you and it will probably poison your relationship. The only thing that you need to say is that you are unable to help them financially because you need to take care of your own family, and you will give them moral support. No other explanation or detail is necessary. In fact, the less you say here, the better. It is healthy to set boundaries and just say no.

You do not need to feel guilty for not being willing to jeopardize your well-being or your children's. You have no obligation, even to other family members, that is more important.

# BY DEFINITION

*"Everybody has a heart. Except some people."*
—BETTE DAVIS

The saying goes that the best defense is a good offense. In your case, this is going to be particularly true. I do not mean face-to-face confrontation, which would be not only pointless but also risky. You are not ever going to win that battle, so do not even try it. What I mean is that it is best if you are well prepared and informed before you leave your husband, and before he even suspects you might leave him. This pretense may be difficult for you, but it is justifiable and necessary to protect your physical and mental well-being as well as your children's while you are under the same roof as your abuser.

Many men become dangerous or threatening if they feel that they are losing control of their spouses or families. Finding out that you are leaving your husband may not result in a full-blown divorce psychosis, but if he is abusing you, you can be sure that you will be transformed immediately into his enemy.

It is said that divorce brings out the worst in people. I think that divorce just brings out what is already there. He is your adversary, your opponent, and your worst nightmare. Accept this and figure out what steps you need to take to protect yourself and the children. Try to read Chapters 8–10 before taking any action, unless you feel that you or your children are in imminent danger. As soon as you start to feel unsafe, you know that you must get out immediately.

Deception is a strategy that seeks to deceive, to trick, or to fool the enemy and to create a false perception in a way that can be leveraged to create an advantage. Try to gather as much information as possible about the marital assets and liabilities, consult an attorney, and start documenting the abuse before you depart. Do your best to make sure that he does not find out. This is a justifiable and prudent use of deception, and your conscience can remain clear. You are doing it for your survival.

Deception is a well-known and sanctioned military strategy. Remember that you are about to go into a heated battle. The element of surprise will have given you time to obtain much-needed information to have an unexpected advantage. Then you must get yourself and your children out of harm's way. You may decide not even to be present when he does find out that you intend to divorce him, which I think is the safest approach.

Once your husband finds out about the divorce, don't engage in discussions with him about anything other than the children. Keep your conversations short, or better yet, don't speak with him at all. Refer him to your attorney if he has questions or wants to negotiate with you to "save money." Suggesting you'll save money if you do not hire an attorney to represent you is a ploy to take advantage of you.

Stay calm if he becomes enraged. Stop talking with him and get to a safe place. Do not engage with him at all to avoid his tactics to scare you. He may threaten to take away the children from you, even though he is an abuser. He will not win if you don't let him. He is trying to wear you down. Shut him out completely, if you can, until the divorce is over.

I became very afraid when my husband threatened to take the children away from me the first time I filed for divorce, even though he had never changed a diaper or taken them to the doctor, prepared meals, done the laundry, and very seldom had washed the dishes or gone to the grocery store. It wasn't entirely rational of me to think that he would succeed, but his tactics instilled fear. I would have weathered the divorce much better if I had shut him out. I also let him waste countless hours of my time in direct negotiations with him. He wouldn't have kept his word no matter what agreement we came to, so this was meaningless.

Please don't fall for intimidation and psychological warfare. Once you file for divorce, your husband is your opponent and he will use whatever tactics he can against you. Don't expect him to behave well or to act ethically. Now is not the time for you to feel sorry for him or to try to reason with him. He doesn't want to be reasonable. After all, this is war!

## BE OBJECTIVE ABOUT THE OBJECTIVE

*"It is fatal to enter any war without the will to win it."*
—DOUGLAS MACARTHUR

If you go to war, you must have the objective to win it. This objective must be defined *and* attainable. Don't expect to get most of the assets in the marriage, as that is not realistic or even fair. Don't waste time in fighting for things that are not obtainable. You probably will get half of the assets that you can find if you fight for them. Don't expect to get half of his inherited assets, or even any of those, unless they were put in a joint account with your name on it.

One of your objectives should be for the divorce to be over in a reasonable period. And that means without unnecessary delays created by you. Your husband will use stalling tactics, so don't make things worse yourself. Don't spend money or time on battles you won't win. Your attorney will help you to be realistic, and you will need to use good common sense as well. Do a lot of research on the internet and read other books besides this one if they help you.

On the other hand, do not give up fighting for what you deserve and do not give in to your husband's unrealistic demands—and yes, he is going to make them—just because you want the divorce to end. That is what your husband is counting on, and it will affect you for the rest of your life.

Use economy of force. Meaning, allocate minimum essential power to secondary efforts. If your objectives are clearly understood (such as custody of the children, child support, alimony to go back to school, and half the assets), let go of whether you also get the leather couch or the flat-screen TV. You can replace furnishings.

Fighting for things you probably won't get is a waste of time and costs unnecessary attorney fees. Now is the time to figure out exactly what is most important that you want to get in the divorce. Keep your eye on the big picture.

Moral ascendancy is the moral right or moral superiority that dominates the events in question. The moral force of your right to be happy and live free from abuse, and to protect your children from abuse, is something that you will be able to lean on to give you strength during the upcoming battle. Your words and actions with your attorney and in court must be truthful and grounded in the firm belief of the righteousness of your cause.

You will need to take measures against your husband's attacks, as I outline below. If you need guidance as to whether a specific action is legal or ethical before taking it, pray for guidance and consult your attorney.

You must ensure the unity of command by making sure that you, your attorney, and his or her legal assistants are on the same page in your combined efforts to achieve your objectives. Unity requires honest and clear communication. Make sure that your objectives are written on paper, discussed thoroughly, and that both you and your attorney have a copy of them. Keep things simple. Ahead of time, you will need to prepare and share clear, concise, and uncomplicated written plans to ensure a thorough understanding of the issues at stake. Once you do, always keep your objective in mind.

## RIGHT MOVES

*"Victorious warriors win first and then go to war, while defeated warriors go to war first and then seek to win."*
—SUN TZU

You will also need to prepare for your husband's countermoves. If he is abusive, he is probably also devious and unethical. His nefariousness is why it is important for you to discover as much as possible about your finances before you file a petition for divorce. Expect him to practice deception by lying and hiding assets as soon as he possibly can.

He may have been hiding assets all along. If he doesn't hide them now, it will be a pleasant surprise. But don't get blindsided or be naive and hope for the best.

Your adversary may use a blockade to attempt to cut off cash, food, and supplies so that you have no choice, but to drop the divorce. Emptying joint bank accounts to punish you should not come as a surprise. Even though this maneuver is not legal, he will count on your not being able to outwait him financially and do it anyway. This tactic is very common, by the way, even when abuse is not a factor.

Having some cash in a bank account that's in your name only before you file for divorce—an account that he is unable to access and drain—has already been discussed (see "Prepare, Practice, Protect" on page 136). You will need to pay your attorney a retainer, and you will need money for current expenses whether you are leaving home or not. You may be able to get a court order requiring him to cover your living expenses, but enforcing the order is another matter. Ask your attorney to file a petition for contempt of court if your husband violates any order to give you funds. He can spend time in jail until he does comply.

My ex-husband had his attorney demand a lot of unnecessary information during the discovery process, only not even to bother to answer many of the questions on his own set of interrogatories. He only partially answered the request for production of documents. I received a blitzkrieg of requests from his attorney for my information, such as copies of our tax returns for the last ten years, followed by a lack of complete disclosure on his part. He failed to provide what I needed most to see.

My husband also used the strategy of distraction. He tried to cancel a life insurance policy I held on him during the divorce, which is a prohibited action once a petition for divorce has been filed. He failed to make mortgage payments. Also, he started a new and very risky business and committed a lot of money and debt to the venture. We will discuss this type of prohibited activity in more detail in "Not My Business" (see page 227). His lawyer advised him that he needed to keep the insurance in force after I had my attorney write a letter to insist on it.

If you think your husband capable of canceling your life insurance or medical insurance coverage against your will, you may need to contact the companies involved directly to ensure that those policies stay in effect. It may mean that you will have to pay the premiums yourself temporarily, but it is necessary that you protect your family in case of an accident, injury, illness, or the death of an income provider.

I was also responsible for my attorney's fees for defending against the continuous and prolonged attacks, or siege warfare, of my abuser's many ridiculous motions to the court. I lost quite a bit of time at work to confer with my attorney on defending against those motions and to appear in court as well. If you have substantial marital assets, it is critical to prepare for this possibility. My husband tried to bring me to the point of exhaustion, a tactic to erode my will and resolve.

I share this incident only to illustrate how you must pay attention, anticipate what your husband might do, and act proactively in your defense. Since your husband may consider your divorce to be a life-or-death situation, you must take measures to protect yourself and your family against his tactics. You are a lot stronger and smarter than you may think—or that he thinks you are. Use that to your advantage.

I sincerely hope that at this point you don't care what he thinks, not only because it really doesn't matter, but also because it is a distraction that you just don't need while you are at war. Don't let your compassionate heart make you vulnerable to his connivances.

I had finally reached a tipping point or the point beyond which there was no going back when it had been almost two years since I had filed for divorce with little progress to show for it. I finally insisted that my attorney schedule a time for mediation as well as for a judge to hear the divorce case, in case the mediation was unsuccessful. My attorney vehemently argued to try to put me off, so I became insistent and would not take "not yet" for an answer any longer. There was no reason not to schedule a court date, and I told him that I was not willing to accept any more delays. I was ready to do battle if my husband was not reasonable in mediation.

This ended up being a good tactic in that it showed my ex-husband I meant business. I wish that I had done it sooner. Until then, I had made the mistake of relying on my attorney to schedule the mediation and court dates at the appropriate times.

In my opinion, most successful attorneys are overbooked and will schedule court dates for the most pressing matters and the most vocal clients. If you're a people-pleaser by nature, you need to push yourself out of your comfort zone and insist that your case gets attention.

The whole purpose of this chapter is to prepare you for the fact that, more often than not, divorce is an ugly and contentious battle. Not something to be afraid of, just to be prepared for. In reality, few divorces are friendly. Abusive men tend to escalate their bad behavior during a divorce because aggression, manipulation, and dirty tricks have worked so well for them in the past. I believe that many women leave too much on the table to just be over and done with the whole ugly mess.

In general, men make a lot more money than women do and they tend to do much better financially after divorce than their ex-wives. Do not let your husband walk away with much more than he is entitled to just to be nice or to avoid conflict. You don't get points for niceness. In fact, niceness is not appropriate in this situation. Your husband won't appreciate it if you let him have more than he's entitled to receive. He just won't respect you. This is not new, as he already doesn't respect you.

Remember, your divorce *is* a conflict. You need to be reasonable and strong. You *don't* need to be nice. One of your main goals is to get custody of the children. Keep in mind that you must fight the good fight not just for yourself, but also for them. Be realistic about what is possible and then fight like hell to get it.

Do your best to anticipate what your ex is probably going to do, and prepare your countermoves in advance, if possible. Keep your focus on the battle at hand and have faith that peace and happiness await you after you win the war.

# HIDE AND SEEK

*"Man is not what he thinks he is; he is what he hides."*
—ANDRÉ MALRAUX

Many spouses try to hide their assets by transferring ownership temporarily to someone else, getting paid in cash, hoarding cash, deferring income, or failing to bill customers until after the divorce, grossly overstating business accounts payable, overstating business accounts receivables as "bad debts," moving personal property to undisclosed locations, overpaying bills or taxes to get a large refund later, failing to disclose the existence of accounts, as well as paying for items or groceries at the store with a debit card while getting large sums of cash back. A few hundred dollars here and a few hundred dollars there over a period of many months can add up significantly.

If you find receipts lying around the house or in your husband's pockets, examine them. See if you can use them as evidence. I know of one case where substantial funds were withdrawn from an account to make a mutually agreed-upon quarterly tax payment on a joint tax return, and the tax payment wasn't ever made.

You may need to hire a forensic accountant, which is advisable if you suspect that there is a lot of money involved. Take into account that this will be expensive and ask your attorney to advise you as to whether your situation merits the cost involved. Even if you know your husband is hiding money, it may be very difficult to prove or stop it.

Some men will destroy or hide vital evidence, so it is important that you keep a copy of everything you find, including the financial and legal documents, in a safe place, preferably outside the home.

# UNCOVER WHAT IS HIDDEN

*"I got my own back."*
—MAYA ANGELOU

If your husband has lied to you about how he has treated you or what he said, then you must assume that he is lying to you about other things as well. This is why it is important that you investigate your joint financial matters, his emails, his Facebook page, and his phone records to protect yourself.

One of my clients found out that her husband had not filed tax returns for the last five years of their marriage. She only found out when the IRS seized one of her bank accounts. They were holding her as liable as he was for any underpayment of taxes. As a result, she faced a penalty for failure to file as well as interest charges, and these two items exceeded the actual amount of taxes owed.

Even after the divorce, my client's ex-husband refused to produce his W2 forms, and she had to hire a certified public accountant to help her through this mess. The CPA had to order copies of the W2s from the IRS. In the meantime, interest and penalties continued to accrue. The man's wages had been garnished several years before by the IRS for unpaid taxes, and there was an IRS lien on their home. She was unaware of any of it. Her husband had hidden mail received from the IRS, the real property assessor's office, and his pay stubs from her for years. She also found out that he'd had another bank account in just his name for years during their marriage. I wonder what else had he been hiding?

Another client of mine had only suspected infidelity after her husband started paying more attention to his appearance and losing weight. After being encouraged to investigate his activities, she found communications to a mistress posted on his Facebook wall, as well as receipts for lingerie and other inexplicable expenses. It cemented her decision to file for divorce.

## HE WILL NOT BE FAIR

*"Men occasionally stumble over the truth, but most of them pick themselves up and hurry off as if nothing ever happened."*
—WINSTON CHURCHILL

Do not expect decency from your husband in the divorce if he has not been decent to you in the marriage. Many men punish their wives for divorcing them by trying to give them as little as possible in the settlement, even if it means that their children will live in poverty. You have an obligation to look out for your children and yourself, so do not be generous with your husband in the divorce, as you will soon regret it for years to come. Take whatever you are legally entitled to and remember that what you get affects your children as well as you. You need to make your priority taking care of the children and yourself. Later, if your husband fails to pay, it is your responsibility to take him back to court. Do not let him get away with anything. It is not fair to your children or you.

There is a very good chance that he will try to threaten and intimidate you, but you can protect yourself. He may try to insist that you do not hire a separate lawyer to save money or that you settle without attorneys. Both are terrible ideas as the two of you have conflicting interests, and ethically I believe that no divorce lawyer should represent both parties in a divorce. If your husband tries to get you to work it out yourselves to save money, remember that he is a bully and you will end up with very little if you go along with him to avoid additional conflict. The more that you give, the more he will demand.

Now is the time to stand up for yourself and get your own legal advice, especially since you may not understand all of your rights. You will need to educate yourself and get professional advice that is not biased against you. Do not negotiate with your husband about keeping the house or the retirement assets or anything else. If your husband presses you, tell him that his lawyer needs to talk with your lawyer, and you have been advised not to discuss it with him. Do not negotiate directly. If you do, you will lose.

CHAPTER EIGHT

# THE DIVORCE PROCESS

## LAW LESSONS

*"We must be willing to let go of the life we planned so as to have the life that is waiting for us."*
—JOSEPH CAMPBELL

To find a good divorce attorney, consider a referral from friends and trusted relatives. You may also contact the American Academy of Matrimonial Lawyers (see Resources) for a recommendation. Do a Google search of your state bar association and follow the links to check your potential attorney's record for disciplinary action.

When you meet with the attorney, find out what his/her fees and hourly rates are, how often you will receive bills, court costs to expect, and what he/she charges for a *retainer,* which is a deposit against the total cost of the divorce. You will pay for other expenses related to your case, among them appraisals, filing fees, faxes, postage, copies, delivery services, experts, and travel. The attorney should give you an estimate of the total cost in writing and an idea as to whether you will be able to get your spouse to pay for some or all these expenses. Some attorneys will work with you on a payment plan, so be sure to discuss this in the first meeting if you need one.

Read the fee agreement carefully before you sign it and make sure that you completely understand it. You should take it home with you so that you can review it while you are under less stress and can focus your attention on it. The time to ask questions about this contract is before you sign it, not afterward.

The attorney also should tell you how long the divorce will take and what your chances are of getting what you want. Find out how long it takes for him or her to return phone calls and what his/her procedure is to handle emergencies.

You may want to consider interviewing more than one attorney before hiring one. Trust your gut in making your decision and avoid aggressive and egotistical types. If the lawyer you meet is a poor listener, keep looking.

When you first meet with the attorney, bring a brief one- or two-page background of your marriage and family life with you. Include the names, birth dates, and social security numbers of all family members, the date of your marriage, whether any of your children are from a previous marriage, or if any prior marriage ended amicably. This description will be very helpful, even in a no-fault divorce state. No fault divorce is a divorce that is granted without a requirement by the court to show evidence of wrongdoing by either party.

Some states require grounds for divorce. If your state is one of these, bring as much evidence as you can that shows your husband is not a fit husband, including names of witnesses to your husband's behavior, photographs, and police reports. If your husband has been unfaithful, bring any proof, and testimony from your private investigator, if you hired one. Bring any information that you have about any conviction or sentence of imprisonment.

Take a financial statement with you of all your known assets and liabilities (debts) to your first or second appointment (see page 172 for a list of what to include). If you have a prenuptial or postnuptial agreement, bring a copy of that too. Once you decide that the attorney is right for you, give him or her this information. If you do not have a financial statement, do the best you can to make a list of what you own and what you owe. Let your attorney know about the things that you do not know. Bring a copy of your tax returns for the last three to five years and your most recent annual social security statements, if you have them.

If you have limited assets and income, contact your local Legal Aid Society (see Resources) to see if you qualify for free or reduced-fee legal assistance. Read books or research answers to your basic questions about divorce in your state on the internet, so that you don't need to call your attorney on them. He is going to bill you for his time, so use it wisely.

If your husband is in control of all your money, be sure to tell the attorney up front to make sure that he is willing to work with you and get a judge to order your husband to pay your legal fees. If you need to borrow money from family members to pay your legal fees, it is important to let your attorney know that the money received for that is to be treated as a loan, rather than a gift. Have a written loan agreement with your family, even if you think that the loan may be forgiven after the divorce is final.

Find out at the meeting whether the attorney feels comfortable in serving as your trusted adviser, as opposed to being the decision maker, as you will be living with the consequences. You must be the decider. Some attorneys have big egos and will make unilateral decisions that affect their clients for the rest of their lives.

The attorney for a client of mine was not a good listener and was very insistent that she receive all the retirement assets and give her husband the house. This was most expedient, as it was what her husband wanted.

My client had prepared a budget of what her income would be after the divorce, so she knew that she would not be able to afford to keep the house herself. Her attorney neglected to inform her that the retirement account was all "before tax" money and the state laws in our state do not differentiate between "before tax" and "after tax" assets in the division of assets. There will be more on the topic of taxes in "Stocks, Bonds, and Cash" (see page 199) and "Retirement Protection and Disability" (see page 206).

My client was in sales, so she had a variable income, and she only had a very small emergency reserve fund. She was under age fifty-nine and a half, so if she had to sell part of the retirement account in an emergency after the divorce, she would have had to pay federal income taxes as well as a 10 percent penalty on the amount withdrawn. She also would not have received enough cash in the settlement to afford to buy a house of her own. While it is true that retirement assets grow faster over time because of tax deferral, the attorney helping my client was disregarding her specific financial needs.

Fortunately, my client stuck up for herself and said that she was unwilling to take more than half of the assets in the retirement account and that she was entitled to receive the cash value of half the equity in the home. She ultimately got what she wanted.

Make a list of questions to bring every time that you meet with your attorney so that you get the answers and advice that you need without having to contact him or her multiple times. Every time that you call costs money, so don't involve the attorney in every disagreement with your spouse. Only call him or her when there is a crisis or when you need specific advice. You should try to speak to the attorney's secretary or paralegal first on matters that do not require legal advice. Remember that the paralegal's time costs money, too.

Follow your attorney's instructions and give him or her the information that he or she requests promptly. Make sure that it is organized well! Do not use your attorney as your therapist or for small talk, as it will be very costly if you do. If you do not have all the paperwork that you need for the appointment, reschedule the appointment and make getting the necessary documents a priority.

Let your attorney know if you plan to move during or after the divorce. If your state requires a consent form and you are unable to get your former spouse to sign one, your attorney will send a letter with your intentions to move to the court as well as to opposing counsel. If your physical safety is an issue, your attorney will explain that your new address must remain concealed from your abusive ex-husband in the change of address letter filed with the court.

Limit chitchat with your attorney, but do tell him or her about any problems or important issues so that you can deal with these issues up front. It is not necessary or helpful to go into a lot of the details, but be sure to give the important ones. It will be very helpful for you to give some thought to these issues and to write these things down to refer to before the meeting. Be completely truthful about important information, even if the information doesn't always put you in the best light. You want to avoid having your attorney blindsided later, which may cost you dearly. Remember that the attorney is there to give you counsel, not to judge you.

Be sure to write or stamp "Attorney-Client Privilege" on any documents you give your attorney in a meeting.

Your attorney will file a petition or application for divorce, which lists what you are asking for as the petitioner, or plaintiff, and explains the reasons for the divorce. Your spouse will have an opportunity to respond by having his attorney file an answer or schedule an appearance. The paperwork can be served to you by a process server or by the opposing attorney.

A court date will be set for an initial appearance, and both you and your husband must appear in court at that time. If you are requesting a temporary order regarding an issue such as where the children will live, if child support will be paid and how much, or who will live in the home, that business may also be handled at this time. The lawyers may meet out of court to try to reach a settlement, or the court may suggest that you and your husband go to mediation. In some states, protocol requires a couple to go to mediation before going to court.

Mediation is a way of resolving the dispute between the parties that is facilitated by a neutral third party called the mediator. It increases the control that the parties have over the resolution, rather than having a judge make an arbitrary decision. It is less costly and takes less time than going to trial (see "Mediation" on page 185). If you do not settle in mediation, a trial date will be set. You are entitled to your day in court, and it is your legal right to appear before a judge. A trial may be unavoidable if your husband is unreasonable in mediation.

I live in a no-fault divorce state, but in some states, it is possible to argue that fault grounds, such as abuse or adultery, should influence the division of assets and whether alimony is justified. Be sure to ask your attorney about the laws in your local area.

The next step in the legal process, whether you go to court or do mediation, is *discovery,* a process whereby essential information is gathered to prepare for trial. Early in the process, your attorney will send his attorney *interrogatories*: a list of questions your attorney wants to be answered about finances, facts, allegations, and evidence. He will also send a request for documents, which may include, but is not limited to, bank and brokerage statements, phone records, deeds, mortgage statements, W2 forms, 1099 forms, and tax returns. Your spouse's attorney will also send interrogatories and a request for documents to your attorney.

You may need to press your attorney to send these official mailings, especially if he or she is busy with other cases. If your attorney hasn't told you the mailing date, I would advise you to send an email to your attorney, with a copy to his paralegal, requesting that they send out interrogatories that week or the next, and to notify you of the date afterward. These forms are standard, so be sure to get a very good reason from his paralegal if there is going to be a delay.

A week after the due date, if your husband has not responded, send your attorney's paralegal an email that your husband is in contempt of court and request that they send the opposing counsel an email that you will be filing a petition for contempt very soon if you don't receive a response within days. Answer the interrogatories that you receive as soon as possible. Prompt response will help move the divorce process along. In my state, the opposing party has sixty days to respond to an official request.

There will be a lot of paperwork that your attorney will have you sign, and you will have to swear that the facts in those documents are true. Be sure to read each document very carefully and double-check it for accuracy before signing. Make sure that the numbers in the financial statements are correct and that everything you know about is included. Let your attorney know of any inaccuracies, untruths, or misstatements you see in your husband's documents as well.

It should be possible to get a divorce within a year of filing, but this may not happen unless you press the issue. After the interrogatories and requests for documents have been answered, give your attorney a list of some reasonable dates with the instruction to get the date set for mediation and trial.

Be prepared for *depositions,* sworn testimony given in the attorney's office and transcribed by a stenographer. The attorney will ask the opposing party questions to help prepare for trial. When it is your turn to give your sworn testimony, and be questioned by your ex-husband's attorney, observe the same protocol that you would when going to court (see "Proper Protocol" on page 176). Get a good night's sleep the night before the deposition, and have a coaching session with your attorney beforehand if you are nervous about how you will come across.

If you have a common-law marriage, you will go through the same divorce procedure as if you were officially married. If you haven't met your state's requirements for a common-law marriage, you can just separate, as a legal dissolution of marriage is unnecessary. A family court will handle the custody and child support issues and the division of assets will probably occur in small claims court. An attorney can guide you through this process.

Here is a list of things you need to check on when gathering your financial information. A downloadable and printable copy of this list may also be found at www.breakingbonds.com/blog/.

## BALANCE SHEET

**ASSETS:**

Checking accounts
Saving accounts
Credit union accounts
Money markets
Certificates of deposit
Savings bonds
Bond certificates
Stock certificates

Dividend reinvestment plans
Brokerage statements
Individual retirement accounts (IRAs), simplified employee pension (SEP) IRAs, and Roth IRAs
Pension plans and profit-sharing plans
401(k) plans
Non-qualified deferred compensation plans
Stock purchase plans
Stock option or restricted stock plans
Business interests (contracts or ownership)
Health savings account balances
Loans or promissory notes owned by you or your husband
Lawsuits filed by you or your husband
Potential claims (filed and not yet filed), including small claims as well as other lawsuits, regardless of court venue, over benefits such as disability and social security, insurance claims, and more
Annuities
Life insurance (type, face amount, owner, beneficiary, premiums)
Health, dental, vision, and disability insurance
Trusts
Inherited assets or gifts
Motor vehicles (cars, trucks, RVs, boats, motorcycles, and so on)
Real property (home, vacation home, rental, unimproved, commercial)
Timeshare interests
Leases
Receivables
Livestock inventories
Patents, copyrights, trademarks, and royalties
Creative works, both in progress and completed

Cemetery plots
Frequent flier accounts, airline and hotel rewards, credit card points
Club memberships (country, social, dinner, sports, and fitness)
Season tickets
Antiques, collectibles, and collections (note if a gift, owned before marriage, or inherited)
Equipment (sporting, electronic, and hobby related)
Firearms
Furs
Jewelry (note if a gift, owned before marriage, or inherited)
Safe deposit box contents
Storage facilities
Home furnishings and appliances (note if a gift, owned before marriage, or inherited)
Expected tax refunds or other refunds
Accrued vacation benefits
Expected inheritances
Assets held by others

**LIABILITIES:**

Mortgages
Auto loans
Credit card debt
Margin loans or security-based loans on brokerage accounts
Loans against 401(k)
Student loans debt
Other loans or promissory notes
Payables: Debts owed by a business, whether incorporated, sole proprietorship, or a limited liability company (LLC). This includes payroll, income and social security taxes, money owed for supplies, inventory purchases, and so on

Tax liens, overdue and currently owed taxes
Pending lawsuits against you

This list is by no means all-inclusive, so be sure to include anything that I may have left out. Make sure that your attorney is aware of any asset that is not marital property, such as inherited assets or personal gifts. If your separate assets were used to purchase property, include a copy of the settlement statement from when you bought it.

Let him know if you used separate funds for a remodeling project and how much. Bring the most recent statements, receipts, or copies that you have.

Remember that your husband may remove important records from your home as soon as he is aware that you plan to divorce him. You may never see them again, *even* with an official request for documents in a divorce proceeding. You are legally entitled to this information, but abusers do not feel that they need to play by the same rules as the rest of us. You can find out a lot of information by reading the tax returns, looking through file cabinets for statements, emails, computer files, desk drawers, sheds, storage units, and safe deposit boxes.

## DIVIDE AND CONQUER

*"It is important for a woman to be able to control her finances."*
—MARIA BARTIROMO

You need to put thought into what is best for you financially. Do not assume that your attorney will know these answers. For example, taking possession of the family home makes no sense at all if you can't afford to maintain it after the divorce. Get recommendations from your financial advisor and your accountant as well as your attorney. You will get a different perspective from each of them, and these differences will be invaluable in making your decision.

Once you have a very clear picture of which assets you want to receive in the divorce, tell your attorney what you have decided and provide a list in writing. Be sure to read this chapter and the next two first, as you will want to make a fully informed decision.

## EMAILS ARE E-TRAILS

*"In words are seen the state of mind and character and disposition of the speaker."*
—PLUTARCH

Be careful in all your emails and your email responses to your husband, both during and after the divorce. They may be used as evidence in court against you. Do not ever react in anger to emails and texts, and if you must respond at all, be truthful. You are not required to answer them, so only do so by choice. Your emails are not private and can become "Exhibit A" in court!

It would be better if you limit your email responses to the bare minimum, and only discuss the children. Do not take his phone calls if possible. He is going to try either to guilt you into taking him back or to make you feel bad about yourself. He may say he has changed. He hasn't, and he won't. Your husband may change temporarily, just long enough for you to drop the divorce petition, but you wouldn't have gotten to this point if he sincerely meant it.

Your best and safest strategy is to avoid his emails and phone calls, which will have the sole purpose of trying to wear you down. Do not engage in recriminations back and forth. He is not sorry, so save your energy for yourself, your children, and your job.

Be careful what you say on the phone or in letters, too, as these may be used against you in court as well. It is better to have your attorney handle the case and stay away from your husband's negativity.

I finally divorced my husband after my children were adults, but I continued to receive emails from him for over two years afterward. These emails were usually a toxic and crazy combination of conciliatory and hostile remarks. They did nothing for my self-esteem or our relationship, which should have ended with the divorce.

It was empowering to me to email him one last time to tell him that I was blocking his emails and phone calls from then on and that he could reach me through one of the children if there was an emergency. Then I did just that.

## DOCUMENT DETAILS

*"We store away clues, details that may be useful to us later."*
—DANI SHAPIRO

You may want to find out if it is legal to record conversations with your husband without his permission in your state. If it is, record them as a matter of course. If it is not, take detailed notes, recording the date and time of each one. Keep a phone log of your calls with him.

Of course, it is better for your well-being to keep these conversations limited or to eliminate them entirely, but if you must talk to him, use those interactions to your advantage in court. Your husband will try to get under your skin and manipulate you or scare you in the conversations. Write down as much as you can word for word right after the call, or as soon after it happens as is possible.

Write down whatever details you can recall about incidents in the past that would affect custody or that could be used to support your settlement. Procrastinating in making such records may result in faulty records or missing details, which will undermine your case.

Gather any documents that can support you in your divorce proceedings, including letters, emails, Facebook posts, receipts for gifts purchased for a lover, and detailed records of incidents or visitations. Record when your husband is late or he cancels or fails to show up for a scheduled visit with your children. This behavior could have an impact on custody.

Remember to hide your records documenting calls and other interactions with your husband in a secure location. Whatever you do, do not let your husband know that you are documenting what is going on. You will need to continue keeping records even after the divorce decree is signed, as some men will sue for custody after the divorce is final.

## PROPER PROTOCOL

*"Judgments prevent us from seeing the good that lies beyond appearances."*
—WAYNE DYER

Chances are very high that your divorce will be negotiated between the attorneys you and your husband hire or through mediation. But you need to be prepared to go to trial in a courtroom in front of a judge, just in case you cannot agree on terms.

Even if you come to terms on financial matters, you may need to go to court to ask for a restraining order or to handle custody issues. Here are some tips on how to behave and what to expect in court.

Get a good night's sleep before court appearances, and have a coaching session with your attorney beforehand if you are nervous about how you will come across in court.

Bring your well-organized accordion file with your copy of all the important documents to court with you, just in case there is something that your attorney is missing. Although he or she will probably bring all the necessary paperwork, my attorney forgot to bring a document that was crucial on one occasion. Fortunately, I had my copy on hand (See "Organize to Optimize" on page 181).

Also, bring a notepad and pen to take notes and to write your attorney a message in court if one is needed. Be sure to let your attorney know immediately if something is said in court that is untrue or if the attorney gets some facts or dates wrong—but do it quietly.

If you bring a friend or relative for support, they will not be allowed to sit at your table, and you should not look at them or talk with them during your proceedings. It would be much better for you to avoid bringing them in the first place in case they make you nervous. You do not want to be distracted. If they offer to come, please say no thank you and be firm about it.

Avoid proximity to your spouse in the hall or waiting room to prevent conflicts. If he insists on arguing with you, call security. If your attorney is not there when you get to court, he or she probably has other cases scheduled close to the same time. When your case is called, let the bailiff or court clerk know. They will call the attorney or postpone the court date.

There will be a court stenographer present who will transcribe everything that is said, although some cases are tape recorded rather than transcribed. It is possible that your first court appearance may not be in front of a judge, but rather a matrimonial referee, a law clerk, or another court-appointed person. As they are acting in an official capacity, it is important to be as courteous and truthful with them as you would be with the judge.

At trial, each attorney makes an opening statement, which is a summary of the case. The plaintiff's attorney then calls witnesses to testify and presents evidence. If you filed for divorce, then you are the plaintiff. In some states, this individual is called by a different term.

Opposing counsel then cross-examines the plaintiff's witnesses. Afterward, opposing counsel calls the defendant's (your husband's, if you filed) witnesses and presents evidence. The plaintiff's attorney has the right to cross-examine them.

Closing statements will then presented in court by each attorney. These state what each side is requesting in the divorce and how they want the judge to rule. Make sure that your attorney has your wishes spelled out in writing, and preferably typed, as those notes ultimately may be incorporated into the divorce decree.

Most judges do not tell you their decision at the trial. In fact, you may have to wait several weeks for a final decision on the divorce settlement. Your attorney may then have to file additional paperwork to get the divorce finalized.

If there is an appeal, only issues of law, not issues of fact, will be reviewed. An appellate court can only decide if the trial court applied the law properly. You have a certain period in which to file an appeal, so be sure to let your attorney know if you think that the decision was wrong or unfair as soon as possible after you read the decision. Appeals are lengthy and expensive, so be sure to get a realistic idea from your attorney as to whether you should pursue one.

Remember the following when going to court.

- Be prompt. Make sure that you are always on time for appointments with your attorney, your mediator, and especially for court appearances. Allow plenty of time for traffic issues, finding the location (including getting lost), parking, and passing through a security line at the door to the court. Security is a lot like airport screening.

- Dress the part. Wear conservative clothing, such as a simple dress or a nice jacket and skirt. Dress modestly. Jeans and shorts are not respectful of the court or the gravity of the situation. Leave vanity at the door and go easy on the makeup and jewelry. Cover up any tattoos and only wear one pair of pierced earrings at a time. Remove nose rings and ear cuffs. If you don't have a nice outfit and don't have the money to buy one, go to a used clothing store. I have found designer brands that had never been worn at some of these shops, as they still had price tags attached. You don't want to look too affluent, but you do want to look presentable and respectful. The judge may be older and conservative. He or she will probably be affected by your appearance and demeanor, whether you like it or not. Now is not the time to take a stand on your mode of dress. The outcome of your case is just too important.
- Be respectful. You want the judge to be on your side. Address the judge directly as "Your Honor." Stand whenever the judge stands and when the judge is giving a decision or order regarding your case.
- Answer only "Yes, sir/Yes, ma'am" or "No, sir/No ma'am" to yes or no questions. If you don't know the answer, say, "I don't know." or "I don't remember." Do not guess.
- When you are questioned on the witness stand, keep your answers short and to the point. Answer only the question that was asked. Do not try to be helpful by elaborating your answer as you could hurt your case in doing so poorly. If you bring up other issues in your answer, you

may end up hurting your case. The judge could perceive you as wasting the court's time.

- Only speak when asked a question. Never interrupt the judge. Pass a note or whisper quietly if you must communicate with your attorney while you are in the courtroom— which is only if there is something important you need to tell him or her.
- Stay calm and do not get emotional on the stand. Do not let your husband's attorney goad you into losing your temper.

Tell the truth. If you don't, it will cost you. Committing perjury is a felony, and you could end up with a substantial fine and jail time if you lie under oath.

## DIVORCE CONFIDENTIAL

*"Trust in yourself. Your perceptions are often far more accurate than you are willing to believe."*
—CLAUDIA BLACK

Please keep in mind that any conversations you have with friends, family, or in-laws are not confidential in a divorce proceeding. They could be subpoenaed to divulge this information in court by opposing counsel, or they could accidentally let something slip that you need to be kept private. It is best that you only share details of your marriage that could affect you adversely with your attorney and your therapist because these are confidential relationships.

If you have a close friend whom your husband does not know, feel free to vent—but only if you are certain that this individual is completely trustworthy, discreet, and nonjudgmental of you. Only share your negotiation strategy with your attorney and your trusted financial advisor. You will need to make sure that you do not have regrets later about your having had a lack of discretion in the divorce.

Do not violate an important boundary and rely on your children for emotional support. Do not confide details of your marriage that would be best discussed with your therapist to them. It is bad enough that they have seen or heard abuse in the home. You need to put your children's needs before your own. You will have a better relationship with them afterward if you remain in a neutral parental role throughout the divorce.

Badmouthing your husband will poison your relationship with your children, so avoid doing it. If your husband is a real manipulator, it may have been necessary for you to inform them of what is going on, but please continue to choose your words carefully. Avoid name-calling, as this may make your children defensive and protective of their father and resentful of you, which is not what you want to accomplish.

Say that what their father *did* is not acceptable, rather than *he* is not acceptable. It will help to reduce the emotional burden of your divorce on your children, who are already coping with overwhelming feelings.

Feel free to call him a *pathological liar, abuser,* and *devious manipulator* to your therapist and best friend. Vent to the right person.

## ORGANIZE TO OPTIMIZE

*"Tis skill, not strength, that governs a ship."*
—THOMAS FULLER

Organization can save you. Having a checklist and detailed notes will help to reduce your level of stress. Keep:

- A phone log of calls with your spouse. Record the date, time, and content of each of your calls.
- A separate phone log of calls and messages that you have left for your paralegal and attorney.
- Copies of all documents that you have given to your attorney in case he/she cannot locate an important item. Make sure that you organize the documents you give to the attorney so that you are not billed by his/her office to put them in chronological order. I set up file folders for my attorney, labeled for different topics, such as Assets & Liabilities, Bank Statements, Brokerage Statements, Credit Card Statements, Household Inventory, Appraisals, Interrogatories, Tax Returns, Evidence and Abusive Emails, Receipts, and Division of Assets. I then put them in an accordion file, which I handed to the attorney at our second meeting. I kept them updated. Don't assume that your attorney is organized. Help him or her to be more effective by making your items easy to find when needed.
- A record of the date you deposit child support payments.
- Paid and unpaid bills (in separate files).
- A comprehensive calendar of children's appointments and sports events, business obligations, attorney appointments, deadlines, and court dates to avoid booking appointments related to your divorce when you are not going to be available. (This can prove where you or your children were at certain times.)

Also use to-do lists, whether in writing or on your computer or other personal device, so that you don't forget important details. It is essential, for example, that you pay your bills on time before, during, and after the divorce, as you are now creating a credit history as a single person.

Please remember that most people forget important details when they are under a lot of stress and that you and your attorney probably won't be exceptions to this rule. Having a system in place to keep you both organized is essential to reduce the stress and win your case.

## TAKING PERSONAL STOCK

*"We are not interested in the possibilities of defeat. They do not exist."*
—QUEEN VICTORIA

Make an inventory of all your valuable personal property and take pictures of all the furniture, jewelry, paintings, collections, antiques, kitchen goods, tools, electronics, vehicles, and equipment. Make sure that the date and time stamp is working, as it will give you proof of ownership on the date you took the pictures. Or you can email it to yourself at work so that you have dated proof. Make sure that your husband is aware that he won't be able just to cart things off and deny that they existed. Even if they disappear, they will be considered in the division of assets. Make a list of each item, indicating which ones were owned prior to the marriage, gifts, or inherited. Those will be excluded from marital property, so you won't have to get them appraised. Unless your husband is willing to be reasonable in splitting the other items, you will need to get an appraisal of all except the excluded items and prepare a list of which items you want to receive in your share and which items you think that your husband should receive. Indicate on each list whether it was previously owned, a gift, inherited, or your portion or your husband's portion of the marital property. Keep track of the appraisal costs that you incur, as your husband is liable to pay half of those expenses. That is only going to happen if you insist on including it in the checklist of expenses for your attorney.

It will save you and your husband a lot of money if you can agree on how to divide your personal property, so make a list of what is most important to you and what is most important to him. If it is possible, see if you can both agree to use eBay or estate sale values instead of having to get everything appraised. It would be best to communicate this via email. If he is unfair or becomes abusive or uncooperative, then please leave it alone and just hire an appraiser. Make a list of what you think is a reasonable division of personal property and give a copy of it to your lawyer along with the appraisal to present to the court.

## GUARDIAN AD LITEM

*"It is easier for a father to have children than for children to have a real father."*
—POPE JOHN XXIII

If the court appoints a legal guardian or guardian ad litem to represent your children throughout the custody aspect of your divorce case, it is in your best interest to be friendly and cooperative with this individual. A guardian ad litem is usually, though not always, an attorney who represents the children's point of view regarding custody and visitation to the court. Such people are often paid by the state but are sometimes paid by the parents.

In my state, trained volunteers who work as court-appointed special advocates (CASA) represent the children's interests.

You can expect your children's guardian ad litem to contact you to set up a home visit to talk with you about your relationship with each of the children and your point of view regarding custody. They will also speak privately with each of your children and with your ex-husband. The guardian may make a recommendation to the judge about custody. Since this person is very influential, you want the guardian ad litem to be on your side.

Make sure that you and the children are calm and neatly groomed and that the house is as clean and inviting as possible when the guardian ad litem comes to visit.

If there are allegations of child abuse, a state caseworker may be assigned to investigate. Notify your attorney as soon as you are aware of any investigation, and share copies of any documents with him.

## MEDIATION

*"You don't notice the referee during the game unless he makes a bad call."*
—DREW CURTIS

Mediation (aka arbitration) is a way of resolving a dispute between two parties with facilitation by a neutral third party known as a *mediator.* Most divorce cases get settled in mediation without ever going to trial. Do not assume that mediation will work to your benefit just because you have been the victim of abuse. Although it is true that mediation is less expensive than going to trial, you could end up with a lot less than you would by going to court and paying the extra costs to pay the attorney to represent you there. If your husband doesn't budge, you must be prepared to go to court.

Some states require divorcing couples to try mediation first before going to court. In theory, mediators are neutral, as they work for both the husband and the wife. If your husband is fair regarding custody and assets, mediation can be a cooperative and beneficial experience. It will not work well for you, however, if you are fearful for your physical safety, if your spouse will not compromise, if you get upset easily, or if you have difficulty standing up for yourself. Remember that the mediator's job is to negotiate a settlement, not to be your advocate.

In my case, my husband was kept with his attorney in a separate room from the room that I was in with my attorney. Even though it creates extra expense for you, do not go into mediation without your lawyer present. Bring a complete and updated list of assets and liabilities with you along with a list of what you expect to receive. Give copies of these lists to your attorney at a meeting before mediation and right before the first mediation session starts, and tell him that you want him to fight for this settlement. Be sure to double-check it against what is included in the divorce agreement before you sign it.

Don't forget about child support and alimony when you are indicating your important goals. Research the laws in your state ahead of time and insist that they are honored.

Be realistic in what you expect to get out of the divorce. Remember that any assets that your husband had before the marriage belong to him, so do not expect to get a part of those assets. But by the same token, do not agree to give him part of the assets you inherited or acquired before the marriage and kept as separate assets.

You might not get as much from the settlement if you signed a prenuptial agreement. Be sure that you discuss the terms of the prenup with your attorney to determine what you are entitled by law to receive. In most cases, each spouse receives 50 percent of marital assets in the divorce, although you may be entitled to more.

Some states require an equitable distribution, not an equal one. Judges have a lot of discretion in dividing property in states where the law dictates equitable distribution, as what is equitable is a subjective determination. Your judge may consider such factors as fault, the different earning capacities of the spouses, whether one spouse supported the other one while obtaining a degree, the health condition of the spouses, the length of the marriage, and separate property. Judges have biases, just like other people do, and going to trial may work in your favor, or it may not.

Your attorney should be able to give you some insight ahead of time into how the judge assigned to your case treats women. If you insist on a lot more than half of the assets, you may lose in court, so be sure to get some direction from your attorney.

Your attorney may advise you to ask for more than he or she expects you will get in the end as a negotiation strategy during the mediation. It will be vital that you get as complete an accounting as you can of all the assets immediately before going to mediation.

The attorneys at my mediation took the first several hours of mediation time just to draw up a list of the assets together. This was something that they already had, and I believe that it had no purpose other than to increase their hourly fees. Puffing up fees is not uncommon. Please make sure you avoid this tactic by insisting with your attorney ahead of time that he or she come to the meeting prepared and that you will be in mediation for two or three hours tops. Alert your attorney and the mediator that you plan to walk out after the appointed time and go to trial. Make a show of setting a timer at the start, which will be a very effective way to limit fees. I sure wish that I had done that. My outcome would have been quite different. Protect your interests.

As most divorces never go to trial, be prepared during mediation to settle. If you do go to trial, it is important to know that a judge decides most cases, not a jury. Appeals are expensive and rare. Remember during mediation that you may not get all you want if you go to trial and that it is going to be stressful and expensive.

Staying strong and being firm about what you want during mediation may be your best bet. Stay calm and be objective about the objective.

CHAPTER NINE

# MONEY MATTERS

## CREDIT COUNTS

*"Credit is an 'I love debt' score."*
—DAVE RAMSEY

Before you file for divorce, obtain a credit card in your name alone. You may not be able to get credit based on your income alone, so make an application and get the card while you are still married so that you can qualify for credit based on your joint income with your spouse. As soon as you file for divorce, close any joint credit cards that have a zero balance and freeze the jointly held credit cards. You probably won't be able to close them out completely if they still have a balance, but you can contact the credit card company and prevent any additional charges from being added to the joint debt by freezing the account.

Do not underestimate the importance of taking this step, as you are still responsible for payment of any joint debt that you or your husband incur during your marriage, even debt that your husband will ultimately be responsible for in the settlement. Credit card companies are only concerned with whether you signed for the card (and its related debt), not the terms of a court order. Document all phone calls you make to the credit card companies and send them follow-up letters requesting that the lender report to the credit agencies that each of these credit card accounts was closed at your request.

Late payments and skipped payments will adversely affect your credit score for years to come, so do your best to make sure that payments are made by the due date for any debts you or your husband have incurred while the divorce is still going on. Your credit score will affect whether you can buy a home in your name alone or if you can refinance your existing home to remove your husband's name afterward. It also affects the rate of interest that you will be charged on any loans you apply for in the future. You need to do what you can to protect your credit score.

In many states, you may be held accountable for debts accumulated by your spouse during the marriage even until up to the day that your divorce becomes final. That's a scary thought!

Order a credit report periodically to monitor and protect your credit. You are entitled to one free report each year from each of three major credit-reporting agencies (Experian, TransUnion, and Equifax—see Resources), so order one from each service every four months for at least two or three years after the divorce is final. Keep up this practice indefinitely to protect your credit due to credit fraud.

You may also want to use a credit-monitoring service if you are worried that your husband may borrow money in your name without your authorization. If your name is on the loan agreement and you don't pay the loan off if he doesn't, your credit will be adversely affected.

If your name is on a truck or car loan for a vehicle that your husband drives, insist that he pay off the loan or refinance it. That must be spelled out in the divorce decree, too, so don't let your attorney omit it. Otherwise, you will have to make payments if he doesn't later to avoid having the loan affect your credit score.

You will not be aware that payments haven't been made if the overdue notices are sent to your husband's new address. Monitor your credit after the divorce to make sure that your husband is not continuing to create new problems for you.

After the divorce, make getting out of debt a priority. Credit card debt is extremely expensive, and most people do not pay attention to how much they are paying in interest charges. Check all your credit card statements to find out the interest rate on each one. Then pay the minimum each month on the least expensive ones while you pay as much as possible on the highest interest rate card.

Stop charging on credit cards altogether until all your previous credit card debt is paid off. Some people recommend cutting up your cards, but I think that is too drastic unless you are incapable of self-discipline. If your spending is out of control, put the cards in your lockbox until you get them paid off. You need to keep good credit, so don't cut up the cards unless you absolutely must. Simply pay them off as soon as you reasonably can. You may need to have that credit available to you if an emergency arises.

For most people, it is not necessary to have more than two cards. It makes sense to cut up cards from clothing stores and other specialty credit cards, as these are limited in scope and usually charge higher interest rates. Figure out a repayment plan so that their balance is zero within three years or less. A good rule of thumb is to pay off the credit card with the highest interest rate first while paying the minimum and a smaller extra amount on the other cards so that you don't incur expensive late fees or adversely affect your credit rating. Keep just two credit cards for emergencies, and make small essential charges each month on at least one of them, making sure that you pay it off by the due date each month to avoid interest charges. Being careful with your credit cards will improve your credit score over time.

## REGARDING BILLING

*"You can't be in debt and win. It doesn't work."*
—DAVE RAMSEY

Find out if the utility bills for your home are in joint name or individual name.

If you are moving out of the house you share with your husband, be sure to have your name removed from these accounts, or you will continue to be financially liable to pay them. The court will look unfavorably on you for turning utilities off if your spouse is still living there, so be fair and have them transferred into his name alone if you have moved out.

If you are staying in the house, transferring the utility bills to your name alone will prevent your ex-husband from turning off service, but then you will be solely responsible for payment. Ask your attorney how to handle this as soon as possible first, in case the court orders your husband to continue to pay the utility bills. Ask your attorney to request that your husband make the checks payable to you instead of directly to the utility companies so that you can keep track of them and put the utilities in your name. If he keeps the utilities in his name and is not living at the house, he may "forget" to pay them, and you might wake up one morning without water or electricity.

If he doesn't pay them when he's been ordered, you will have to take him back to court, and you will have to keep paying these bills yourself in the meantime. There will also be a charge to turn the utilities back on if they get cut off, and the utility companies may now require a deposit from you. You need to hold onto your resources for other expenses.

## ENSURE RESTRAINT

*"Keep a diary and someday it'll keep you"*
—MAE WEST

In most states, neither you nor your spouse may conceal or destroy assets, take on substantial debt, start businesses, open each other's mail, destroy records, cancel utilities or insurance coverage, or change beneficiaries once one of you has filed for divorce. An automatic restraining order is activated in these states as soon as the petition for divorce is filed. Make sure to discuss this issue with your attorney, to find out the law in your state, especially since there is a strong possibility that your husband will be vindictive and do things that he isn't allowed to do by law.

Many people are either unaware or claim ignorance of the law. Do not assume that your husband ought to know the law or that his lawyer will inform him. Take responsibility yourself and inform your spouse immediately that he cannot do certain things and that you will make sure that he is held in contempt of court if he does them so that he will be unable to claim ignorance.

My ex-husband tried to cancel a valuable life insurance policy, and I had to petition the court to ensure that it wasn't canceled, even though we lived in an automatic restraining order state. He claimed ignorance and then refused to continue paying the premiums even with a court order to do so, claiming that he could no longer afford to pay them. I had to pay them myself to ensure that the policy did not lapse. There will be times when enforcement is possible, and other times where you simply must make payments yourself to protect your family.

Do not hide assets or cancel life insurance if you want to have the judge on your side. Remember that after you file for divorce, you are not allowed to change the beneficiary on any assets until the divorce is final, either. Tell your husband yourself as soon as you file that he cannot legally cancel medical insurance and life insurance, or change beneficiaries—and do it in writing via email so that you have documentation that you gave him notice.

Also spell out that he will be required by the court to replace any medical or life insurance that he cancels, probably at a much higher cost. If he understands the consequences, he will be less likely to cause you financial harm.

Send a backup copy of the email to your attorney, so that he has proof that your husband was notified. You may also decide to back up the email by sending a printed copy of the email to your husband return-receipt requested. Because he may refuse to accept delivery of such a letter, you can ask your attorney to serve the letter to him at the same time as the divorce papers.

## MUST HAVE MEDICAL

*"It is health that is real wealth and not pieces of gold and silver."*

—MAHATMA GANDHI

If you have medical insurance available to you at work, try to get your attorney to specify in the divorce decree for you to carry the children on your policy and have your ex-husband reimburse you for it rather than allowing him to carry the children on his policy. A divorce is a qualifying event that will allow you to obtain coverage yourself for you and your children on your policy at work if you haven't done so already. Even if the coverage is more expensive than letting your ex-husband keep the children on his company policy, it is better to switch them to yours than to worry about whether he will cancel the coverage at some point in the future.

Even parents who love their children sometimes do irrational things out of spite to get back at their former spouses.

The amount of the insurance premium that your ex-husband is liable for should be added to his child support payments and garnished from his wages. If you don't work or have access to medical insurance at work and you are worried about your husband canceling his family insurance coverage, notify your attorney to address the situation immediately. If you are not employed and your husband's group family policy has covered you, you may apply for three years of COBRA medical insurance coverage without having to get a physical or needing to worry about pre-existing conditions. A requirement is that you file for coverage within sixty days of the divorce with the human resources department of his employer.

To retain this coverage, you must be sure to make the first payment within forty-five days of the election, even if you don't get a bill from the insurance company. This coverage will be a lot more expensive than it has been under the group medical plan, as you will now also be paying the company's share of the cost of the insurance. It may cost a great deal less than you would pay for medical insurance that you could find on your own, and give you better coverage than other available plans. Be sure to compare available plans.

It is unclear what type of insurance policies will be available in different states in the future. At the time of this writing, you may still be able to obtain coverage under the Affordable Care Act. Check out www.healthinsurance.org,www.affordable-health-insurance-plans.org, or the healthcare exchange in your state for information. It is impossible to predict what changes will be made by the legislature going forward on health care, so be sure to get current advice on what is available in your state.

Do your homework on costs and coverage under different options well before the divorce negotiations are finalized to make sure that you have a course of action planned for the near future. Include the amount that it is going to cost you in your budget for negotiating alimony and child support. You may need to adjust this from year to year.

## COST OF LIVING

*"Budgets are nothing if not statements of priorities."*
—JEFF MERKLEY

Make a detailed budget for your monthly expenses and your periodic expenses so that your attorney can determine how much alimony and child support to ask for in your divorce negotiations. Many women underestimate their monthly costs by failing to include such things as the cost of home repairs, gas and car maintenance, auto and homeowner's insurance, health insurance deductibles and copayments, home repairs, education, unexpected expenses, state income taxes, inflation, and more. Allow for discretionary expenses as well, such as travel, birthday, and Christmas gifts—just be sure to make the amount those reasonable.

You and your ex-husband will need to come to an agreement on who pays for the children's school tuition, music lessons, sports fees, school trips, clothes, back-to-school costs, cell phones, internet service providers, phone carriers, college search trips, gas, car insurance, and college expenses, such as books and dormitory housing.

Look at your bank account statements for at least the last year to see where the money in your household has been going. If you haven't done so already, prepare a budget of what your expenses will likely be after the divorce based on what your joint spending patterns have been, as you will need to give this to your lawyer. Free printable budget worksheets are available online that you can revise periodically to reflect your spending accurately. Guessing is not a good idea in such a serious matter. You can get forms at: https://www.smartabout money.org/ Tools/Budget-Wizard.

Alimony is no longer tax deductible from the payer's income and taxable to the recipient for divorce or separation agreements signed after 2018, so you will not need to take into consideration taxes on alimony payments you receive when you do your budget.

You may have to make estimated tax payments on your income now that you will be a single filer to avoid penalties. Check with your accountant to get an estimate. To avoid filing quarterly payments, you may prefer to increase your tax withholding at work.

If you earn more in annual income than your husband, you may owe him alimony and will need to factor that amount into your budget plan.

## STOCKS, BONDS, AND CASH

*"Life isn't fair. Everybody has their issues. It's how you handle your issues that distinguishes you."*
—MARIA SHRIVER

Cash that is in savings accounts, checking accounts, and money market accounts is *liquid,* or readily available. Besides covering expenses incurred during the divorce, you need to receive an adequate portion of the remaining liquid assets in the divorce settlement for emergencies, to possibly buy a home, or to pay for going back to school. Find out if the accounts are in single or joint name, if there is overdraft protection, or if there is a payable on death designation on each of these accounts. Your attorney will ask you for this information, so make sure that you have it.

Certificates of deposit (CDs) have penalties if you cash them in before their maturity dates unless they are held at a brokerage firm. CDs held at a brokerage firm do not have penalties, but they may be sold prior to maturity at a gain or at a loss, depending on what interest rates are doing at the time of sale. You will need to find out who owns them, whether there is a listed beneficiary, and, if they are bank CDs, if they have been pledged as collateral for a loan.

Brokerage accounts may include cash, money market funds, CDs, stocks, bonds, mutual funds, annuities, and other securities. You will need to find out who owns them, if there are any named beneficiaries, and if there are any loans against the accounts. It will be important to get the cost basis and date of purchase for each of the securities that are still owned in accounts that are not retirement accounts. The cost basis may be provided on the brokerage statements.

This information will be important in deciding which nonretirement assets to ask for in the division of assets. You do not want to receive all the investments with a low-cost basis while your husband receives the investments with a high-cost basis. That would not be fair to you because the low-cost basis investments will incur more taxes when sold. If there is no agreement between you and your husband on the division of securities, you may want to insist that they are divided down the middle as much as possible. Municipal bonds are sold in increments of $5,000, so an exact down-the-middle division with a bond portfolio may not be possible.

Get help from your financial advisor in deciding what to ask for in the division of assets.

Employee stock options and restricted stock (stock that is not transferable until certain conditions are met) have vesting schedules for when the employee acquires ownership in them after they have been granted. The transfer of ownership to the employee is contingent on their continued employment with the company for a certain period. For example, these securities may become 25 percent vested after one year, 50 percent after two years, 75 percent after three years, and 100 percent after four years. If some of the vesting occurs outside the period of the marriage, then that portion of the investment is not considered marital property. Your attorney may need to hire an accountant to determine the marital value of vested and unvested securities. Employers do not allow a former spouse to own options and restricted stock in their companies, so it will be necessary for your spouse to buy out your share at the time of your settlement. Do not consent to a court division of the options or restricted stock, as your spouse would be in control of managing the options and stock for you, and you would have no way of knowing when the securities are sold post-divorce unless your husband provides you with that information. It will also likely be difficult to obtain your share of the proceeds from him. Take half of the current value in cash instead to avoid this issue.

Make sure that you get statements going back several years on all bank and brokerage accounts. Check Schedule B and the K1s for your tax returns for the last few years to make sure that you do in fact have all of them. Go through the account statements to see if you can find any suspicious-looking withdrawals. That will be a good way to find out if your husband has been hiding money from you

If there are U.S. savings bonds in your portfolio of stocks and bonds, you will need to find out the ownership, face amount, series, rate of interest, and whether the bonds are still accumulating interest. If they aren't accumulating interest any longer, they will need to be cashed in and the proceeds divided or allocated in the divorce decree. The U.S. Treasury has a website where you can calculate the value of federal government bonds (See Resources). Some of the older bonds may be in paper certificates, so be sure to keep them in your lock box in case of fire.

## LIFE INSURANCE AND ANNUITIES

*"If a child, a spouse, a life partner, or a parent depends on you and your income, you need life insurance."*
—SUZE ORMAN

If you are to remain the beneficiary of your husband's life insurance after the divorce, please be aware that many states automatically revoke spousal beneficiary designations after a divorce is final. If your husband owns the policy, it will probably be necessary for him to redesignate you as the beneficiary of the policy after the divorce. If you don't ensure that he does this, the insurance may not be paid to you. Your attorney should insist that a provision is included in the divorce agreement that gives you access to information about the policy so that you can periodically check with the insurance company and verify that you are still the beneficiary and that the premiums have been paid on time. If he doesn't designate you as beneficiary, you may have to go back to court at your own expense. The owner determines the beneficiary and can change the beneficiary at any time.

I believe that it is prudent to insist that there be a change of ownership of the policy to you as part of the divorce agreement, and for you to pay the premiums yourself after the divorce to make sure that the policy stays in force. Include these premiums as part of your budget for determining alimony.

If your husband has a group term policy at work, only he can be the owner, and it will be canceled if he switches jobs anyway, so it may not be worth fighting over. There is no cash value for term insurance.

Get advice from a financial advisor regarding any annuity policies that are marital property so that you become fully informed of the details of each specific policy in your portfolio to determine the best way to handle each one in the divorce. An annuity is a contract that guarantees that the insurance company must pay benefits to the owner or the beneficiary upon certain conditions. Just like life insurance, the owner has control of the policy and can change the beneficiary at will.

The annuitant, the person on whose life the policy is written, usually cannot be changed until death. When the annuitant dies, the proceeds are paid to the beneficiary. The owner and the annuitant may or may not be the same person. The owner and the beneficiary may or may not be the same person; keep in mind that the owner can change the beneficiary at any time.

Fixed annuities guarantee a fixed rate for a limited term. There may be penalties if you cash in an annuity before the maturity date. The surrender period may be longer than the term the rate is guaranteed for, so you need to find out the details. If the policy has been annuitized, it may guarantee periodic payments for a definite period or the lifetime of one or both of you.

Variable annuities are invested in sub-accounts that may have a guaranteed option as well as in money market funds, stock funds, and bond funds. Their values are subject to daily market fluctuations. There are internal expenses in variable annuities called mortality and expense charges, as well as internal expenses for the mutual funds. There may also be income riders or death benefit riders, which may be quite valuable. If you take out more than the guaranteed amount from these funds in a given year, you could lose valuable income guarantees, if they apply.

There can be substantial taxes and penalties if annuities are cashed in as part of the divorce, so it is important to find out:

- If there is a surrender period and when this period ends.
- The cost basis if it is not held in a retirement account.
- Whether it is more prudent for you to divide any policies between you and your ex-husband rather than to cash them in. This could mean changing the ownership and the beneficiary. Remember that in most cases, you will not be able to change the annuitant.

Some annuities are held in an individual retirement account or IRA, which means that they are subject to IRA rules and are fully taxable. Others are nonqualified assets, which means that they have a cost basis. This point is very important because the cost basis in a nonqualified annuity is not taxable. Retirement accounts, including IRAs and ROTH IRAs, will be discussed in the next section, "Retirement Protection and Disability" (see page 206).

Keep in mind that there are income tax consequences to pulling periodic payments from all annuities, whether they are in retirement accounts or not. All the assets in a retirement account, apart from the ROTH IRA, will be subject to taxation at ordinary income tax rates when withdrawals are made. The IRS treats withdrawals from nonqualified annuities (except annuities from one insurance company that I know of) as taxable interest first. This means that all the interest must be taken out and subject to ordinary income tax first before you can pull out the "tax-free" return of principal, or cost basis. Also, there is a 10 percent penalty on the portion of the withdrawal that is considered income if you are under age fifty-nine and a half unless you qualify for one of the exceptions listed in the next section.

It might be better to negotiate for a lump sum payment for your share in the annuities that have been annuitized rather than having to depend on receiving a check every month from your ex-husband and having to worry about taking him back to court. Personally, I would rather take a discount than 100 percent of nothing, which is still nothing.

I believe most abusers will not honor agreements, even legal ones. Be realistic about how your husband will behave based on past behavior, not on sugary promises. The fewer times when you must rely on his goodwill, and the less contact you have with him after the divorce, the better.

If your husband is in the military, you may be able to get an annuity through the Survivor Benefit Plan. Janice Green states in *Divorce After 50*, "In divorce situations, timing regarding the SBP is crucial. State courts now have the authority to order a military member to designate a former spouse as a beneficiary, as part of the divorce judgment."[1] The election of a beneficiary does not happen *until* the military member is eligible for retirement, which means that this designation must be handled very carefully. You must file the signed divorce decree specifying that you are to receive the annuity with the Defense Finance and Accounting Service (DFAS) within one year of the divorce, as well as inform the DFAS to activate the deemed election for survivor benefits at the time he is eligible to retire. Both these steps are necessary to ensure that a subsequent spouse does not become the beneficiary and leave you with nothing.

Send the DFAS the documents by certified mail, return-receipt requested, so that you have proof in the future that the DFAS receives the notification. Follow up with a phone call requesting written acknowledgment from them.

If your attorney is taking care of this matter for you, make sure that you are provided copies of all correspondence and the return receipt. You may need to produce it to the DFAS in the future (at the time of your ex-husband's death) to be able to collect your survivor benefits. Make sure that you follow up if you don't receive the written acknowledgment.

## RETIREMENT PROTECTION AND DISABILITY

*"Retirement protection is often compared to a three-legged stool supported by social security, employer-provided pension funds, and private savings."*
—SANDER LEVIN

Most company-sponsored retirement accounts are defined contribution plans, 401(k) plans, 403(b) plans, or simplified employee pension (SEP) plans. These accounts, which are called qualified assets, grow tax deferred. There is a greater compounding effect over time than with after tax assets, called non-qualified assets, because of the tax deferral. Keep in mind that you will have to pay federal income taxes on any portion of the retirement assets that you withdraw from the account. Also, you may also have to pay state income taxes on withdrawals, depending on where you live. If the withdrawal occurs before age fifty-nine and a half, you will have to pay an additional 10 percent federal tax penalty unless you qualify for one of the exceptions listed below. Some employers offer a ROTH 401(k) or 403(b) option, where contributions do not qualify for a tax deduction, but the funds grow tax-free if the rules are followed.

Find out if your state considers the taxability of an account when assets are divided. Cash and unappreciated securities in taxable accounts have already had taxes paid on them and are for that reason worth more than the same amount of retirement dollars that have not yet been taxed. In many cases, the sensible thing to do is to split the accounts. However, your trusted financial advisor will advise you as to what is in your best interest given your particular situation That person will guide you on how to do an IRA rollover of your portion and to reallocate the account for you after the divorce. Individual retirement accounts (IRAs) are discussed below.

A *qualified domestic relations order* (QDRO) is a court order that your attorney may need to prepare to protect your interests in your husband's retirement plan if the divorce decree from the court alone does not give you the protection that you need. The QDRO will give instructions on paying your share of these benefits to the administrator of the retirement plan for your husband's company.

If you husband has a defined benefit or pension plan that pays a future fixed monthly amount, your attorney may have to hire an actuary to figure out how much you are entitled to receive. These plan payments are based on complex actuarial factors and assumptions related to compensation, years of service, inflation, interest rates, and life expectancy.

A QDRO is not used to protect marital interests in military or government pensions, which are covered by other laws. Your attorney will advise you regarding this issue. If he is not an expert on such plans, you may need to hire one to make sure that your rights are fully protected if there is a substantial sum involved.

Make sure that your attorney asks for a copy of the plan document, plan summary, and statements for the last several years to date for your spouse's 401(k), 403(b), or other retirement plan accounts. Please don't assume that your attorney has reviewed the pension fund restrictions, because he may not have even thought of this. Bring it to his or her attention and keep a checklist of all the details to cover in the divorce so that important items are not overlooked. Give a copy to your financial advisor to review for you.

You may take a cash settlement or receive half of the retirement assets into an IRA on a tax-deferred basis, or have the right to collect a portion of the payments of your ex-husband's defined benefit pension plan when he qualifies to retire. Find out if you will still be able to receive your share of his pension in the divorce settlement if your ex-spouse dies before his retirement. If the right to any benefit terminates at his death, it is worth nothing to you if he dies prematurely. You should know this important fact in advance of negotiating a settlement.

In drafting the QDRO for a pension plan, make sure that your attorney includes the *cost of living adjustment* (COLA) if one is offered, and that your interest in the plan is stated as a percentage of your husband's pension, not as a specific dollar amount. This is very important, as inflation will eat into the purchasing power of your retirement payments over time.

Make sure that you receive increases in value from accrued earnings, which is income that has been earned but has not yet been paid. If this is not spelled out appropriately in the QDRO, you won't get a share of those increases.

Earned, but not yet distributed contributions to plans should be accounted for as well.

Also, if the plan permits, your attorney should state in the QDRO that your benefits are to become payable at the earliest date that either one of you would be eligible to receive them, and your benefit is not tied only to when your ex-husband actually retires.

You may be better off negotiating a lump sum rather than having to wait until your ex-husband retires to collect a share of his benefits. An actuary will have to figure out the current value of those future benefits. Be sure to get advice from your financial advisor as well. How disciplined you are with large sums of money should be a factor in this decision. If you are a spendthrift, it may be more prudent to receive monthly checks instead.

If your spouse is receiving disability benefits or worker's compensation due to illness or injury, those payments will be considered marital property *if* they replace income that your spouse would have earned during the marriage. If your spouse receives these benefits *after* the divorce is final, they will be considered his sole property; however, the payments may be taken into consideration in setting marital support. If you are receiving those same sorts of payouts, they will also be considered marital property under the same regulations.

If your husband receives military disability or veteran's disability compensation, you are not eligible to receive any part of those payments in a divorce. If your ex-husband is working and then becomes disabled after your divorce is final, he may choose to take disability payments that eliminate any potential retirement pension benefits. This choice would leave you without an enforceable division of those pension benefits, yet another reason that you may want to consider taking a lump sum payment instead. Be sure to discuss this possibility with your attorney.

Different laws apply to military and government retirement plans. It will be very important to have an attorney with experience in such plans prepare the document to avoid problems that could cost you a lot of money in the future, especially if an argument arises as to which spouse (you or someone before or after you) is entitled to survivor benefits. You may need to hire a specialist before you go to mediation if the amount is significant.

In *Divorce After 50,* Janice Green offers a lot of good information about military retirement plans. If you were married for ten years or more while your ex-husband served in the military, you will be able to collect your share of the retirement benefits directly from the DFAS, so long as you are awarded no more than 50 percent of his pension in the divorce. If you are awarded more than 50 percent, you will have to collect the rest directly from your ex-husband.[2]

A *military pension division order* (MPDO), which is like a QDRO, must be in place for you to receive the benefits directly from DFAS (see Resources).

If you have been married to a military spouse for under ten years, you may still be able to receive part of the military pension benefits in the divorce decree, but your spouse will have to be required to forward them to you within a specified period after receiving them.[3] If he doesn't comply, you will have to take him back to court. Your lawyer and/or financial advisor can advise you as to whether it would be better to take a lump sum instead and sever all ties, especially since you are dealing with an abuser.

There are two types of individual retirement accounts, which are also qualified assets. The regular IRA (or IRA) allows an individual to fund a tax-deductible contribution of $6,000 per year plus an additional $1,000 contribution at age 50 and over, subject to eligibility based on income and whether the individual is covered by a corporate plan. The funds grow tax-deferred, so there is a greater compounding effect over time than with after tax assets. Withdrawals are fully taxable and are also subject to the fifty-nine and a half rule.

The Roth IRA has the same contribution limits, but there is no tax deduction allowed. The account grows tax-deferred until you withdraw the funds. If you follow the rules, withdrawals are tax free, which makes these assets quite valuable. There is no minimum required distribution at age seventy and a half, as is required for other retirement accounts. If your husband owns a ROTH IRA, try to get at least half of these assets in the divorce decree, which can be transferred directly into a ROTH IRA account in your name.

With a regular IRA, you can make withdrawals before age fifty-nine and a half, so long as the periodic payments are substantially equal and the payout period lasts for a minimum of five years—or until you reach age fifty-nine and a half, whichever is longer.

There are several methods to determine the monthly amount you will have to withdraw for that period without making any changes. If you do make a change in the amount, a 10 percent federal tax penalty is applied retroactively to all previous withdrawals, so get financial advice before you make any decisions to avoid a very costly mistake.

Income taxes still apply to any withdrawals. The tax penalty may be waived in the case of medical expense, disability, qualified higher education expenses, and a few other limited exceptions that I won't cover here.

It is in your best interest to avoid touching your retirement nest egg until you reach full retirement age even if you are tempted to take it early (see "Social Security Survivor" on page 211). Live within your budget and avoid premature withdrawals.

Do not jeopardize your future by making withdrawals from retirement funds to maintain your children's lifestyle or to pay for their college expenses. Their dad can help them, and they can also help themselves. They can get loans and grants if they want to go to school.

Deferred compensation plans normally have a vesting schedule if there is an annual company matching contribution. They are usually awarded to the spouse who holds the plan. Be sure to get a current statement right before mediation begins or your first court date to get an updated value. Also, be sure to note what time of the year matching awards are made, and vesting occurs. You are entitled to receive compensation for your share of the vested benefits, so discuss what this means in detail with your attorney.

## OTHER FREEBIES

*"Write injuries in dust, benefits in marble."*
—BENJAMIN FRANKLIN

Flexible spending accounts or flex plans (125 plans) allow employees to set aside money in an account before tax to pay for health insurance premiums, uninsured care for an employee or dependent, or for dependent care. The unspent balance used to be forfeited if not used by year end; however, you can now carry forward up to $500 from one year to the next. The balance in an FSA account is part of the marital estate, so there should be a cash buyout of the spouse's share of the remaining balance in the account.

Health savings accounts also allow employees to set aside money in an account before taxes for these expenses, and the unspent balances can be carried forward indefinitely. Make sure this item is on your list for discussions with your attorney and during mediation.

These small items are easily overlooked, but they can add up. You are entitled to a share of them.

Do not forget about upcoming bonuses, which are part of the marital estate. Some bonuses have different names, such as signing bonuses, retention awards, performance awards, and the like. These are all most likely to be considered part of the marital estate unless they are partially earned through work completed after the divorce. In that case, part of the bonus will be allocated to the marital estate based on work completed before the divorce is final.

The value of accrued leave for military service may be a marital asset in your state. Also, commissary benefits and exchange benefits are available for former spouses who had not remarried when the marriage lasted for at least twenty years during which at least twenty years of military service occurred.

## SOCIAL SECURITY SURVIVOR

*"Social security makes up a much larger share of total retirement income for unmarried women than for married couples, unmarried men, and whites."*
—DIANE WATSON

If you have worked, you have a social security earnings record and are entitled to receive full social security benefits when you reach full retirement age, which under present law is between ages sixty-five and sixty-seven. The amount that you will receive will depend upon your age and earnings record.

At age sixty-two, you are eligible to receive 75 percent or less of your full retirement age benefits, depending on your year of birth. I do not recommend that you take benefits early because the checks that you will receive for the rest of your life will be permanently reduced. Do not make that decision lightly. People live longer now, and cost-of-living adjustments to social security certainly do not keep pace with inflation. You won't be able to live on just your social security alone, but you can at least make the amount you get every month the highest possible.

Find out what your ex-spouse's social security benefits are as well, because you will have the option to draw 50 percent of the benefits based on his record if you have been married for at least ten years, and your marriage was valid under your state's law. This includes common law marriage if your state recognizes this category of partnership.

If your benefits will be higher based on his record, and you are close to your ten-year marriage anniversary, you may want your attorney to slow down the process of divorcing him until you have reached that important milestone.

If you remarry before age sixty, you may not be able to collect benefits based on his record unless your subsequent marriage ends.

Once you are divorced for at least two years, you will be able to claim benefits based on your husband's record, even if he is eligible, but is not yet receiving benefits himself. Benefits that you collect on his record will end if he dies or if you become entitled to social security at the same or a higher amount based on your personal record.

If your ex-husband dies, you may be eligible to receive survivor benefits of 100 percent of his benefit if you:

- Were married for at least ten years,
- Are at least sixty years old (or at least age fifty if you are disabled),
- Are not entitled to retirement benefits that are equal to or greater than his,
- Have not remarried before age fifty and are at least age sixty (or at least age fifty, if you are disabled) when you file.

If you have been collecting social security benefits based on your ex-husband's record, you can switch to receive survivor benefits at his death if they are higher. Your benefits will not affect the dollar amount of the benefits your children receive.

If you will receive a government or foreign employment pension and are not eligible for social security benefits, it may affect your ability to claim on your husband's record. Check with the Social Security Administration (see Resources). I recommend that you also consult with an attorney who specializes in these matters, as some of my clients receive unreliable or incomplete information when they contact SSA. Their office can be extremely difficult to reach by phone.

Social security laws may change in the future, so please discuss which strategy will be most beneficial to you with your financial advisor. You may obtain a copy of your social security earnings records at www.socialsecurity.gov. Make sure that you get a copy of your husband's record as well. Your attorney also should request it in the formal request for production of documents during discovery. Remind your attorney that this needs to go on the document request list if you don't already have a copy of it.

CHAPTER TEN

# FINANCIAL DECISIONS

## YOURS, MINE, AND OURS

*"I do not wish for women to have power over men, but over themselves."*
—MARY SHELLEY

Almost all property acquired during a marriage, except for inherited property or gifts, is considered marital property regardless of who owns it or how it is titled—unless you have a prenuptial agreement specifying otherwise.

By contrast, any property you owned before the marriage, inheritances you received before or during the marriage and kept in your name alone, the pain and suffering portion of a personal injury judgment, and personal gifts are considered your separate property in most states. If you commingle separately owned property and jointly owned property, it is usually considered marital property.

In some states, passive and active appreciation during the marriage on separately owned property is considered marital property. *Passive appreciation* is appreciation in value that occurred due to factors such as inflation and market value increases.

*Active appreciation* of your separately owned property requires a contribution by your spouse, such as a cash infusion to help you to grow your business.

Community property states view both spouses as equal owners of all property and require a 50/50 split of all marital property.

Equitable distribution states do not require a 50/50 split, but the distribution should be fair and just. Many factors are taken into account to determine fairness and justness, including the length of the marriage, the financial situation of each party, the standard of living of each party during the marriage, the income and earnings potential of each spouse, the needs of the custodial parent of minor children, and the contribution of one spouse to the education or earnings capability of the other spouse. Debts are divided as well.

Community property and equitable distribution states have different laws regarding the division of property, so please ask your attorney to clarify the laws in your state for you. It is very difficult to predict what the outcome would be if such a case is tried in court by a judge, so more than 95 percent of all divorces settle out of court.

In some states, income produced by separately held property during a marriage is considered marital property. This income may include rental income, interest income, earned income from business interests, and dividends.

Also, if your spouse earned a professional degree during the marriage, the degree may be considered an asset—meaning, you may be entitled to a share of its value.

If you have commingled separately held bank accounts or brokerage accounts, some states will conclude that those assets are now considered marital assets, while some other states will allow you to trace the funds back and allocate the withdrawals to be reimbursed.

If you bought a home during the marriage using joint and separate property, some states would require the spouse who contributed separate property to be reimbursed, while in other states it is all marital property.

If separately held funds (inherited or acquired before the marriage) were used to improve the marital home or to pay off the mortgage, reimbursement might be required in the division of assets. Your attorney will inform you of the laws of your state.

One of my clients told me that his daughter was getting divorced and that her attorney told her that she would have to give half of the brokerage account that he had funded for her many years ago to her husband in their divorce. The account had been kept in just her name all those years, and no funds had ever been added to the account by anyone other than her father. In her state, that is not considered to be marital property. The husband argued that he had contributed to paying taxes on the account. But he did not acknowledge the fact that his father-in-law had loaned him and his wife the down payment on their home and that they had never paid him any interest or principal on that loan. The daughter stood up for herself and argued that her ex-husband was not entitled to any part of the brokerage account, and she received the account as separate property during mediation.

Although you probably won't get more than half of the marital assets, you *do* have a say in which half of those assets you get. You may not get everything that you want, but you do need to get a lot of what you want. Don't take what you don't want. For example, you can't be forced to take the house if you don't want it or can't afford to make payments on it, especially since you would have to pay all the closing costs to sell it instead of splitting those costs with your husband if he doesn't want the house either. You can't be forced to take only the retirement assets if you also need cash for emergencies and to buy a house eventually. You are only required to take half of the retirement assets even if your husband doesn't want them.

If neither you nor your husband wants the house, it should be spelled out in the divorce agreement that it will be sold and you will both split the net profits, but only after all expenses and debts are paid—both yours and your husband's. Spell out in the agreement that the escrow agent or title company for the sale is to make checks payable for your net portions of the sale after these bills are paid directly to each of you. If the house doesn't sell within a certain period, require that it be auctioned. You don't want to have to deal with this unwanted real estate indefinitely.

Now is the time to fight for yourself and your future. Remember that the attorney's job is to give you good legal advice, not to decide the settlement for you. You also need to make sure that the attorney protects you from your husband's present and future bad behavior. Do your best to anticipate what he will do and then discuss those dangers with your attorney. If these issues are not addressed appropriately in the divorce agreement, you won't be protected.

## ALIMONY DOESN'T LAST

*"An investment in knowledge pays the best interest."*
—BENJAMIN FRANKLIN

Alimony is a temporary fix to allow you to get back on your feet. It will be very important to discuss this issue in detail with your attorney, as it varies from state to state. If you and your husband are not able to come to an agreement on the amount, the judge in your case will make a determination based on the circumstances of your situation. Factors taken into consideration include the length of the marriage, whether you have children, your employability, age, medical condition, needs, customary lifestyle, and the ability of your husband to pay. Please also note that if your income is higher than your ex-husband's the judge may instruct you to pay him alimony.

Some judges take a hard line against abusers by making them pay significant alimony, even though marital support is not supposed to be punitive. This approach is understandable, as chronic long-term abuse can affect a woman's ability to function. The cost of undergoing therapy to recover from abuse and the cost of job training are factors that should be raised by your attorney, especially if your husband did not let you work during the marriage in order to maintain control over you. Consult with a psychiatrist or psychotherapist to see if a diagnosis of PTSD is appropriate and to assess your current ability to work without extensive treatment for it.

The guidelines of individual states determine the level of child support.

Alimony doesn't last forever, so it is incumbent upon you to become self-supporting as soon as possible. Have a plan, get the therapy and education you need, and get a job. If you are at a loss as to what to do, get job counseling and take aptitude tests. Most alimony has an end date, or it ends if you remarry or cohabit, whichever comes sooner. Please make sure that you know what the rules are. Your husband may petition the court for a modification of the alimony payments due to changed financial circumstances for either one of you. If you're spending a lot of time with a new boyfriend after the divorce, a judge might view this as cohabitation.

Make sure that you have protection for your alimony payments. Alternatives include buying a life insurance policy to replace this support if your husband dies, a lien on real estate that he is awarded in the divorce, or a clause in the QDRO for your husband's pension if he is expected to retire before your alimony terminates. Discuss strategy with your attorney. If you can garnish your husband's wages, this would be preferable to having to take him back to court to comply.

## WHAT IT'S WORTH

*"What you risk reveals what you value."*
—JEANETTE WINTERSON

Many divorcing couples argue over property and business valuations. Keep in mind that assessed values for property taxes are well below the actual market values and that you will need to get your home appraised. Make sure that the appraiser is impartial and provides recent comparative sales in the appraisal to justify the appraised value. If you can't both agree on an appraiser, the court will appoint one for you.

If you or your husband has a business, use an objective professional business appraiser, rather than the regular accountant, to value the business. If your husband has been paying the accountant for years, that person may be biased against you. There are several different methods that may be used in valuing a business. Keep in mind that the *cost/asset method* frequently produces the lowest valuation. The *market method,* which compares the business to other similar businesses, may not be useful if your family business is a small business.

Some things that affect valuations include the financial condition of the company, goodwill and other intangible assets, poor collection rates for receivables, nonrecurring items, buy/sell agreements, liquidity, and restrictions, among others. Sit down with your attorney and the independent business appraiser and discuss the appraisal in detail to make sure that you understand it and agree with it. You may even want to get a second opinion.

If you must accept a note for the buyout of your husband's business, make sure that you get collateral to back the note, either a lien on business assets or real property. It is preferable to get a lien on real estate (real property), as it is fixed in place, and cannot be sold out from under you, unlike inventory or equipment.

You will be able to force a sale of business assets if he does not make the agreed-upon payments. You do not want to be an unsecured creditor if the business runs into trouble.

Better yet, if there is cash available to buy you out at a fair price, take this instead. If there is no cash available, try to get him to take out a loan to buy out your share. If not, you will likely have a problem later getting paid and you might have to take your husband back to court. That will cost you more money—money that you may not have.

You will be much better off if you do not continue to be a partner with him in anything.

## BIRD IN HAND

*"Personal experiences affect the facts judges choose to see."*
—SONIA SOTOMAYOR

We have all heard the saying "a bird in the hand is worth two in the bush." In any settlement, you need to consider the *time value* of money. Any money that you have right now is worth more than the money you are promised in the future because the money you have right now could be invested and earn interest or grow. So, in the division of assets, you will have to discount payments promised to you in the future to the level of their present value.

*Inflation*, which is the increase in the cost of things from one year to the next, reduces the purchasing power of cash value over time. Thus, time value and the anticipated rate of inflation are very important factors in determining present value, as well as the rate of return that your money could have earned if it had been paid as a lump sum to you in the divorce. A certified public accountant will usually do a valuation.

There is also the question of *opportunity cost*. You don't have the opportunity to spend cash or invest it now if you don't receive it until some later date. Not having the cash in hand (being illiquid) reduces your flexibility. Therefore, if you do agree to receive payments over time, make sure that you get enough cash in the settlement for emergencies or other anticipated major expenses. Keep in mind that in making this decision you may not ever get those future payments. Your husband may make that very difficult, if not impossible.

Remember the character of the man making the promise. An abuser is not to be trusted and is likely to stop making payments just out of the need to control or for spite. You will then have to take him back to court to get the money. You may not be able to afford to the expense of taking him back to court, and he may be counting on that.

Also, what if he loses his job or his business goes sour, and he is then unable to make the payments as promised? Think long and hard before you agree to take payments over time.

Your attorney may not have the same perspective as I do regarding the reliability of abusers if he or she has not had the experience of dealing with a psychopath or narcissist personally. In my experience, it is usually better to receive less money now than promises that will be very difficult to enforce. If you can't trust him now, how are you supposed to trust him ten years from now with your financial future? If it is at all possible, insist on getting cash in your hand now!

# GET IT

*"Distrust and caution are the parents of security."*
—BEJAMIN FRANKLIN

Insist that your ex-spouse's wages be garnished for child support and alimony or you may never see it. He probably will not make all payments on time or even at all unless he is compelled to do so. He may selfishly try to punish you by withholding money needed to support the family.

Many states automatically require wage garnishment for child support, but this can be bypassed with a legal agreement if you give your consent. Do not agree to this under any circumstances, and do not fall for the excuse that the reason not to garnish wages is that it would be embarrassing to him or might get him fired from his job. You may end up not receiving support for years, if ever, without the garnish. Please don't worry about his feelings. He didn't worry about yours while he was abusing you. Many companies already garnish the wages of some of their divorced employees, so don't fall for this tactic.

I recommend you keep a spreadsheet of every child support payment due you, noting when each is paid and the running balance.

Keep another spreadsheet for medical reimbursement requests, which includes the date a request is sent for reimbursement and when it is paid. Send you ex-spouse such bills via certified mail or priority mail so that you have proof that they were received.

Be sure to keep copies of any bills sent to your ex-husband and keep a running balance of what he owes on them. Stay well organized so that you can give all the proof you need to your attorney and the judge in case you find it necessary to take him back to court.

# HELP!

*"It's not about perfect. It's about effort."*
—JILLIAN MICHAELS

Temporary Assistance for Needy Families is a wonderful government resource that assists women financially to care for their children if deserted by their father or if the father dies. It is there for you to take advantage of, on behalf of your children, if you qualify for it (see Resources).

The most important thing to consider right now is providing for your children's care, so please view it as a necessary measure to survive rather than as a handout. We all pay taxes on our earnings to provide a safety net for people who are temporarily suffering through hard times. That is why it exists.

If I knew you personally, I would reassure you that I feel it is my moral obligation to pay taxes to help other women who are suffering so that they may feed their children and to empower them to get back on their feet after a divorce or the death of a spouse. If you have too much pride to ask for help for yourself and your children, you deny me, and others like me, the opportunity to help someone in need. Give us this chance to give you a helping hand, and provide your family with the assistance that you need and deserve. Open your heart and be willing to receive support from others. Difficult circumstances can happen to anybody.

If you qualify for aid to dependent children because your husband is not making his child support payments, be aware that most states have computerized data sources to locate a missing parent. They then use various enforcement methods, such as wage garnishment or intercepting tax refunds, to collect what is due. Your ex-husband even could get arrested and spend a night or two in jail to compel him to live up to his obligations. You will have to sign a form authorizing the state to get reimbursed from your husband if your children are to receive state aid. Sign it without hesitation.

The money is coming from government funds when he should be making the payments. He has a legal and moral obligation to support his children, so do not feel sorry for him or allow him to shirk his duty to support them. For more information, contact your local Health and Human Services office (see Resources). The HHS office can also give you information on food assistance programs. Do whatever you must do to survive.

I do not recommend that you hire a private child support collection agency, as their fees can be very high, up to 35 percent of payments, even for payments that come in which they did absolutely nothing to collect. Their contracts are notoriously difficult to terminate. Essentially, you will have to gather and give them the same information that you would give to your state agency for their search.

By contrast, your state will probably charge a 5 percent or less administrative fee, and most states are efficient in using computerized data sources to track down deadbeat fathers. (For more information, see Resources.) If your state is unable to locate your ex-husband, try hiring a private detective.

## NOT MY BUSINESS

*"I thank God for my failures, maybe not at the time but after some reflection. I never feel like a failure just because something I tried has failed."*

—DOLLY PARTON

It is not legal in many states for a spouse to start a new business during a divorce proceeding. Please be sure to check with your attorney about laws in your state if your spouse starts a risky business that could put your financial future in jeopardy and subject you to substantial additional debt. I had to get a temporary restraining order (TRO) when my husband mentioned that he had started a new business venture and that he had committed to invest a substantial amount of money that he didn't have. His plan was to expand the business dramatically during the divorce by ramping up production and taking on a lot of debt. He figured the timing was good because he could make me pay for it against my will. He had lost large amounts of money in the past, and the risks of this project were huge.

Even though I told my ex-husband that what he was doing was illegal, he refused to stop the project. He had committed to the purchase and installation of a very large and expensive piece of equipment to get the business started. As soon as I found out about this purchase, I immediately called my attorney to get a restraining order. I also had the presence of mind to call all the vendors in Florida to find out where he had made a substantial deposit. I found the vendor, who was antagonistic to me even after I explained that I was a co-owner in the business and that my husband had illegally committed to buying the equipment from him during a divorce proceeding. He rudely told me that it was not any of my business. I then informed him that he would not be paid if he made delivery and that I was merely giving him a courtesy call to inform him that I was planning to fax him a copy of the restraining order the next day. He changed his tone with me immediately and thanked me for the call. He did not deliver the equipment.

My ex-husband and I both suffered equally financially from the loss of the deposit, which was not fair to me because he made the payment illegally. However, I would have lost a whole lot more than that if he had continued with the project. I might have ended up in bankruptcy court because of bad investment decisions *he* was making even after I had filed for divorce. He was aware that a bankruptcy would have affected my reputation, and that could have wrecked my career as a financial advisor. I believe vindictiveness was involved in his choice to engage in risky behavior, as well as incompetence and an outsized ego.

To make matters worse, his attorney filed a petition to have the restraining order set aside, only to drop it after conferring with my attorney while we were waiting outside the courtroom. This move was very costly for me, as well as for my ex-husband. His attorney should have known before filing the appeal that his client was breaking the law. Instead of researching the matter beforehand, he chose to take me to court instead, which was a waste of my time and racked up additional legal fees for both of us from our attorneys. My ex was furious with me, even though he was the one who had behaved unethically.

In the state where I live, one party to a divorce is responsible for debts incurred by the other party until the time that the divorce is declared final. Unfair, but this meant I was responsible for debts that my ex-husband incurred after I filed for divorce until such time that the judge signed the divorce decree.

The underlying point here is that you must act to protect yourself wherever possible. Keep an eye on your husband during and after the divorce. If you don't, this lesson will keep turning up in your life until you finally learn it. Some people never do, and they stay in the role of unhappy, passive victims their entire lives. This is not what you want for yourself or your children.

## MUCH OBLIGED

*"Credit card interest payments are the dumbest money of all."*
—HILL HARPER

Debt can be a real minefield. Creditors don't care which partner in the settlement is supposed to pay off the marital debts—they just want to get paid. A court order does not affect your obligation to a creditor if you also signed for a loan. They will go after you to pay the loan if your ex-husband doesn't. This kind of obligation includes, but is not limited to, income and property taxes, mortgage payments, car payments, and credit cards.

I received a notice shortly after my divorce was final that several checks had bounced on a joint checking account that my husband had set up online. The bank informed me that I was responsible for paying those checks even though I did not authorize the account. To protect myself, I took a copy of my divorce decree to the bank and demanded to see the bank manager, who reluctantly removed my name from the account. When I confronted him, my ex-husband said it was all a big mistake. But in my opinion, he knew exactly what he was doing.

Follow up after the divorce to make sure that your name is removed from all your husband's bank accounts in case he bounces checks so that you are not held liable for them.

Avoid keeping assets secured by loans that he is obliged to pay for over time, as he may fail to continue to make the payments. If you are to get the car, either refinance it exclusively in your name, or make the car payments on your own if the ownership is left in both names. Make sure that your divorce decree specifically protects you from your ex-husband's debts or you may be legally responsible for paying them if he files for bankruptcy, even after you are divorced.

It will be helpful to include an indemnity provision in the divorce decree that gives you the right to sue your ex-husband to reimburse you for debts that you paid that were rightly his. But remember that it will be expensive to take him back to court, and there is a possibility that he may no longer be able to pay his debts. Try to minimize the risk of this as much as possible by dividing the debts in a way that protects you as much as possible in the divorce agreement. Also remember to request that a provision be included that states that joint assets will be used to pay off all joint debts completely before being divided and distributed to you and your husband.

If your husband is keeping any real estate and you are unsure if he will be able to refinance the property exclusively in his name, make sure that your divorce decree states that the quitclaim deed for the home that you will be required to provide him will be held in escrow by your attorney or the closing agent until the refinancing actually takes place. Otherwise, if he fails to close, your name will remain on the debt while you will have signed over your ownership rights in the property. He will then own the property outright while you still owe his mortgage.

Make sure that the divorce decree states that he must obtain financing in his name, if needed, within a specified period, such as ninety days. If that is not done on time, the decree should state that the property will be auctioned and the mortgage paid off.

If the mortgage is left in both names, you will be required by the lender to pay if he doesn't, and it will affect your credit rating. Even if he does make timely payments on the mortgage, it may be very difficult for you to buy a home in your name alone after the divorce, as the loan will show up on your credit report as *your* debt and will affect your ability to borrow additional funds of your own.

Before you decide to keep the home, check with your bank to make sure that you will be able to qualify to refinance the mortgage in your name. If you don't qualify, you must reconsider. If you and your husband decide that the property is to remain in both your names so that the children can be raised in the family home, make sure that it is in the decree so that you do not have problems later with the IRS. If you sell the property within six years of the divorce, transfers between spouses are not taxable.

I think that this is a terrible idea, as it means that you will continue to have a lot of contact with your former abuser. Decide what is important to you and your children. Your home is wherever you and your children are; it is not a physical house. It may be much better for you to start somewhere new anyway, in a place where you don't have bad memories.

If your husband files for bankruptcy, he will still be obligated to pay alimony and child support, but the amount may be modified in bankruptcy court. If he is unemployed and can't pay, he may go back to court and get the amount of spousal support modified to account for his reduced income. The court cannot make any change retroactive to before the date he files a request for modification, so each month he delays filing is another month he owes you the old amount.

If you filed joint income tax returns and owe back taxes, or you get audited within three years of filing a return and are assessed additional taxes, the IRS can come after both of you for all the taxes, regardless of what your divorce decree states. If you are married for an entire calendar year during the divorce proceeding, you may decide to file joint returns or separately for that tax year.

I filed my return separately during the divorce as soon as I found out from the business appraiser that my husband had misrepresented information on his business tax return. I was not willing to sign a tax return "under penalty of perjury" when I suspected that he might be cheating on his taxes. My ex-husband was angry because it cost him more to file separately than jointly with me, but that didn't bother me at all. I was divorcing him and intended to protect myself.

If you are concerned about your husband being untruthful on tax returns that he filed when you were together, make sure that the divorce decree holds him solely responsible for any income taxes, interest, or penalties assessed for prior year tax returns after the divorce.

## DEATH AND DIVORCE

*"I paint flowers so they will not die."*
—FRIDA KAHLO

Read your will and trusts to verify the names of the beneficiaries. Also, remember to find out who the listed beneficiaries are, if any, for your bank and brokerage accounts, insurance policies, and retirement accounts.

If one of you dies during the divorce proceeding, customarily the survivor inherits as if a divorce petition was never made. Ask the estate attorney how your marital and separate assets will pass in your state if you die before the divorce is final. Your husband will probably get to manage your estate if you die without a will. In most cases, children live with the surviving parent if the custodial parent dies while they are still minors. Discuss putting a guardianship clause in your will with your attorney if you need to avoid this from happening.

You may be prevented from making changes in your will once you file for divorce, as the laws of your state may include automatic restraining orders. Therefore, consider changing your will before you file for divorce so that your husband doesn't inherit everything if you die. Even if your husband is entitled to claim an elective share in your estate if you die first, as most states won't allow you to completely disinherit him, taking this step will prevent him from getting everything that is in your name alone.

If you've already filed for divorce and must wait until the divorce is over to change your will, set an appointment with an estate attorney for as soon as possible after the date of your final court hearing. The purpose of this meeting is to draft a new will and other related estate documents for you to remove your ex-husband completely.

Remember that changing your will does not automatically change beneficiaries listed on life insurance or retirement accounts, so make sure that you take care of that as well once the divorce is final. Make taking care of this a priority and put it on your calendar. I have heard of too many people forgetting to do this, with disastrous results.

In many states, an ex-spouse is unable to inherit if his or her name accidentally is left as a beneficiary. Then the asset must go through probate. You can avoid this if a beneficiary update form is signed. If the estate is the beneficiary or default beneficiary of a retirement account, income taxes are due on the entire account value within one tax year.

Designating a person as a beneficiary allows that person two other options: the option of taking the proceeds of the retirement account over a five-year period and paying the tax liability over five years, or taking the account as a "stretch" over their lifetime. If they take this asset as a stretch over their lifetime, they will end up with a lot more money over a much longer period. The taxes will be on a much smaller distribution amount each year, and the major portion of the account will continue to grow tax deferred over time.

In some states, an ex-spouse can still inherit if his or her name is left as a beneficiary after the divorce. You need to take care of this important issue in any case to protect your children.

If you have signed a power of attorney and a health care power of attorney giving your ex-husband authority to handle financial affairs and make health care decisions for you, have new ones prepared to change that as soon as possible and destroy the old ones. Shred them ASAP. Mail a copy of your new powers of attorney to any company that has the old ones on file.

Review these new proxy documents with your attorney to make sure that you are using the correct forms for your state.

## MAKING MISTAKES

*"All human beings make mistakes. We make choices and judgments that have nothing to do with the truth of who we are."*
—IYANLA VANZANT

You will make your share of financial mistakes during your divorce. None of us is perfect, so expecting oneself to be perfect is counterproductive and unrealistic. I acquiesced to some things in the mediation room that I deeply regretted later, and it took me quite a while to forgive myself for having been so weak. I succumbed to being attacked by the mediator as being "unreasonable," which I was not. One of the problems was that we were in mediation for too long—over ten hours in a row.

When I felt bullied and that my wishes were being overridden, I should have gotten up and walked out, or said that I needed to sleep on it. It was abusive, and my attorney did nothing to stop it. Because I was exhausted and wanted to get the divorce over with, I caved.

In many cases, divorce professionals (attorneys and mediators) just want a deal, and they don't know or care about their clients. It's nothing personal, and that is the problem. Your case is just a case, a business deal for them—one of many. There are some attorneys and mediators who do care, but I don't think you should count on them to take care of all the important details. Even the best attorneys make mistakes or fail to anticipate unintended consequences.

Years later, I am still dealing with the long-term consequences of not standing up for myself in that one meeting. I learned this lesson the hard way. But as angry as I once was about it, I had to forgive them for what they did, which was a lot easier than forgiving myself. It is too late for me to undo the damage, so I had to let it go. I have no choice if I want to be happy.

Be your own best advocate. It is too important to delegate responsibility for your well-being to someone else, no matter who they are or where they got their degrees.

# PART FOUR

# THE NEXT CHAPTER

*"I didn't get there by wishing for it or hoping for it, but by working for it."*

—ESTÉE LAUDER

CHAPTER ELEVEN

# LIFE AFTER DIVORCE

## RECOVERY ROAD

*"Real power comes when we stop holding others responsible for our pain and we take responsibility for our feelings."*
—MELODY BEATTIE

If you have been a victim of abuse, you probably have post-traumatic stress disorder. Symptoms of PTSD may include a lack of appetite, insomnia, flashbacks, fear of intimacy and other relational problems, panic attacks, and ongoing anxiety.

The hippocampus in the brain processes a traumatic event when it occurs. Then the memory of the event—including sensations and perceptions—is stored in the neocortex. Memories normally become more distant with the passing of time. Our brains process some trauma differently. With PTSD, trauma continues to be reactivated in the hippocampus so that we experience it over and over as if an event just happened. The passage of time has little effect.

Traditional counseling can help you to process your trauma and suffering. While anti-anxiety medication or sleeping pills help some people to cope, drugs may not be enough to alleviate your symptoms without producing unacceptable side effects. Therefore, you may wish to explore additional, complementary therapies, such as hypnosis, acupuncture, eye movement desensitization and reprocessing (EMDR), emotional freedom technique (EFT) or tapping, or the rewind technique. These have been shown to greatly reduce or eliminate symptoms of post-traumatic stress by helping move stored memories from the hippocampus to the neocortex, bringing a sense of resolution to the trauma.

If your symptoms are severe, please get guidance from your doctor as to which treatment or combination of treatments will be most effective for you. If you try one of these therapies and it doesn't work, try another. Don't give up. Deep breathing techniques, meditation, and yoga will also help you to relax. You need to get relief from the suffering. Please make this a priority.

Try saying the affirmation "I am safe" several times right before bedtime each night so that it has a chance to affect your subconscious mind while you are sleeping. This may help to alleviate feelings of fear and insecurity. As previously mentioned, affirmations may be more likely to work if you also write them down right before bedtime several times in a row. Give the new belief a few months to settle in.

In fact, do whatever you need to do to feel safe again. For example, you may want to take a self-defense class or get a dog for protection. To improve your sense of security at home, if your house doesn't have an alarm system, get one and use it. Personally, I also like to visualize archangels wrapping their wings around my children and me and guarding each of the doors to my home. I thank them for keeping us safe.

# TRUST THE PROCESS

*"A woman is just like a teabag. You put her in hot water and she just gets stronger."*
—ELEANOR ROOSEVELT

It is going to take you a while to recover from both the abuse you suffered and your divorce. I recommend that you wait to jump back into the dating game until you have taken the time you need to heal. How much time to take is different for each divorced woman. My healing took longer than three years. It is still a work in progress. Divorce can change you into a bitter person who feels cheated, a needy woman who is constantly looking for a partner to make her happy, or a liberated woman with all life's possibilities ahead of her.

One of the lessons of my recovery was to learn not to derive my happiness outside of me, as I already have everything I need to be happy. I am not talking about material things. I am talking about loving myself and trusting my own capabilities. Now I no longer look for a partner to make me happy or to be whole, but for companionship. Making myself happy is my responsibility. Nobody else could make me happy if I didn't feel good about myself or grateful for what I have right now. Living in the past mentally only kept me a victim, and I no longer wish to stay there. Because I am content already, I want to be in a relationship with a man who is already content with his life. I trust that I will know when it is time to open my heart in a new relationship.

It is important to figure out what gives you joy as you engage in your life. I find a lot of delight in a cup of tea, a relaxing bath, taking a long walk in nature, listening to the birds, hearing my children's voices, and hugging a friend. Simple things. Our connections with other people and ourselves are what bring us happiness. It will help to reconnect with family and develop strong friendships with other women during your recovery.

I recommend that you read a lot of books on personal development. You also may want to read the Bible or books on spirituality. Question everything.

You are entering a new phase of your life and this transition gives you an opportunity to expand the possibilities of what you want to do, have, and be. I began researching and writing this book to help other women heal and to heal myself. Writing has now become an important part of my life. Perhaps you would also enjoy writing. Start a journal.

Do your best to view your divorce as the beginning of a new chapter in your life. Take some classes, try new things, exercise, and travel. Get out of your comfort zone. Take an evening course at your local high school, join a book club or a runners' group. Go back to church or try a new one. Go to a Meetup group that seems interesting to you. Volunteer. Now is the time for you to rebuild your life and self-esteem. If you want to be happily married to someone else in the future, you must first learn to care for yourself and be content with your life while single. Enjoy your freedom by using it to find out who you are, what you like, and what truly makes you happy. It will make your life more interesting and make you a more interesting person.

## STAND UP

*"The most common way people give up their power is by thinking that they don't have any."*
—ALICE WALKER

The lesson of having to stand up for my interests has turned up time and again since the divorce. If this is one of your issues, it is going to turn up repeatedly for you as well until you finally learn the lesson. A couple of years after my divorce, a large tree branch fell off in my front yard. I got a couple of verbal bids to remove the branch and the tree from my yard, and both quotes were high. The bid that I accepted was from someone who had done a lot of work for me in the past. He had already come in and removed the tree branch without asking before he gave me his bid. He then padded the bill by a considerable amount, claiming that he had done two jobs—removing the branch and removing the tree.

In the past, I would have just paid the bill to avoid conflict and then allowed myself to feel victimized. But I had been taken advantage of so many times that I was done being passive. I remained calm and polite and was emphatic that I had requested a quote for the whole job, and that removing the tree, including the branch, was one job, not two. He tried to argue, but I stood firm, and he finally acquiesced. I then sent him a check for the amount of his original bid.

Some people will keep pushing you until they know what your boundaries are. If you don't set boundaries, you are going to be unhappy, because people will take the space you give them. It's not personal. This is just the way human beings behave. So, get used to it.

By the way, violating people's boundaries is not good for anyone. Those who do it will lose respect not only for you but also for themselves for not being strong enough to resist taking advantage of you. You aren't doing them any favors by not standing up for yourself.

When you feel someone is crossing a line, give yourself permission to speak up. Just be respectful, firm, and fair in doing so. You do not have to explain or defend yourself. A simple no will do and is best in most cases. This also applies to boundaries you set with your children.

We are all here, in this life, to learn lessons, and to give and receive love. We all make mistakes and have a lot to learn throughout our lives; I believe that is the reason why we are here. Don't expect to be perfect or feel bad because you aren't because you never will be. Nobody else is, either. You are enough just as you are.

Self-acceptance in itself is a lesson. You must accept and love yourself as you are if you are going to make any progress. Of course, it is nearly impossible to do this if someone in your life is belittling and criticizing you at every turn—including you.

No one is coming on your behalf to save you from challenging people and circumstances. You can and must learn to do it for yourself. On a spiritual level, the greatest gift you can give to your ex-husband is to show him there are consequences to not being a loving and supportive spouse and consequences for violating your boundaries. The sooner that happens, the sooner that he will learn his lessons. You both deserve to be free of each other.

Your needs, your value, and your happiness are just as important in God's eyes as anyone else's. You also deserve your forgiveness and compassion for having made mistakes. Master potters from Japan intentionally mark well-made pieces of pottery to give them a flaw, so that they will be beautiful, not perfect. Wabi-sabi is the name for this aesthetic or worldview, which comes from the Buddhist philosophy of imperfection, impermanence, and incompletion. Being human means being imperfect and our uniqueness makes each of us beautiful and precious.

## DISENGAGE

*"Success is a state of mind. If you want success, start thinking of yourself as a success."*
—JOYCE BROTHERS

As much as is possible, try to avoid or limit contact with your abusive ex-husband after your divorce. He likely will try to continue to abuse you. You may need to get a legal restraining order to prevent him from contacting you. Unless you absolutely must maintain some form of contact with him for the children, I recommend you change your phone number and block his emails. If he must have your phone number, listen to messages that he leaves you instead of answering the phone and engaging in upsetting conversations. You can respond briefly by text if you must. But in many cases, the best response is no response at all. He is trying to elicit a reaction from you.

If you have a home or other real estate that must be refinanced or sold, you won't be able to stop dealing with your ex-husband entirely for a while after the divorce. But let the bank, the realtor, or the attorney handle the real estate transaction as much as possible. You do not have to be in contact regularly with your ex-husband to take care of the matter.

If your ex-husband was abusive to your children during the marriage, you might be able to limit their contact with him to supervised visits or eliminate contact entirely if you can prove to a judge that this is in their best interest. Remember to document his behavior, identifying specific dates and occurrences of verbal and physical abuse, so that you can sue for sole custody. Request the court to do a psychological evaluation of him for anger management issues or other psychological problems because you have concerns about leaving your children alone with him.

Other reasons that warrant restricted visitation include the threat of parental kidnapping, a history of drug or alcohol abuse, suicide threats, or criminal convictions. If your ex-husband has a substance abuse problem, see if the court is willing to order weekly testing. If he has been abusive to you, it is possible that he will begin to be abusive to your children if you are no longer there to be his punching bag. Look at their faces when they come home to see what kind of time they had with their father. Ask them a lot of questions about meals, their treatment, and whether they were left unsupervised or in someone else's care during visits with their father. And be on the lookout for bruises.

Document when your ex-husband does not show up for planned visitation so that you can have his right of visitation revoked after a reasonable period—let's say after three months. Your children do not need him to subject them to any more disappointment and unpredictability.

Meanwhile, be sure to spend plenty of one-on-one time with each of your children, engaging in enjoyable activities. Ask them about their feelings. Their world has just changed forever, and they need to know that you will always be there for them.

## SAY WHAT YOU MEAN

*"While we try to teach our children all about life, our children teach us what life is all about."*
—ANGELA SCHWINDT

Years ago, The Moody Blues wrote the song "Say What You Mean, Mean What You Say." Adhering to this principle of healthy communication can be much more difficult than it seems.

You probably have had a problem with setting boundaries for a very, very long time, or else you would not have been in an abusive relationship. Throughout your marriage, it was not safe for you to say no. It was not safe for you to express your feelings and needs. It was not safe for another person to be angry with you and for you to be OK with that.

Now that you are divorced, you need to start saying no and to stop worrying about other people's feelings when you do. There is a lot of power in that little word: *No.* It's a whole sentence in two letters. Try to use it without defending or explaining yourself. See how that feels. Initially, it may feel awkward to say it, and then very empowering. Practice makes perfect.

Start saying no to your children, and be consistent. Tell them that your financial situation has changed and there are limits to what you can give them and what they can do. If you were too permissive in the past, explain that things are going to change now. They may not like everything this means. Tell that that it is OK for them to get upset or even angry, but that they will still need to respect your wishes as you are in charge and doing the best you can.

Your children need boundaries. Do not give in if you have said no or there will be constant arguments to turn every no into a yes. Make sure that they learn how to deal with negative emotions appropriately. They will only treat you with respect if you demand it. Tell them that you love them and that no still means no. Initially, they likely are going to push your buttons. My children knew just how to push mine. But I guess that I had finally reached the point where enough was enough. I have a much better, more authentic relationship with my children now that I stand up for myself. They respect me more. Give yours the opportunity to realize that you are just another human being, and you have needs and rights, too. They will become better people for this lesson, not selfish, as they may have been trained to be by their father. I was surprised at how quickly my children came around and accepted the new me when I said no.

It is time to change your relationships with other people as well. Stop saying yes to every request for your time, money, or attention. While you are in transition, you need to focus on taking care of yourself and your children. Just say, "I can't help you, but thank you for thinking of me." No excuses, no explanations. If they ask you why not, don't answer. It's not necessary.

Sometimes when people ask me a question that I think is inappropriate, I will respond, "Why do you ask?" Other times, I just smile and don't answer it. The way I see it, I don't owe them anything. Neither do you. They should respect your right to say what you mean.

## FOLLOW UP

*"The way to right wrongs is to turn the light of truth upon them."*

—IDA B. WELLS-BARNETT

Once the divorce is final, it is *your* job to make sure that your husband's name is removed from titles, deeds, credit card accounts, investment accounts, and any other accounts that you receive in the divorce settlement. Submit updated beneficiary designation forms on your retirement plan, stock purchase plan, deferred compensation plan, annuities, and life insurance policies as soon as possible after the divorce is granted. Then make sure that the changes were made.

Organize your records. If you have a financial advisor, ask for help. Provide him or her with a certified copy of the divorce decree signed by the judge. Do not expect your attorney to take care of changing titles for you. He or she may be willing to prepare quitclaim deeds on your real estate, or refer you to a real estate attorney to prepare and record these documents. It is up to you, however, to follow up and make sure that these things are taken care of properly.

Also, don't forget to keep ordering and carefully reading credit reports on your credit history every four months so that you can address any issues that may arise.

Set the appointment with an estate attorney to update your will as soon as possible, as well as your power of attorney and health care power of attorney, if you haven't already. You will need to use an attorney who specializes in estate law to prepare all three of these documents.

Have a lock box in your name at the bank to secure your important legal documents, such as your will, insurance policies, car titles, deeds, and so on. Destroy the old estate documents with a paper shredder. Consider whom you would want as a joint signer on the lock box in case something happens to you.

Change the locks on your doors if you will remain in the family home and haven't done so. Install a fireproof safe in your home to hold your power of attorney, health care power of attorney, a copy of your will, and copies of your insurance policies and other documents. Keep an updated list of your assets and liabilities, including bank account and brokerage account numbers, credit card account numbers, and online passwords in your fireproof safe. Indicate on the list if you have any bills automatically paid from your bank accounts. If you have a separate safe for jewelry and your bank lock box keys, indicate the code for it on the list. My adult daughter knows where the key to my safe is so that she has access to it if something should happen to me.

Do not leave the originals of your power of attorney or health care power of attorney in your lock box at the bank, as they will not be accessible when most needed. Keep both of these documents in your fireproof safe and make sure that the person you have designated to be your proxy decision maker knows where to find them. Bring the health care power of attorney with you if you go to the hospital. The administrators will make a copy of it for their files. It won't do you any good sitting in the bank if you are in a serious accident or have a sudden illness.

Although you may be able to change your legal name back to your maiden name in the divorce decree, you may want to wait at least a year before you make that decision. You don't want to make a drastic change that you regret later, so you should be completely sure that is what you want to do. It takes a lot of work to change your name on everything, and there are many other, more important things that you must take care of first.

Put all your ex-husband's emails and your emails to him, and emails to and from your attorney in a separate archived email folder. Keep these for at least five years, just in case he decides to take you back to court. It is important to keep them segregated so that you don't accidentally open one. Don't look back unless you must.

Put all emailed PDF documents and spreadsheets related to the divorce in a separate folder on your computer, so that you have all those items in one place, in case you need to revisit them. Keep in mind that you could have an IRS audit of a previously filed joint tax return, so you will need to keep tax-related or employment records for up to seven years.

Put all the paper documents related to the divorce in waterproof plastic containers and store these in the basement or garage. Ten years from now, they can be shredded and forgotten. Keep a copy of the divorce decree and any pension information with your other important papers, just in case they are needed.

# BUDGET BASICS

*"Do what you can, where you are, with what you have."*
—THEODORE ROOSEVELT

The chances are that your financial picture has changed with the divorce, and not for the better. So be careful about making big splurges to pamper yourself for the time being. If you can't afford it, you are going to regret splurging later. I took a short, inexpensive trip after my divorce decree was final, which was something I knew that I could reasonably afford to do.

Please also wait at least a year before you consider plastic surgery, liposuction, or other expensive cosmetic procedures so that you avoid making decisions that have unintended consequences. If you are thinking about having an expensive elective surgery out of insecurity over your appearance or at the prospect of living alone, you would be better served spending money on a good therapist. The real work that you need to do is on the inside, not the outside.

Make sure that any financial assets you received in the divorce settlement last as long as possible and are invested to help you achieve your short-term and long-term goals. Prioritize these goals to see what is most important and realistically achievable. Set up and then live within your new budget. Taking control of your money will make you feel calmer and more empowered. Consult a financial advisor for help with budgeting, retirement planning, insurance planning, and college savings. Before you make a big expenditure, consult with your advisor to see if you can afford the expense based on your other needs and goals.

It amazes me how easily I can fritter away money without realizing it if I don't consistently pay attention. Debit cards, as well as credit cards, are an easy way to get into trouble since many people don't keep as close track of what they spend as they do when paying with cash. If you need to make cuts in spending, then you must track where your money is going. Eliminate snacks and processed food. It is much better for your health to allocate your food dollars to fresh fruits and vegetables.

Bottled water is wasteful, bad for the environment, and costly. Get a water pitcher with a Brita filter instead. Eliminate sodas; they are harmful to your family's diet and your teeth. Diet sodas cause cravings for sugar, so eliminate them as well.

Use cash instead of mindlessly using your debit or credit cards for discretionary weekly spending, which can easily get out of control. When the cash runs out, stop spending until the next week. Clip coupons or print them online and make a grocery list every week before you go shopping. Only buy what is on the list. Make a game of going through the coupons in your Sunday paper with your children to see how much you can save. You will be teaching them invaluable lessons about money as a limited resource that they must allocate wisely.

Remember, the less money you spend on groceries, the more you will have to spend on other things that your kids may need or want.

Cook on the weekends, and freeze leftovers for meals during the week. Or cook every other day, and have leftovers every other night. Plan menus for the week before you go to the grocery store. Buy bags of apples and store-brand cans of low-salt almonds for healthy snacks.

If you can afford to take the children out to dinner once a week or once a month, order water instead of soda at the restaurant. It is not only healthier, but your restaurant bills will be a lot lower. I go out to lunch or dinner occasionally with a friend or a client, and I notice a big increase in my credit card bill if I overdo it, especially if I have a glass or two of wine.

Take control of your spending. Like all of us, you have a limited amount of resources, so be aware of how you spend yours. Find a way to live within your new budget and start saving for your retirement. Nobody else is going to do this for you.

Do your best to anticipate upcoming expenses, such as birthdays or insurance payments. Plan for such expenses in your budget. Delay large purchases for several months or wait to buy big-ticket items until you can pay for them in cash.

Instant gratification can have a large price tag. But it will be easier for you to make minor adjustments and cutbacks rather than to stop going out entirely until the credit card debt is paid. Consider going to the movies once a month instead of every week. Matinees are cheaper and just as fun as late-night shows. Skip the pricey concessions and bring along a plastic bag with low-salt almonds or other nuts, as a snack. Have a pizza night and watch a movie at home with the children on a Friday or Saturday night. Make conscious decisions about how you spend your money.

Of course, you need to have some fun in your life, so make changes in moderation, and you will have a greater likelihood of being successful. There are many things you can do, such as having a picnic, bowling, visiting a park, or playing cards or games as a family, which cost little or no money. Bring your lunch to work. Not only will this help you keep off weight, but it will also save you money. Your children should bring their lunches to school as well.

Limit how often you eat out by marking it on a calendar. Consider going to some less expensive restaurants when you do. I occasionally have potluck suppers with friends. It is less expensive than going out, and we have a better time, too. Also, I go to my local used bookstore frequently and trade in books that I no longer wish to keep for new, used ones.

Cancel unnecessary magazine and periodical subscriptions. Shop at discount stores like Sam's Club and Costco for paper products and dry goods, which are considerably cheaper if you buy them in bulk. Be willing to try more store brand products as many of them are manufactured by brand-name companies, anyway. And be careful not to buy things you don't need just because they are on sale. Remember that you are still spending money when you buy them.

Consider sometimes going to used clothing stores or designer used clothing stores for part of your wardrobe. In concession stores, I sometimes find items that still have the price tag on them. I don't buy used shoes, but I have bought several slightly used coats, jackets, and leather handbags over the years for a fraction of what they would have cost at a department store.

Your children pay attention to how you handle money, so do it wisely. My good spending habits have been ingrained since childhood, as my parents had limited resources. I believe I recovered financially from my divorce more quickly because of that.

Stop buying the children gifts out of guilt for Christmas or birthdays. Set a dollar amount that you can afford to spend for each child and do not exceed that amount. Set realistic expectations. If necessary, explain to your children that there is a limited amount of money this year and that you hope it will be better next year. It is important for them to realize that they are not entitled to get everything that they want when they want it. Teach them that happiness does not come from having everything that they want, but from being happy with what they have. It is not your job to give your children things that other children have, but to give them what they need, which is mostly your attention.

For your siblings and their families, send a family gift instead of one for each member. Or better yet, draw straws and send only one family a family gift. Let them know beforehand that your customary gift giving is going to change.

Build up an emergency reserve fund of six to nine months of living expenses in a bank savings account, and then start saving for your retirement, if you haven't already. Fund your retirement plan at work as much as you can afford it. It will come out of your paycheck and won't be as painful as you think because it is being taken before taxes. Have an additional bank draft from your checking account to an investment account scheduled for shortly after your paycheck is deposited. It is a great way to build up a nest egg over time. You will be more successful if it is set up to happen each month automatically rather than writing a check for it. Something will invariably come up every month so that you either don't do it or forget about it. Make the decision once on a bank draft for an amount you can afford, and it's done. You will feel better if you are taking care of yourself and making progress. So, do it. Every time you get a raise, increase the percentage that you invest in your 401(k) plan or 403(b) plan until you reach the maximum allowed amount.

Your marital status as of year end, December 31, will determine your filing status for that tax year. Filing a joint return does give you added tax benefits, including eligibility for certain tax credits and deductions. Normally, income drops after the divorce, but the tax rate as a single filer is usually higher than as married and filing jointly. Once you are divorced, you may be able to file as head of household instead of as a single person, a status that has a few potential benefits. There are several requirements for this, so consult your tax advisor.

Alimony you receive is no longer considered to be taxable income. As a single filer, you still may need to either make estimated quarterly tax payments or increase your withholding on your income from work to avoid penalties for underpayment of taxes. Ask your tax person.

Child support payments are not taxable, so you do not have to report them on your tax return. You can claim a child as a dependent if you have legal custody. You may be able to release your right to claim your child as a dependent for tax benefits to the noncustodial parent, but you should have a very good reason for doing so if you do. You may also be eligible to claim a child tax credit if you claim your child as a dependent.

## MONEY MAKER

*"If you can dream it, you can achieve it."*
—ZIG ZIGLAR

If you receive alimony, remember that it lasts for a limited amount of time, so you need to become self-reliant as soon as possible. You must figure out how to support yourself and your children. You may have set aside your career to raise your children and take care of your husband, a decision that has taken you out of the full-time workforce for years. The good news is that you are still capable of getting a job or starting your own business, and earning money. Your future is up to you, so give serious thought about what you would like to do for a living, and then act. Update your resume and make it happen. Becoming independent will do wonders for your self-esteem.

Do you have the education you need to get the job you want? The higher the level of education you possess, the more marketable your skills are likely to be and the higher your income. If you don't have a high school education, contact your local YWCA for general educational development (GED) classes, which are available during the day, in the evening, and on Saturdays. A GED diploma is considered the equivalent of a high school diploma.

Or you could train for a specific trade or craft. Trade schools take a shorter period to complete than college, are less expensive, are more flexible in scheduling, and usually have job placement available at the end. With trade schools, you earn a certificate of completion. If you eventually want to get a job that requires a college degree, consider going directly to college instead of trade school, even though it may take longer to complete it.

You will probably qualify for financial aid for a two- or four-year college degree if your resources are limited. Try to get some on the job training in your field before you graduate. Many part-time internships are available that can improve your skills. Community colleges offer classes for working adults looking to change careers. You may also find free online classes.

Do your homework and find out the income level and job opportunities in your areas of interest. You want to get a degree in a field where you will be able to find a job and support yourself and your family. It may take a while, but it is worth the investment of time and money that you put in.

In general, women are better listeners and communicators than men, so many have the inherent ability to excel at careers in sales, which tend to offer higher-paying jobs. Although the income is less predictable than salaried jobs, you can make a very good living if you work hard, have talent, and are willing to be patient. Some sales jobs also provide a base salary.

You may be entrepreneurial and want to start a company of your own. If you need guidance, one way to discover your natural strengths is to take an online career aptitude test. Please keep in mind that the results will only give you tendencies and that you will need to make up your mind what you want to pursue. If you are an older woman, don't let your age stop you from deciding where you would like to go, and making a change. You will need to take positive action if you want to see positive change in your life. The nonprofit association SCORE (www.score.org) offers free business mentorship to people setting up small businesses.

In *Grit,* Angela Duckworth convincingly argues that success is due more to a combination of passion and perseverance in the pursuit of a long-term goal than to intelligence or natural aptitude. Those who consistently invest more time and effort working toward long-term goals tend to achieve them. Over thirty years ago, senior management seriously considered firing me for mediocre short-term performance, but my local manager at the time insisted that they give me a chance to prove myself. He told them that I was very hard working and persistent, a good recipe for long-term success. I had a family to support and was determined to make a living. To this day, I remain loyal to my company because they gave me the opportunity to prove myself. I have consistently been one of their most productive employees for well over thirty years.

If you run into roadblocks, don't give up. Find a way around them. If things don't work out, commit to something else. People who are successful have had failures; they just kept trying. Work hard and don't give up. Believe in yourself, and you can change your world for the better. Nobody said it would be easy. It isn't. But it is possible if you have determination.

## ONLY THE LONELY

*"Trust has to be earned, and should only come after the passage of time."*

—ARTHUR ASHE

Starting a new life can be either exciting or scary. You may be longing for a partner who appreciates you and treats you well.

Recently divorced women can be vulnerable in new relationships. Some women are so used to being abused that it feels comfortable and familiar, and they continue to attract men who abuse them. Despite your desire for companionship and love, it's important for you to do everything you can to end the cycle of abuse in your life.

Reading self-help books, using positive affirmations, and going to a good therapist to find out why you were vulnerable in the first place will help you to make necessary changes in yourself so that you can attract a worthy partner. Repeating affirmations, such as "I am enough," "I love myself," "I am ready to give and receive love," and "I deserve a healthy relationship with a good man," after your divorce is final will help you program yourself to bring something much better into your life. If you want something different, you need to become someone different.

Take it slow. You do not have to confide all your past hurts in someone you barely know. Make sure that you get to know the man you date as a person and be sure you like him first. You are not obligated to answer all of his questions, especially if you feel uncomfortable or feel that it is too soon to divulge personal information. A strong attraction can make some people forget that they don't know another person all that well. We tend to project our good qualities on people who may not necessarily have them.

When you date a man, think with your head as well as your heart. Pay attention to what he says *and* what he does. How do you feel when you are around him? Does he make you feel comfortable and good about yourself? If not, don't see him again. Your body doesn't lie, and it will tell you that there is a problem by giving you warning signs.

Does he make you nervous or on edge? Do you get a sinking feeling in the pit of your stomach? Do you feel happy in his presence? Can you relax with him? Does he keep promises? Is he reliable? Does he tell the truth? Pay attention and practice discernment.

Dating websites are popular now, but please exercise care here. I found that several men I encountered on one popular dating site were not truthful. I stopped dating them as soon as I became aware of it. I also noticed that one of my former clients, who was an attorney, had joined the same website and lied about his age by five years. While age is certainly not as big a deal as some other things, like marital status, one of my friends was subjected to a scam on a dating website by a man from another country pretending to be someone who lived in a nearby city. He used a picture of a very handsome man to lure her in. She was initially swept off her feet by gifts of candy and flowers that he mailed to her from where he was supposed to have been living. She had never met him, but she still got caught up in the excitement of a budding romance. After several weeks of this whirlwind courtship by email, he urgently pleaded with her to wire money to his bank account, claiming that he was on a trip overseas and his wallet and luggage were stolen. She offered to help wire him money from his bank account, but he declined, insisting that she needed to loan it to him and that he would reimburse her. In that moment, she realized she had been caught up in a scam. My friend was heartbroken and felt violated by this predator. She is a private banker and an accomplished and intelligent woman. Still she had fallen quickly for a total stranger online.

A scam can happen to anyone. Please be careful, use your common sense and intuition, and protect your heart and your assets. If you are meeting someone for the first time, choose a public place to meet during the day. I prefer to meet for coffee in the morning before work at a busy local coffee shop. I can get away easily by just saying that I need to go to work. There are a lot of good and kind men out there; recognize and screen out the ones who are not.

Like many recently divorced women, you may consider having a fling after your divorce is final. Honestly, it is not worth it. Risky behavior like one-night stands may result in a sexually transmitted disease or violence. If the man you sleep with is a total stranger, you are allowing yourself to be vulnerable to someone who may or may not be a good person. When you sleep with someone, you sleep with every partner he has ever slept with as well, so please be very careful to use protection. Remember, condoms may not necessarily protect you from all types of sexually transmitted diseases, or even pregnancy. There is a success/failure rate printed in small type on every box.

Avoid married men, as that story can never end well, no matter what lies he tells you. Someone who is disloyal to his wife and lying to her to see you will not be loyal to you and will lie to you as well, no matter what he says to the contrary.

Do not ever give a loan to someone you are dating, regardless of the sob story he tells you. It does not make you a cold or ungenerous person. You need to protect yourself, and it is not your job to rescue other people. The fact that someone you are involved with has asked you for money should set off a red flag. You should firmly say no and strongly consider ending the relationship.

## BE HAPPY

*"People are just as happy as they make up their minds to be."*
—ABRAHAM LINCOLN

A wonderful, well-thought book on how to be happy is *Be Happy* by Robert Holden. In it, he explains that happiness is a choice, a state of mind that you can actively choose every day, and it is not based closely on anything outside of yourself. It is a feeling of being content with who you are, and at peace with any actions you have taken.

You must be authentic to be happy. So be the person who you are, and enjoy and appreciate what you have now. Practicing gratitude attracts more wonderful things into your life, and also helps you to put things in perspective and stay grounded. There may be some people who have more than you do, but there are many others who have less, too. It is not always apparent whether someone who has more than you has suffered a major loss or catastrophe. Therefore, it's best not to judge or compare yourself to others. It's unproductive and a waste of your time.

People-pleasing is a habit you can no longer afford, as the demands of others can be insatiable and leave you feeling exhausted and empty. It will be liberating for you to let that go. You are not here to be popular; you are here to make a difference, to share your gifts with others, and to enjoy your life. Pace yourself and get rest when you need to, take care of your health. Set boundaries and say no when it is appropriate. You do not have to justify yourself to anyone. You deserve to be happy and to make your own choices. Pleasing yourself leads to happiness.

You can't change the past, but you can learn from it and transform it into something greater by allowing yourself to be more compassionate, kind, and loving to yourself and others. Like a ripple in a pond, one act of kindness inspires another. It can make you happy.

CHAPTER TWELVE

# LIFE LESSONS, FORGIVENESS, AND PURPOSE

## LIFE LESSONS

In *"Mistakes are part of the dues one pays for a full life."*
—SOPHIA LOREN

divorcing your abusive ex-husband, you have taken back your power to choose how you are treated, the thoughts you allow yourself to believe, and the actions you are going to take to change your life. What you have experienced has made you a wiser, more confident woman. Make a list of the many lessons that you learned in the marriage and during the divorce, give thanks to God for them, and promise that you will not repeat them. Claim for yourself that you do not have to experience those lessons again. Then light a match and burn the list! Doing so will help you put the experience into perspective and lift your spirits.

I believe God puts people in our path to teach us what we need to learn. The adage "When the student is ready, the teacher appears" never really hit home with me until I truthfully analyzed my relationship with my parents and my spouse. Healing will take place if you look past the personality and dynamics of the drama to see the gift given to you for personal growth. Sometimes that growth is very painful, but it also can be very beautiful if you will look at it with your heart.

I now view my ex-husband as one of my greatest teachers. From him, I learned that I couldn't get love by being perfect (or trying to be) or by doing things for others that compromise my needs or values. I learned that I needed to set better boundaries and accept responsibility for the way that I allow people to treat me. I learned that unless I loved and valued myself, nobody else would, either. My deeply wounded parents were long dead and I was an adult, so I couldn't stay stuck in my old childhood wounds forever if I wanted to be happy. I had to learn each lesson and then let it go. I still have a lot to learn.

Let the lessons you've learned inform your decisions and behavior going forward, but let go of your memories of incidents that have happened which make you feel sad, angry, or unloved. Every time that you think about an incident with emotion, you re-traumatize yourself. Every time that you ruminate on what your husband did to you, you inflict another wound on yourself.

If you refuse to forgive or to wish happiness for everyone else, including your abusive former spouse, you will inadvertently block your own happiness. Unresolved anger and unforgiveness affect you spiritually, emotionally, mentally, and physically. When you have angry thoughts about someone else, your mind doesn't know how to keep your body calm and healthy. Your anger and lack of forgiveness affect *you* and not the other person, who may be completely unaware of how you feel, or not sorry. People with chronic anger have a much higher risk of coronary artery disease and heart attack. Some scientists believe that chronic anger is more dangerous than either smoking or obesity as a risk factor that could lead to an early death.

## FORGIVE AND REMEMBER

*"To be a Christian means to forgive the inexcusable because God has forgiven the inexcusable in you."*
—C.S. LEWIS

Whether you are a Christian or not, I include the preceding quote from C.S. Lewis because of its universal message. We forgive to free ourselves as much as others. Before you are able to be happy, you will have to forgive your ex-husband. Forgiveness will not be easy, as he may not ever acknowledge what he has done, much less be sorry for it. You will also have to forgive yourself for allowing the abuse to happen and for continuing to allow it to happen.

Your initial reaction to this last assertion may be that this is unfair. How are you to blame for what happened to you, you may ask? Or that it is your fault for attracting this relationship? He was so charming and deceived you, so how are you responsible for that?

It took me a long time to acknowledge that if I'd had a higher regard for myself, I would have noticed much sooner that he was unreliable and selfish. I would not have started a long-term relationship with him in the first place.

It will take time to forgive yourself and your ex-husband; you may have to forgive day after day over and over for a long period. Consider the time that you spend on this intention to be an investment in your freedom.

It is a common opinion that you must forgive yourself first before you can forgive others. I found that it was much more difficult to forgive myself, as I frequently felt responsible for everything that happened. This was the case even when something that went wrong was beyond my control. This type of reaction is typical for women who have sustained long-term abuse because it is what our abusers tell us. I was hard on myself, as I kept hearing a critical voice in my head that originally came from my parents and was reinforced by my abuser. I found it much easier to forgive others first.

There are several things that you will need to do to be able to move on with your life. You need to:

- Acknowledge what happened: what he did and that it was wrong.
- Feel the emotions in your body regarding the abuse.
- Accept that what happened is reality.

For me, facing some of the things I needed to acknowledge was too hard, so I shut down and numbed myself by eating whatever I could get my hands on. Because I felt unsafe showing emotions or feelings as a child, my anger and grief about my marriage felt so overwhelming that they were scary. It felt as if a bottomless pit would swallow me whole. Gradually I felt safer to feel and allowed myself to sob, to cry, and to hit things—I took up boxing for a short time—to release the negative emotions from my body and to heal. A good therapist can help you navigate through this process.

You also need to acknowledge your part and forgive yourself. Accept responsibility for what you did wrong in the relationship. No relationship is perfect, and you may have antagonized or enabled the situation. I know that I did.

My ex-husband was unhelpful and demanding at the same time. I would nag, and my ex would become passive aggressive, only agreeing to do the smallest of things, and then he would never do them. When I brought it up, he became mean and angry. I finally gave up and stopped asking him to do anything at all, feeling powerless, unsupported, and unloved. He would frequently criticize what I did, tearing me down. I would argue, eventually give up, and then sink into a deep depression, hating myself. I would withdraw and shut down. He would get frustrated, and then get needy and controlling. He told me that I was cold because I no longer wanted to be affectionate with him. He never thought that his behavior could be the reason. Everything was my fault. He made me responsible for his happiness, and I would always come up short. He never considered my happiness because it just wasn't important to him.

I allowed this unacceptable pattern to continue to happen and unconsciously played the martyr. I lost respect for him and for myself because I did not leave this very unhealthy relationship. I tolerated his bad behavior for way too long. I did my children no favors by staying just to keep our family intact. My intentions were good but wrongheaded. But once the divorce went through, I needed to forgive myself so I would be able to move on.

If I could forgive myself, you can, too. Remember, if it gets overwhelming, you can just give it to God. We are not meant to be perfect.

In forgiving my parents and myself, I came to be at peace with the fact that they were both alcoholics and my mother did not protect me from my dad's verbal and physical abuse. My parents were flawed, as we all are, and they made some good choices and some very bad choices. As have I. My mistakes were just different ones. My ex-husband could have done things better or differently, but he made his choices. I needed to let that all go to set myself free.

Forgiveness does not mean that bad things did not happen to you or that you were not hurt. It does not excuse anyone's actions or mean that you must reconcile with that person, only that you release them and release yourself so that you are not held prisoner by the past.

It helps me to try to separate the person from their actions; I forgive them and yet do not accept, excuse, or condone their actions in any way. I frequently ask for divine grace to help me, as I sometimes do not feel that I am a big enough person to do it alone. The quickest progress that I have ever had with forgiveness was in saying the following variation of the indigenous Hawaiian Ho'oponopono prayer during daily meditation for thirty days in a row. It goes like this:

*I am sorry.*
*Please forgive me.*
*I forgive you.*
*Thank you.*
*I love you.*[1]

While you are sitting with your eyes closed, visualize any person, living or deceased, who either you hurt or who hurt you, sitting in front of you, and then say this prayer to them. It is a powerful prayer of connection, and you may feel a lot of emotion in your body as you say the words the first several times. Let yourself stay connected with your feelings while you keep breathing deeply into your abdomen. You will probably feel much lighter afterward, as if a burden has been lifted.

The Forgiveness Prayer in the Jewish prayer book known as the *Siddur,* reads:

*I forgive all those who may have hurt or aggravated me either physically, monetarily, or emotionally, whether unknowingly or willfully, whether accidentally or intentionally, whether in speech or in action, whether in this incarnation or another, and may no person be punished on account of me.*[2]

It is very good for your health to release any toxic emotions from your body. These charged feelings get trapped and then become triggered by traumatic memories. True forgiveness may not be possible until you can release these trapped emotions from your body. Tears are very therapeutic for that reason.

If you have PTSD, it may be extremely difficult, if not impossible, to forgive traumatic events that you are still reliving in your mind, with all the corresponding emotions, as if they just happened. It may be necessary to treat the trauma *first* with EFT, EMDR, or some other method that works for you to release these stuck emotions. You will then be able to remember an incident calmly with detachment. This will give you the freedom to forgive the other person and truly be at peace.

In *Healing Everyday Traumas* by Lynn Karjala, simple tapping exercises are given to discharge the trauma and help reduce and eliminate negative feelings and beliefs, using emotional freedom technique (EFT) and thought field therapy (TFT). These exercises work by stimulating the flow of vital energy along the meridians, a set of pathways in the body that are associated with specific organs.[3] This technique, called acupressure, is like acupuncture, but without the needles.

Remember that forgiveness is a gift that you give to yourself as well as to others. We are all connected in Spirit, and God does not play favorites. His love is all encompassing and impersonal. God is love and love is God. As difficult as it may be to accept at first, God loves your ex-husband as He loves you. Expressing compassion for yourself, as well as for your ex-husband, who must be a very sick person to have done those horrible things, is in order.

Better to leave judgment to God.

Forgiveness is not rational, but it is very necessary if you are going to be a happy person living your best life.

In *Anatomy of the Spirit,* Caroline Myss states: "In the life and teachings of Jesus, forgiveness is a spiritual act of perfection, but it is also a physically healing act. . . . Forgiveness is an essential spiritual act that must occur to open oneself fully to the healing power of love. Self-love means caring for ourselves enough to forgive people in our past so that the wounds can no longer damage us—for our wounds do not hurt the people who hurt us, they hurt only us."[4]

Be vigilant about your thoughts. You could miss out on a lot while you look backward. Living your best life is up to you. Now is the time for you to liberate yourself from your old life and create a new and exciting one. You get to choose.

## SELF-REGARD

*"Sometimes God allows what he hates to accomplish what he loves."*
—JONI EARECKSON TADA

Your husband brainwashed you into thinking that you have no value and your needs are not important—possibly over a period of many years. He may have told you that you are incompetent, unattractive, unintelligent, incapable of anything worthwhile, and without options over and over. He may have screamed horrible epithets at you or demeaned you into thinking that those dreadful things he said were true, or both. He may not have bothered even to answer you when you tried to talk to him, which is another form of abuse.

Anyone who tries to demean you and reduce your sense of self is not worthy of you. You must come to the point where you realize that the real reason your husband has been telling you these lies is to keep you powerless and afraid. Remember that it is going to take time for you to recover and believe deep down that you are not those awful things he said you were. You may continue to need self-esteem work for many months, if not years, after your divorce. Be patient with yourself. A good counselor, as well as the company of nonjudgmental friends, will continue to be extremely helpful in your recovery.

Another means of improving self-regard is mirror work. As described by Louise Hay in *You Can Heal Your Life,* this technique helps to mend the fabric of the mind and boosts self-esteem.[5] Here are a few basic instructions on how to do it.

Very simply, say: "I love you, I *really* love you _______________ (your name)," while gazing into your own eyes, ten times twice a day. This one practice can do wonders for you. The first time or two that you do it, it may bring up some strong emotions for you, which is a sign that it is working. I cried the first time that I did it.

Yes, it's awkward and seems silly, but you will get used to it. It works if you will do it daily for weeks, months, or whatever period it takes for the message to sink in.

Many people look outside themselves for self-esteem, to such things as material or job success, popularity, dress size, and so on. Using external factors to determine your self-esteem will set you up for failure, as these things are temporary and fade away. You have an intrinsic worth as a child of God that is not attached at all to what you do or how you look. Use the affirmation "God loves me as I am, I am enough." right before bedtime to help it seep into your subconscious mind, where the repair work needs to take place. When negative thoughts and doubts appear, choose not to believe them. Gently dismiss them as old, limiting thoughts that no longer serve you and repeat your positive, esteem-building affirmation.

Ironically, one of the best ways to boost your self-esteem is to think about yourself just a little bit less and think about others more. An obsessive pursuit of self-esteem to the exclusion of other objectives may prevent you from pursuing other important goals, such as continuing your education or helping others. Yes, you do need to work on yourself, just not all the time. There is a balance. I usually feel very uncomfortable in large groups. I feel calmer if I try to set someone else in the group at ease by showing genuine interest in how they are and asking them unobtrusive questions about themselves. Most people appreciate genuine inquiries.

Give to others what you want to receive, such as patience, respect, and kindness. Make this a daily practice. Ask in prayer each morning, "What shall I say, what can I do, who can I help today?" The more love that you give, the more you will feel connected to others.

The Kabbalah, an ancient Jewish mystical practice, states that we are all connected and that we are here in this life to receive in order to share with others. Accept help with gratitude when it is offered. Be willing to receive so that you can recover and heal. Feel valued and worthy of receiving assistance and love. You will also feel better about yourself if you help someone else. It can be a smile, a kind word, a willingness to listen, or something more concrete. All the ways you can give of yourself are valuable.

Of course, you have an obligation to take care of yourself. Do not ignore or forget to honor your own needs when you are giving to others. Jesus rested when he needed to. See *Mark 6:31, Matthew 8:21, Matthew 11:28–29,* and *Matthew 26:45* regarding the topic of rest. The divorce process may leave you feeling depleted on occasion. Rest when you need to and take care of yourself.

# A WONDERFUL LIFE . . . IS A MEANINGFUL LIFE

*"Follow your bliss."*
—JOSEPH CAMPBELL

In looking for a way to patch the holes in my heart left by my parents and ex-husband, one of the many things that I have learned is that my past has made me a kinder, more thoughtful, and more compassionate person. Not a perfect person, by any means, but I hope a better one. I can pick up nonverbal cues when someone is hurting and trying not to show it. I can reach out to them and offer a little kindness willingly, as I know how much it means when someone offers it to me.

The main purpose of life is to give and receive love. No judgment, no condemnation, just pure, unconditional love. We are all intimately connected to each other and God, so when you act in a loving way to someone else you also are showing love to yourself.

Regardless of your religion, please look at the prayer of St. Francis of Assisi.

*Lord, make me an instrument of your peace.*
*Where there is hatred, let me sow love.*
*Where there is injury, pardon.*
*Where there is doubt, faith.*
*Where there is despair, hope.*
*Where there is darkness, light.*
*Where there is sadness, joy.*
*O Divine Master,*
*Grant that I may not so much seek to be consoled, as to console;*
*To be understood, as to understand;*
*To be loved, as to love.*

*For it is in giving that we receive.*
*It is in pardoning that we are pardoned,*
*And it is in dying that we are born to Eternal Life.*
*Amen.*

I have recited this prayer hundreds of times without fully understanding on a spiritual level why it is in giving that we receive or in loving that we are loved. But it is. We are connected to one another as one in Spirit so that giving to someone else is the same thing as receiving ourselves. Give what you need to receive. Also, be receptive to receiving love and support; know in your heart that you are worthy of it. You must be able to receive in order to be able to give. Many women turn away offers of assistance so as not to impose on others, out of pride, or due to a false belief that they do not deserve it. Others are then denied the opportunity to give when it is needed. Offer help when you can and remember to accept help as well. Giving and being of service is our ultimate purpose.

## THE END IS THE BEGINNING

*"Change and renewal are themes in life, aren't they? We keep growing throughout life."*
—SUSAN MINOT

Some women feel as if their lives are over when they get a divorce. Grieving the end of a marriage sometimes feels like a death. Allow yourself to grieve for the marriage that you should have had, then let it go. Your life is going to change. Do not be afraid of change; embrace it. You now have the freedom to make important decisions on your own regarding your lifestyle, home, career, and relationships. When the fog clears, you will realize that you saved your own life. You cannot change the past, but you have learned many lessons in your marriage and divorce that you will not repeat. You get to start over.

You now have the tools to practice self-care and to improve your self-esteem. The life ahead of you is rich with possibility. You have proven that you are a survivor and that you are a stronger person after having gone through the ordeal of leaving your abuser and the abuse behind. That is a real accomplishment. You can survive and thrive. Make good choices, ask for help when you need it, and have determination. Give thanks. Take one day at a time and do the things that you know you need to do to improve your life and be happy. You deserve it.

# CONCLUSION

*"Believe you can and you're halfway there."*
—THEODORE ROOSEVELT

How you fare in the divorce is up to you to a large extent. Be your own best advocate by educating yourself, being realistic in your expectations, deciding in advance what you want to achieve, and standing your ground with your attorney and the mediator—if you're using one—if they don't seem to be acting in your interest or try to make decisions for you. The outcome of your divorce proceedings will affect you and your children for the rest of your lives, so hold firm. Don't let any mistakes made in the past or during the divorce stop you from asserting your right to receive what you deserve.

Needing to avoid conflict by going along with aggressive men during mediation when it wasn't in my best interest was a very costly mistake I made. From this, I have learned that it is not always possible to avoid conflict. Sometimes you must fight. I didn't, so I lost. Be confident in the righteousness of your cause, as there is a lot is at stake and you don't get to hit the repeat button.

I learned to trust my judgment and do my research during my divorce. Understand that just because your attorney is intelligent does not mean that he or she will be able to take the time to research the issues that you feel are vitally important to you.

Busy attorneys can't be expected to be as invested in the outcome of the divorces they negotiate as their clients are.

Remember that it is extremely important for you to be prepared to stand up for yourself in the final hour of negotiations. Read the agreement carefully before you sign it. This is your responsibility.

Remember to pray, prepare, and act. Let go of the things that are out of your control and move on. Forgive yourself for having made mistakes, and acknowledge that you will continue to make them in the future, as all of us do. Hopefully, you will make different mistakes because you have already learned from the ones you have made.

Take good care of yourself through this ordeal so that you can stay strong. You deserve freedom from abuse. You deserve to be fairly treated in the divorce. You deserve to be happy and at peace. Remember that you don't have to go through this alone. I am in your corner. Many other people are willing to help you. Just ask.

*"Good luck and Godspeed."*
—LAUNCH CONTROL TO THE CREW OF APOLLO 11

## ACKNOWLEDGMENTS

I could not have written this book without a lot of help from others.

Thank you to all the women who willingly shared their experiences with me.

Thank you to my therapist of many years, Jerry Campbell, LCSW, whose constructive advice and insights helped me to heal and to pursue a more spiritual life.

Thank you to my patient and tireless editor, Stephanie Gunning, for her sense of humor, valuable feedback, and many necessary revisions.

Thank you for many happy memories to my dear childhood friend, Laurie Miller Spencer, who loved being an emergency room doctor and tragically lost her young life to gun violence from a former partner.

I am grateful to both my father and my ex-husband for having been my two greatest teachers. They helped me to become a better person. The lessons that they taught me may be of great benefit to my readers as well, which is a bonus.

The author will donate a portion of the net proceeds of this book to New York Institute of Technology Laurie Miller Spencer Scholarship Fund and the YWCA.

# END NOTES

The biblical references in this book are all drawn from the King James version of the Bible.

## Chapter 1 The Truth about Him


1. William Hirstein. “What Is a Psychopath?” Psychology Today (posted January 30, 2013). Available at: www.psychologytoday.com/blog/mindmelding/201301/what-is-a-psychopath-0.
2. Eleanor D. Payson. *The Wizard of Oz and Other Narcissists: Coping with the One-Way Relationship in Work, Love, and Family* (Royal Oak, MI.: Julian Day Publications, 2002), p. 21.
3. Ibid, p. 50.
4. Callie Marie Rennison. “Intimate Partner Violence 1993–2001” Bureau of Justice Statistics, U.S. Department of Justice (February 2003). Available at https://www.ncjrs.gov/app/publications/abstract.aspx?ID=197838.
5. M.C. Black, K.C. Basile, M.J. Breiding, S.G. Smith, M.L. Walters, M.T. Merrick, J. Chen, and M.R. Stevens. “The National Intimate Partner and Sexual Violence Survey: 2010 Summary Report” National Center for Injury Prevention and Control, Centers for Disease Control and Prevention (November 2011)). Available at: http://www.cdc.gov/violenceprevention/pdf/nisvs_report2010-a.pdf.

6. Shannan Catalano. "Intimate Partner Violence in the United States" Bureau of Justice Statistics, U.S. Department of Justice (revised December 19, 2007; accessed August 3, 2017). Available at: https://www.bjs.gov/content/pub/pdf/ipvus.pdf.
7. Ibid.


## Chapter 2 The Truth about You


1. Barbara Roberts. *Not Under Bondage: Biblical Divorce for Abuse, Adultery and Desertion* (Victoria, Australia: Maschil Press, 2008), pp. 25–6, 46, and 50.
2. Neale Donald Walsch. *What God Wants: A Compelling Answer to Humanity's Biggest Question* (New York: Atria Books, 2005), p. 190.


## Chapter 3 Body


1. "When Men Murder Women: An Analysis of 2014 Homicide Data," Violence Policy Center (September 2016). Available at: http://www.vpc.org/studies/wmmw2016.pdf.
2. Robert Preidt. "More Women Killed by Someone They Know in States with High Gun Rates," HealthDay News (January 28, 2016). Available at: https://consumer.healthday.com/public-health-information-30/violence-health-news-787/more-women-killed-by-someone-they-know-in-states-with-high-gun-rates-707449.html.
3. "Connection Between Mouth Bacteria, Inflammation in Heart Disease" Science Daily (April 16, 2015). Available at: www.sciencedaily.com/releases/2015/04/150416132205.htm.
4. *The Complete Book of Water Healing* by Dian Buchman (New York: Contemporary Books, 2001), pp. 11, 159–61, and 224–30.

5. Institute of Medicine, "Sleep Disorders and Sleep Deprivation: An Unmet Public Health Problem, Washington, D.C., The National Academies Press, 2006.
6. William D. S. Kilgore, E. T. Kahn-Greene, E.L. Lipizzi, R.A. Newman, G.H. Kamimori, and T.J. Balkin. "Sleep Deprivation Reduces Perceived Emotional Intelligence and Constructive Thinking Skills," *Sleep Medicine, vol. 9, no. 5* (July 2007), pp. 517–26.
7. Bruce McEwen and Ilia N. Karatsoreos. "Sleep Deprivation and Circadian Disruption: Stress, Allostasis, and Allostatic Load," *Sleep Medicine Clinics,* vol. 10, no. 1 (March 2015), pp. 1–10.

## Chapter 4 Mind

1. Eckhart Tolle. *The Power of Now: A Guide to Spiritual Enlightenment* (Novato, CA.: New World Library, 1999), p. 57.
2. Karl Deisseroth. "A Look Inside the Brain," *Scientific American,* vol. 315 (September 20, 2016), pp. 30–7.
3. Louise Hay. *You Can Heal Your Life* (Carlsbad, CA.: Hay House, 1984), pp. 75–82, and 91–5.
4. Byron Katie. *Question Your Thinking, Change the World: Quotations from Byron Katie* (Carlsbad, CA.: Hay House, 2007), p. xvi.
5. Dimitri A. Christakis, Frederick J. Zimmerman, David L. DiGuiseppe, Carolyn A. McCarty. "Early Television Exposure and Subsequent Attentional Problems in Children" *Pediatrics,* vol. 113, no. 4 (April 2004). Available at: http://pediatrics. aappublications.org/content/113/4/708.short
6. Tian Dayton. *Trauma and Addiction: Ending the Cycle of Pain Through Emotional Literacy* (Deerfield Beach, FL.: Health Communications, Inc., 2000), pp. 7–9.

7. "Addiction Risk Factors," National Institute on Drug Abuse (January 2017). Available at: https://easyread.drugabuse.gov/sites/default/files/node_pdf/34-addiction-risk-factors.pdf.
8. "Cycle of Addiction," Recovery Connection (January 1, 2011). Available at: http://www.recoveryconnection.com/cycle-addiction.
9. "Jane Fonda on Perfection." Oprah's Master Class, Episode 201, OWN Network January 2012.
10. Geneen Roth. *Women, Food, and God: An Unexpected Path to Almost Everything* (New York: Scribner, 2010), p. 211.
11. Phillippa Lally, Corneila H.M. van Jaarsveld, Henry W.W. Potts, and Jane Wardle. "How Are Habits Formed: Modeling Habit Formation in the Real World," *European Journal of Social Psychology,* vol. 40, no. 6 (October 2010), pp. 998–1009.

**Chapter 5 Soul**

1. Gregg Braden. *The Divine Matrix* (Carlsbad, CA.: Hay House, 2007), p. 55.
2. Luke Timothy Johnson. *The Creed: What Christians Believe and Why It Matters* (New York: Doubleday, 2003), pp. 34–5.
3. Rollin McCraty, Raymond Trevor Bradley, and Dana Tomasino, "The Resonant Heart," Shift: At the Frontiers of Consciousness (December 2004–February 2005), pp. 15–9. Available at: https://www.heartmath.org/assets/uploads/2015/01/the-resonant-heart.pdf.
4. Frederica Mathewes-Green. *The Jesus Prayer: The Ancient Desert Prayer that Tunes the Heart to God* (Orleans, MA.: Paraclete Press, 2009), p. 76.

5. Father Thomas Keating. *Intimacy with God: An Introduction to Centering Prayer* (Spring Valley, N.Y., Crossroad Publishing Company, 1994), p. 18.
6. Rav P. S. Berg. *The Essential Zohar,* (New York, Three Rivers Press, 2002), p. 59.
7. Caroline Myss. *The Power of Prayer: Guidance, Prayers, and Wisdom for Listening to the Divine* (Louisville, CO.: Sounds True, 2011). [Audio]
8. Michael D. Lemonick. "Music on the Brain," *Time* (May 28, 2000). Available at: http://content.time.com/time/magazine/article/0,9171,46157,00.html.
8. Robert J. Zatorre and Isabelle Peretz, editors. "The Biological Foundations of Music," *Annals of the New York Academy of Sciences,* vol. 930 (June 2001), pp. ix–x, 436, 452–456.
9. Peggy Peck. "ASH: Daily Doses of Bach and Breathing Lower Blood Pressure," MedPage Today (May 23, 2008). Available at: http://www.medpagetoday.com/meetingcoverage/ash/9597.
10. Marloes J.A.G. Henckens, Erno J. Hermans, Zhenwei Pu, Marian Joëls, and Guillén Fernández. "Stressed Memories: How Acute Stress Affects Memory Formation in Humans," *Journal of Neuroscience,* vol. 29, no. 32 (August 12, 2009), pp. 10111–19. Available at: http://www.jneurosci.org/ content/jneuro/29/32/10111.full.pdf.
11. Kim E. Innes, Terry Kit Selfe, Dharma Singh Khlasa, and Sahiti Kandati. "Meditation and Music Improve Memory and Cognitive Function in Adults with Subjective Cognitive Decline: A Pilot Randomized Controlled Trial" *Journal of Alzheimer's Disease,* vol. 56, no. 3 (February 2017), pp. 899–916. Abstract available at: http://www.j-alz.com/vol56-3.
12. Sarka-Jonae Miller. "The Surprising Health Benefits of Humming," Natural News (December 7, 2013). Available at:

www.naturalnews.com/043157_humming_stress_reduction_heart_health.html.

13. Jennifer Crocker and Jessica J. Carnevale. "Self-Esteem Can Be an Ego Trap," *Scientific American Mind,* vol. 24 (September/October 2013), pp. 26–33. Available at: https://www.scientificamerican.com/article/self-esteem-can-be-ego-trap.
14. Marc Allen. *Tantra for the West: A Direct Path to Living the Life of Your Dreams* (Novato, CA.: New World Library, 1992), pp. 39–47.
15. Denzel Washington. 2015 Dillard University Commencement Speech [Video]. Available at: https://youtu.be/ua7kS-o3Vi4.

## Chapter 6 It Takes a Village

1. "A Domestic Violence Awareness Resource Guide for Alpha Chi Omega" (September 15, 2013). Available at: https://www.alphachiomega.org/getmedia/6fb4e862-b2ad-4088-b5de-fc71126f30ad/Domestic_Violence_Awareness_Resource_Guide_public.pdf;.aspx.
2. C.M. Sullivan. "Domestic Violence Shelter Services: A Review of the Empirical Evidence", Harrisburg, PA. (October 2012). National Resources Center on Domestic Violence. Available at: http://www.dvevidenceproject.com.
3. National Center for Injury Prevention and Control. "Costs of Intimate Partner Violence Against Women in the United States," Centers for Disease Control Prevention, Atlanta, GA. (March 2003). Available at: https://www.cdc.gov/violenceprevention/ pdf/ipvbook-a.pdf.
4. "When Men Murder Women: An Analysis of 2013 Homicide Data," Violence Prevention Center (September

2015). Available at: http://www.issuelab.org/resource/when_men_murder_women_ an_analysis_of_2013_homicide_data.
5 Henry Weinstein. "High Court Shields Police Who Fail to Enforce Restraining Orders," *Los Angeles Times* (June 28, 2005). Available at: http://articles.latimes.com/2005/jun/28/nation/na-police28.

**Chapter 9 Money Matters**

1. Janice Green. *Divorce After 50: Your Guide to the Unique Legal and Financial Challenges* (El Segundo, CA.: NOLO, 2010), p. 160.
2. Ibid, pp. 159–60.
3. Ibid, p. 159.

**Chapter 12 Life Lessons, Forgiveness, and Purpose**

1. Joe Vitale and Ihaleakala Hew Len. *Zero Limits: The Secret Hawaiian System for Wealth, Health, Peace and More* (New York: John Wiley & Sons, 2007), pp. 205–6.
2. Rabbi Benjamin Rapaport. "The Forgiveness Prayer: Tools for Dropping the Toxic Baggage," Aish.com (February 2, 2013). Available at: http://www.aish.com/ci/s/The-Forgiveness-Prayer.html.
3. Lynn Mary Karjala. *Healing Everyday Traumas: Free Yourself from the Scars of Bullying, Criticism and Rejection* (Roswell, GA.: Psychology Innovations Press, 2017), pp. 129–42.
4. Caroline Myss. *Anatomy of the Spirit: The Seven Stages of Power and Healing* (New York: Three Rivers Press, 1996), p. 204.
5. Louise Hay. *You Can Heal Your Life* (Carlsbad, CA.: Hay House, 1984), pp. 19–23, 45–6, 56–7, and 82.

# RESOURCES

For more information about the book, to purchase your copy, to connect with Rosemary Lombardy, and to access a library of free resources, visit www.BreakingBonds.com. Also connect with us with on the following social networks for exclusive news, features, and updates.

www.facebook.com/xbreakingbonds
www.twitter.com/xBreakingBonds
www.linkedin.com/in/breakingbonds

The additional resources listed below may prove helpful to you during your marital crisis and divorce. I am not providing an endorsement here for any of them. It is your responsibility to determine if they are beneficial and appropriate for your situation. Phone numbers and web addresses given were accurate at the time of publication. Resources are grouped in categories that are organized alphabetically.

If you're in danger, call the National Domestic Violence Hotline: 1-800-799-7233. Also see the "Emergencies and Safety" section that begins on page 295.

## CHILDREN AND TEENS

**Child Help National Child Abuse Hotline**
1-800-4-A-CHILD (422-4453)
www.childhelp.org/hotline

**National Center for Missing and Exploited Children**
1-800-THE-LOST (843-5678), 24-hour hotline
www.missingkids.com

**National Runaway Safeline**
1-800-RUNAWAY (786-2929)
www.1800runaway.org

**Office of Child Support Enforcement (OCSE)**
http://www.acf.hhs.gov/css

OCSE partners with federal, state, tribal and local governments and others to promote parental responsibility so that children receive support from both parents even when they live in separate households.

**Resource Center on Domestic Violence: Child Protection and Custody**
1-800-527-3223
www.ncjfcj.org/dept/fvd

**Safe Horizon**
1-800-621-HOPE (4673)
www.safehorizon.org

**Teen Line**
800-TLC-TEEN (852-8336), 6–9 pm Pacific
Text "TEEN" to 839863, 6–9 pm Pacific
www.teenlineonline.org

## DIET AND EXERCISE

**Eating Disorder Hope**
1-888-274-7732
www.eatingdisorderhope.com

**My Fitness Pal**
myfitnesspal.com

**Weight Watchers**
www.weightwatchers.com

**YMCA**
www.ymca.net

## DOMESTIC VIOLENCE ORGANIZATIONS

**National Coalition Against Domestic Violence**
1-303-839-1852
www.ncadv.org

The mission of this organization is to advance transformative work, thinking, and leadership of communities and individuals working to end the violence in our lives. Their website has a state coalition list, which you can use to obtain support and advice appropriate for your situation.

**No More Project**
www.nomore.org

This national nonprofit organization, founded by business leaders, is dedicated to reducing and eliminating the costs and consequences of partner violence in the workplace. They provide education, initiatives to raise awareness and help prevent domestic abuse, information, materials, and advice.

**National Network to End Domestic Violence**
1-202-453-5566
www.nnedv.org
This social change organization is dedicated to creating a social, political and economic environment in which violence against women no longer exists.

## EDUCATION AND CAREER

**Kolbe Corp, Career Aptitude Assessments**
www.kolbe.com/assessments/ opgig-career-program/

Career guidance is provided based on natural strengths and interests. Kolbe Corp has several assessment products that you may find helpful in planning your education and career.

**SCORE Free Business Education and Mentoring**
www.score.org

This national nonprofit association to help small businesses is supported by the U.S. Small Business Administration and a network of 10,000 volunteers.

**Unemployment Help Center**
https://unemploymentapply.com

This website provides unemployment resources, information, and links to apply for unemployment benefits for all fifty states. It is not affiliated with the government.

# EMERGENCIES AND SAFETY

In an emergency, please call 911.

**National Center for Victims of Crimes,**
**National Hotlines and Helpful Links**
Crime Victims Hotline
1-855-484-2846
www.victimsofcrime.org/help-for-crime-victims/national-hotlines-and-helpful-links

**Victim Connect Resource Center**
1-855-4VICTIM (484-8446), 9 am–6 pm Monday to Friday, Eastern time
www.victimconnect.org

**National Domestic Violence Hotline**
1-800-799-7233, 24-hour hotline
www.ndvh.org

Advocates are available to provide crisis intervention, safety planning, and referrals to agencies throughout the United States and in Puerto Rico and the U.S. Virgin Islands.

**National Sexual Assault Hotline, Rape,**
**Abuse & Incest National Network**
1-800-656-HOPE (4673), 24-hour hotline
www.RAINN.org

This anti-sexual assault organization works with local rape crisis centers and provides live and anonymous support on their crisis hotline.

**Safe Horizon**
www.safehorizon.org
1-800-621-HOPE (4673), 24-hour hotline

Safe Horizon is a leading victim assistance organization in the United States.

**National Suicide Prevention Lifeline**
1-800-273-TALK (8255),
www.suicidepreventionlifeline.org

**Veterans Crisis Line**
1-800-273-8255
www.veteranscrisisline.net

**Victim Connect Resource Center**
https://victimconnect.org
1-855-4-VICTIM (484-2846), 8:30am–7:30pm Eastern

This nonprofit organization has a confidential referral program for crime victims in the United States.

**VINE**
www.VineLink.com

VINE is a national organization that helps women search for an offender who is in custody, either by name or identification number, and allows them to register to be alerted if he has escaped or been transferred or released.

# FINANCES

**Allstate Foundation, Financial Empowerment Tools**
http://purplepurse.com/get-empowered/financial-tools

**Defense Finance and Accounting Services (DFAS)**
www.dfas.mil/mypay.info

**Equifax (credit rating agency)**
1-800-685-1111
www.equifax.com

**Experian (credit rating agency)**
1-888-397-3742
www.experian.com

**Federal Agency and State Benefits and Assistance**
http://www.benefits.gov

**National Network to End Domestic Violence**
nnedv.org/projects

The Economic Justice Project at NNEDV provides knowledge and skills to domestic violence survivors to become financially independent.

**Smart About Money Program, Budgeting Tool**
https://www.smartaboutmoney.org/Tools/Budget-Wizard

**National Endowment for Financial Education**
www.nefe.org
An independent, nonprofit foundation committed to educating Americans on a broad range of financial topics and empowering

them to make positive and sound decisions to reach their financial goals.

**Social Security Benefits**
www.socialsecurity.gov

**Transunion (credit rating agency)**
1-800-916-8800
www.transunion.com

**Treasury Direct, Savings Bond Calculator**
www.treasurydirect.gov/indiv/tools/tools_savingsbondcalc.htm

## FINANCIAL ADVISOR BACKGROUND CHECK

**Financial Industry Regulatory Agency, Broker Check Tool (free)**
https://brokercheck.finra.org
1-800-289-9999

FINRA is an independent, nongovernmental regulator for all securities firms doing business with the public in the United States.

## HEALTH CARE AND INSURANCE

**Affordable Health Insurance Plans**
www.affordable-health-insurance-plans.org

**Health Care (U.S. federal government)**
www.healthcare.gov
1-800-318-2596

This is the official website of the Affordable Healthcare Act. Also see your state's local healthcare exchange: Search "Name of your state" + "healthcare exchange" online.

**Health Insurance**
www.healthinsurance.org

**Medicare**
www.medicare.gov

Medicare is a federal health insurance program that pays for hospital and medical care for elderly and certain disabled Americans.

**Medicaid**
www.medicaid.gov

Medicaid is a federal social health care program for families and individuals with limited resources.

**Office on Women's Health, U.S. Department of Health and Human Services**
https://www.womenhealth.gov
1-800-944-9662, 9 am–6 pm Eastern Monday–Friday

## LEGAL ADVICE

**American Academy of Matrimonial Lawyers**
1-312-263-6477
www.aaml.org

American Bar Association, Directory of State and Local Associations.

https://shop.americanbar.org/ebus/abagroups/divisionforbarservices/barassociationdirectories/statelocalbarassociations.aspx

**Avvo**
https://www.avvo.com

Avvo is a legal directory that provides legal guides and articles.

**Divorce Source**
www.divorcesource.com

Divorce Source is a legal directory with informative articles provided by members, a community forum, and divorce blogs.

**Law Help**
https://www.lawhelp.org

This website provides information about legal questions and free legal forms.

**Legal Services Corporation**
www.lsc.gov

Legal Services Corporation is an independent nonprofit that provides financial support for civil legal aid to low-income Americans.

**National Center for State Courts, Marriage/Divorce/Custody/Support Resource Guide**
http://www.ncsc.org/Topics/Children-Families-and-Elders/Marriage-Divorce-and-Custody/Resource-Guide.aspx

**Nolo**
www.nolo.com

Nolo is a legal directory that provides legal articles and products.

**WomensLaw.org**
www.womenslaw.org

This organization provides legal information and online support for victims of domestic violence or sexual assault. Legal forms are available on this site, as well as state statutes, safety tips, where to find help, how to prepare for court, websites for national resources, chats and message boards.

## PEER SUPPORT

**Divorce Care Support Groups**
https://www.divorcecare.org

Divorce Care seminars and support groups are available, along with practical information, videos from experts on divorce and recovery, and free daily email encouragement.

## PHYSICAL RESTORATION

**Face to Face**
1-800-842-4546
www.aafprs.org/face-to-face/national-domestic-violence-project/

This program provides plastic surgery and reconstructive surgery free of charge to victims who have sustained injuries to the face, head, or neck.

**Give Back a Smile**
1-800-773-4227
www.aacd.com/aboutGBAS
Front teeth damaged by a violent partner or spouse are repaired pro bono.

## PSYCHOTHERAPY

**American Association for Marriage and Family Therapy, Therapist Locator Tool**
www.therapistlocator.net/iMIS15/tl
American Psychological Association, Psychologist Locator Tool
https://locator.apa.org/

**EMDR Institute, Find a Clinician Tool**
www.emdr.com/SEARCH/index.php

**Healthy Place**
www.healthyplace.com

A consumer mental health site that provides information, online tests, videos, and other tools on mental health disorders and psychiatric medications.

**Good Therapy**
1-800-843-7274
www.goodtherapy.org

Good Therapy provides help in finding a therapist.

**Mental Help Net**
1-888-993-3112
https://www.mentalhelp.net

Mental Help Net provides comprehensive information on mental health and mental illness, including articles, a blog, and help line phone numbers.

## OTHER RESOURCES

**Not Under Bondage**
https://www.notunderbondage.com

The website provides articles and book excerpts by Barbara Roberts for biblical divorce for abuse, adultery, and desertion.

**Office of Head Start**
https://www.acf.hhs.gov/ohs

Head Start promotes the school readiness, health, and development of young children from birth to age five from low-income families in centers, childcare partner locations, and in their own homes.

**Salvation Army**
www.salvationarmyusa.org

The Salvation Army provides confidential emergency and transitional shelters where women and their children can stay, assistance with steps toward recovery and independent living, food pantries, meal programs, and other resources.

**Temporary Assistance for Needy Families**
https://acf.hhs.gov/ofa/programs/tanf

The four purposes of TANF are to: provide assistance to needy families so that children can be cared for in their own homes, promote job preparation, work, and marriage, prevent and reduce out-of-wedlock pregnancies, and encourage the formation and maintenance of two parent families.

## SUBSTANCE ABUSE

**Al-Anon**
www.al-anon.org

Al-Anon provided support for family members of someone with a drinking problem.

**Alcoholics Anonymous**
www.aa.org

AA provides resources and support groups to someone with a drinking problem.

**Cocaine Help Line, Phoenix House**
www.phoenixhouse.org
1-800-262-2463

**Drug and Alcohol Treatment Hotline/**
**National Institute on Alcohol Abuse and Alcoholism**
1-800-662-HELP (4357), 24 Hour
www.niaaa.nih.gov

NIAAA supports and conducts research on the impact of alcohol use on human health and well- being. Research within NIAAA and grants funded by NIAAA are conducted to develop effective prevention and treatment strategies.

**National Alcohol and Substance Abuse Information Center**
1-800-784-6776 24 Hour
www.addictioncareoptions.com

NASAIC maintains a database of substance abuse centers in the United States. Services are provided free of charge to assist in referrals to an appropriate treatment facility.

**Recovery Connection**
https://www.recoveryconnection.com

Recovery Connection provides information and resources about substance abuse prevention, treatment and recovery. Alcohol and drug addiction recovery tools are provided free of charge.

## RECOMMENDED BOOKS

*Alter Your Life* by Emmett Fox, HarperCollins Publishers, 1931.

*Around the Year with Emmett Fox: A Book of Daily Readings* by Emmett Fox. HarperCollins Publishers, 1952.

*The Brain That Changes Itself: Stories of Personal Triumph from the Frontiers of Brain Science* by Norman Doidge. Penguin Books, 2007.

*Chakra Clearing* by Doreen Virtue. Hay House, 1998.

*Codependent No More: How to Stop Controlling Others and Start Caring for Yourself* by Melody Beatty. Hazelden, 1986.

*The Drama of the Gifted Child: The Search for the True Self* by Alice Miller. Basic Books, 1981.

*The EFT Manual* by Gary Craig. Energy Psychology Press, 2008.

*Family Secrets: The Path from Shame to Healing* by John Bradshaw. Bantam Books, 1995.

*The Field: The Quest for the Secret Force of the Universe* by Lynn McTaggart. HarperCollins Publishers, 2001.

*The Four Agreements: A Toltec Wisdom Book* by Don Miguel Ruiz. Amber-Allen Publishing, 1997.

*Frequency: The Power of Personal Vibration* by Penney Peirce. Atria Books, 2009.

*The Gifts of Imperfection: Let Go of Who You Think You're Supposed to Be and Embrace Who You Are* by Brene Brown. Hazelden, 2010.

*Hands of Light: A Guide to Healing Through the Human Energy Field* by Barbara Brennan. Bantam Books, 1987.

*Harry Potter* by J.K. Rowling. Scholastic Press, 1998.

*Learned Optimism: How to Change Your Mind and Your Life* by Martin. E. P. Seligman. Alfred A. Knopf, 1991.

*One Flew Over the Cuckoo's Nest* by Ken Kesey. New American Library, 1963.

*Overcoming Addictions: The Spiritual Solution* by Deepak Chopra. Random House, 1997.

*The Power of Your Subconscious Mind* by Joseph Murphy. Jeremy P. Tarcher, 1963.

*The Sermon on the Mount: The Key to Success in Life* by Emmett Fox. HarperCollins Publishers, 1934.

*Shame and Guilt: Masters of Disguise* by Jane Middleton Moz. Health Communications, Inc. 1990.

*The Sugar Fix: The High-Fructose Fallout That Is Making You Sick* by Robert J. Johnson with Timothy Gower. Pocket Books, 2008.

*The Ten Things to Do When Your Life Falls Apart: An Emotional and Spiritual Handbook* by Daphne Rose Kingma. New World Library, 2010.

*The Twelve Steps for Everyone . . . Who Really Wants Them* by Jerry Hirschfield. Hazelden, 1975.

*The Wisdom of Menopause: Creating Physical and Mental Health During the Change* by Christiane Northrop, Bantam Books, 2001.

*The Wonderful Wizard of Oz* by L. Frank Baum (1900).

# ABOUT THE AUTHOR

**Rosemary Lombardy** is a financial advisor and portfolio manager with over thirty-five years of experience. Although her professional expertise is in financial matters, her perspective on marital abuse, divorce, and recovery is deeply heartfelt and holistic. She draws on decades of personal experience, as well as the experiences of others who have gone through similar situations, to help inform abused women so that they will become empowered to leave their abusers and begin to heal. Her former background in law, as well as being both a Catholic who has studied the Kabbalah and a Reiki master, has infused the book with practical guidance and spiritual techniques that women can use when they most need them. Her intention with this book is to foster self-awareness, responsibility, empowerment, healing, and forgiveness.

Ms. Lombardy resides in Nashville, Tennessee. Visit her website www.breakingbonds.com.

Made in the USA
San Bernardino, CA
19 January 2020

63373425R00175